TORN FROM OUR MIDST

VOICES OF GRIEF, HEALING AND ACTION
FROM THE MISSING INDIGENOUS
WOMEN CONFERENCE, 2008

edited by

A. BRENDA ANDERSON,

WENDEE KUBIK,

MARY RUCKLOS HAMPTON

University
of Regina

CPRC
P R E S S

Printed and bound in Canada at Friesens.
The text of this book is printed on 100% post-consumer recycled paper.

COVER AND TEXT DESIGN: Duncan Campbell, CPRC.
EDITOR FOR THE PRESS: Donna Grant, CPRC.

PHOTO CREDITS:

The photo of Daleen Kay Bosse on page 34 is courtesy of her family and Sisters in Spirit.

The photo of Amber Redman on page 40 is courtesy of Gwenda Yuzicappi and the University of Regina Photography Department.

The photos of *Bison Sentinels* on page 116, Alexis Johnson on page 126 and the Healing Walk on page 129 are courtesy of the University of Regina Photography Department.

The conference quilt on page 118 and the student art gallery on page 122 were photographed by Tim St. Amand.

The photographs on pages 191–203 are courtesy of Cynthia Bejarano.

Library and Archives Canada Cataloguing in Publication

Torn from our midst : voices of grief, healing and action from the Missing Indigenous Women Conference, 2008 / edited by A. Brenda Anderson, Wendee Kubik, Mary Rucklos Hampton.

Includes bibliographical references and index.
ISBN 978-0-88977-223-6

1. Native women—Crimes against—Canada. 2. Indian women—Crimes against—Mexico. 3. Missing persons—Canada. 4. Missing persons—Mexico. 5. Murder victims—Canada. 6. Murder victims—Mexico. I. Anderson, A. Brenda, 1963– II. Kubik, Wendee, 1951– III. Hampton, Mary Rucklos IV. University of Regina. Canadian Plains Research Center

HV6250.4.W65T67 2010   362.88089'97071   C2010-902588-1

Canadian Plains Research Center
University of Regina
Regina, Saskatchewan, Canada, S4S 0A2
tel: (306) 585-4758   fax: (306) 585-4699
e-mail: canadian.plains@uregina.ca   web: www.cprcpress.ca

We acknowledge the financial support of the Government of Canada through the Canada Book Fund for our publishing activities, the support of the Canada Council for the Arts for our publishing program, and the support of the University of Regina President's Fund.

  Canadian Heritage   Patrimoine canadien   Canada Council for the Arts   Conseil des Arts du Canada   University of Regina

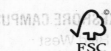

Mixed Sources
Cert no. SW-COC-001271
© 1996 FSC
FSC

To the sisters torn from our midst

*To families who have had to endure not knowing
what has happened to their loved ones*

*To those who have heard what they had hoped
they would never have to hear*

*And to all the strong women, men,
and children who shout out,
"Not One More! Ni Una Mas!"*

CONTENTS

ORGANIZATIONAL RESISTANCE: ACTION FROM WITHIN

SELF-CARE AND THE HEALING JOURNEY

NETWORKING AND STRATEGIZING

Common Themes from Conference Participants
Wendee Kubik—247

Acknowledgements

Friendships that can survive conference planning must be heralded! Thank you to my friend and co-chair, Reverend Carla Blakley. As we initiated the early stages of planning with students, it was our conviction that this work needed to be done through a process of creating bridges, between the academic world and the community, between different spiritualities that may be perceived to be antagonistic, across borders both national and personal. As we struggled together to avoid othering and being othered, we learned much about ourselves, about conference organizing, and about being in community.

Thank you to all who participated in the Conference Core Planning Group, who represented the range of communities working on this conference: Stephanie Balkwill, Mark Duke, Monica Fogel, Wendee Kubik, Jean Kurbis, Myrna LaPlante, Chelsea Millman, Darlene Okemaysim, Nathan Pasapa, Pearl Yuzicappi, Pastor Cheryl Toth, and our guiding Elders, Betty McKenna and Norma-Jean Byrd.

Thank you to conference co-ordinators Bridget Keating and Brittany Matthews, and to my research assistant, Chelsea Millman, all of whom worked tirelessly at the myriad of details that accompany such tasks and brought their own personal analyses of the problems and visions for the solutions. A special thank you is offered to our creative and dedicated videographer, John Hampton.

Over one hundred volunteers flocked to our assistance and, inevitably, names would be missed should I attempt to list them all. So I extend a broad but very sincere thank you to all who contributed to the success of the conference and who continue to shed light on this issue by contributing to these proceedings. Students, faculty, and friends were inspired to step forward to contribute their gifts and skills to this project. Thank you to both Tim St. Amand, our photographer, and Michelle Folk, who together seamlessly orchestrated an evening benefit banquet for the Regina community with Lourdes Portillo. To artist Adrian Stimson, whose work on the *Bison Sentinels* memorial went far beyond our means of remuneration, thank you for making your vision a daily reminder for all at the University of Regina and First Nations University of Canada.

To the Faculty of Arts and to the Women's and Gender Studies Department at the University of Regina, the collegial and passionate support and guidance of all was appreciated. The financial support and wisdom from RESOLVE (Research and Education for Solutions to End Violence and Abuse) was equally invaluable.

Thank you to Dr. Shauneen Pete, acting president of First Nations University of Canada, and to the university's Elders, Ken Goodwill, Isadore Pelletier, and Velma Goodfeather, and the Elders' assistant, Roland Kaye. Thank you to all the staff and faculty at Luther College who worked behind the scenes to ensure that guests were treated well, that finances ran smoothly, and that the conference was a success. In particular, deep appreciation is offered to Academic Dean Mary Vetter for her faith in our work and for her guidance through political and financial matters. And finally, thank you to my husband-turned-registrar-turned-taxi-driver, and to my placard-wielding son, both of whom feel passionately about this topic and are warriors in their own right.

To those who have held to the vision of this book—co-editors and warrior sisters Wendee Kubik and Mary Hampton—thank you and many, many hugs. Thank you, Canadian Plains Research Center, for your confidence in us and in our project, and a special thank you to editor Donna Grant for taking this project on not only as a job but as a personal testament towards making this a better world.

To all who bring their hands, hearts, and minds to this difficult task, we honour you. And, especially, to the families: your courage in telling your stories continues to inspire action and commitment to finding paths to justice and healing.

A. Brenda Anderson

A Blessing

ELDER BETTY MCKENNA

Migwetch great spirit please hear us. We are your children small and weak. In my humbleness I ask for a blessing for mothers who have not returned home, a blessing for the children who years later still wait, a blessing for grandmothers who long for that touch, a blessing for fathers who feel rage inside but keep quiet.

Oh great spirit, a blessing for a young spirit who has joined you too soon, a blessing for a sister whose tears cannot be quelled.

A blessing for a mother who hears her beloved child's voice in the dawn, a blessing for the grandfather who is always looking for her darling face, a blessing for the little brother who will not let anyone sit in her place.

A blessing for the ones who have found their resting places, ones who suffer guilt, ones who suffer helplessness.

Oh great spirit, keep them in your care. Ease their burden day by day. Let the memories of her linger soft as bunny fur. Let the sun shine brighter because she is over there, and whisper gently in her ear that she is loved incredibly. And we whom she has left behind will in prayer forever thank you because you sent her here.

INTRODUCTION

THIS SYMBOL IS USED THROUGHOUT THE BOOK
TO DENOTE TRANSCRIPTS OF PROCEEDINGS
FROM THE CONFERENCE "MISSING WOMEN:
DECOLONIZATION, THIRD WAVE FEMINISMS, AND
INDIGENOUS PEOPLE OF CANADA AND MEXICO,"
HELD IN REGINA, SASKATCHEWAN, CANADA
IN AUGUST 2008.

The Journey from Awareness
to a Conference to a Book . . . and Beyond

A. BRENDA ANDERSON

The Issue

In 2004, Amnesty International cited a Canadian statistic that Aboriginal women are five times more likely than other women of the same age to die as a result of violence. The Canadian government was internationally chastised as having no excuse for not investigating this atrocity.[1]

In February 2009, the United Nations called on the government of Canada to investigate the alarming rise in incidences of missing and murdered Aboriginal women. The UN has requested that the government of Canada report their findings to the UN within a year.[2]

Sisters in Spirit, a research and support group for the Native Women's Association of Canada, has thus far documented 510 Aboriginal women who have been reported missing or murdered in Canada since 1980. Of that number, over 44 percent have occurred in the last nine years.[3]

In the summer of 2008, a group of people from British Columbia walked across Canada to Ottawa to demand justice for their loved ones who have disappeared or been found murdered. They called their effort

BRENDA ANDERSON teaches in Women's and Gender Studies at Luther College, University of Regina. She co-chaired the "Missing Women" conference and has developed courses entitled "Missing Indigenous Women: A Global Perspective" and "Feminisms and Activism: Dancing Through the Minefields."

the "Walk for Justice." Along the way, these women and men and children travelled through Saskatchewan, where that same summer a conference entitled "Missing Women: Decolonization, Third Wave Feminisms, and Indigenous People of Canada and Mexico" was being held at the University of Regina, Luther College, and First Nations University of Canada.

At the time that I write this, two members of Parliament—Anita Nevill of Winnipeg[4] and Todd Russell of Labrador[5]—are calling on the government of Canada to begin an independent investigation into the reasons for such a high incidence of crime and violence against Aboriginal women.

This small sample from recent Canadian history illustrates the growing public effort to create awareness of the fact that brown-skinned women are more likely to go missing than those without brown skin—in other words, to understand, address, and redress racialized and sexualized violence within the historical context of colonization. This is my national context.

I am also part of a global community that consistently tolerates violence against Aboriginal women. Amnesty International has verified over 2,200 brutal murders of Guatemalan women and girls since 2001.[6] Amnesty International also draws world attention to Mexico, and Ciudad Juárez in particular, where the murders of hundreds and hundreds of women have met with deaf ears.[7] The patterns of sexualized violence have become so noticeable that the recent term feminicide (or some use femicide) is now commonly used to describe not only the horrific acts themselves but also the negligence of our governments to address this issue or even protect its own citizens. Mounting cries of frustration and pain are heard more frequently, as families insist on justice; they know there can be no true healing without their voices being heard.

In many ways, investigating this topic as a global affair serves as a mirror to Canada's own complicity in systemic racialized and sexualized violence against Indigenous and Métis women. Most importantly, however, it speaks for the urgent need to link with other academics and activists and family members literally to bridge the borders of our countries. It will become apparent to readers that the same patterns of violence are played out across the globe as a consequence of patriarchal conditioning, historical colonization and current neo-colonialist economic policies, current marginalizing social customs and practices, and assimilative governmental policies.

In this book, we dare five goals: to reflect the spirit and the messages brought to the "Missing Women" conference held in Regina in 2008; to include new voices and new perspectives that were not included at the conference; to reach a broader audience and continue to raise awareness; to offer reflections about the purpose and structure of the conference as a model for future gatherings; and to challenge all communities to be courageous enough to look at the heart of this issue, to recognize the systems that allow such atrocities, and to seek justice and healing for all. It is the hope of the editors that, through understanding some of the root causes that contribute to Aboriginal women being more vulnerable to violence around the world, there will be increased efforts for substantive social change in public sentiment, governance, policing services, and social service resources. We demand no less than a safe world for all.

Theoretical Considerations: Race, Sex, Power, and Identity

The topic of racialized, sexualized violence, specifically towards Aboriginal women, has been highlighted as a human rights issue for decades now. Yet, for the most part, this issue receives little notice in parliamentary debates or budget meetings or on coffee row. Even the terminology is not fully established: do we speak of women as missing, missing or murdered, disappeared, been disappeared? Each has a different emphasis. The word "missing" was used for the title of the conference and for this book, yet many good discussions were held as to the merit of using the term "taken," to connote violent rather than compliant departures. Whatever term is used, the pain and suffering remain the same.

Little work has been done towards linking the range of voices and issues that are necessary to hear if we are to fully understand how we have come to this point where certain people are seen as disposable. Frequently, theoretical questions of epistemology, hegemony, and identity are taken up by academics, but this discourse may not be accessible to or deemed relevant by those outside of academia. This seems problematic to me, for theory cannot be separated from action, just as healing is not possible without first understanding the root causes of violence. We are all theorists because we all hold certain world views. From those social constructs and personal experiences come our actions; thus, theoretical locations and personal actions are contingent upon one another. To understand the connections between colonialism, racism, and sexism, we need to hear personal stories from around the world and in our backyards. We also need to keep our theoretical maps of these world views and paths to justice accessible, understandable, and responsive to all communities.

Bearing this in mind, I suggest we examine the root causes of racialized, sexualized violence, asking: why do perpetrators target brown-skinned women; why are brown-skinned women statistically more at risk to experience violence in general; and, even more fundamentally, why are women targeted for violence? The conference and this book begin by bringing personal stories and theoretical tools together. From these encounters, we may begin to understand and resist the racism and sexism that manifests in violence against Aboriginal women. As we explore these questions, we find that three common categories link the countries—Canada, Mexico, and Guatemala—discussed in this book: their common experiences of racism as perpetrated by a colonialist past and a neo-colonialist present; the social constructions of masculinity and femininity as dominant and passive respectively; and the angry manifestation of these experiences through specific brutalization of brown-skinned women.

Social constructions are based upon patterns of "power over": power of one nation and way of life over another nation and way of life; power over economics, self-governance, and self-determination; and power of one gender over another. Such binaries of differentiated social power are cast as seemingly natural and assumed by those with the power to name and enforce. What each country must deal with now are the voices of those who have been disenfranchised because they are not of the powerful. The marginalized are finding one another within those imposed margins, and their voices grow in number and strength. They are joined by some from privileged backgrounds (whether by colour of skin, gender, economics, nationality, or religion) who choose to partner together to create a society not contingent upon systems of dominance. An understanding of these multiple locations of the privileged and the marginalized and the goal of bridging differences that has emerged from post-colonial and third-wave feminist analyses frame the discourse and approach of the conference and this book.

Reactions to the topic of missing and murdered Aboriginal women are often divided along lines of race, those who are Aboriginal and those who are not. The conference and this book are attempts to bridge the racial gap, to provide space for discussions that are often difficult to have in colonized countries. I want to begin by relating certain real conversations I have had with non-Aboriginal people. I have heard the brush-off—*she deserved it, she was asking for it, she knew what she was getting into when she became a prostitute*—and other such bigoted responses. Not only do I argue that a high percentage of these women and girls who disappear are not in the sex trade, but I question what kind of a world is imagined by people who would make such statements. *Is your world so harsh that you can dismiss someone's life because of what they do,* I ask. And, if this is the case, *do you really think the sex trade was their goal in life, the girlhood dreams of so many? Can you imagine a world where selling your body for sex is your only option for survival, where you were not protected as a child from the violence of drugs, poverty, and hopelessness?*

If I am to give the benefit of the doubt, I believe these callous statements are used as protectionism: *This can't happen to me, I'm a good person, I'm not involved in those activities so I am safe and it's still a good world*—these are divisionary lines created in our minds so that this is someone else's problem. *As long as I feel safe and comfortable in my world, I don't need to worry about anyone else* is a sentiment that divides, empowering some to the disadvantage of others. So I would speak to those who utter such statements and encourage them to think about their embedded racism and sexism, to consider community in a wider context as global citizens, and to set aside sentiments that seem to protect them from horror, yet in the end bring harm to themselves by atrophying their own humanity and capacity for compassion. It seems to me that the first two questions—why do perpetrators choose victims of brown-skin? and why do brown-skinned women experience more violence?—are answered most clearly and simply: because we live in a racist society.

Another side of the story needs to be told. A letter in a local newspaper describes life in "The Hood" in an article entitled "A place where women are stalked." The young Aboriginal woman writes: "It isn't so bad here—except for the cars rolling around, looking for prey: young women, especially native young women, are targeted when walking down a street. . . . I've been followed too many times; I know better than to walk alone. My sister has been cut off by a car; then the man inside tried to grab her. Fortunately, my mom was on that street to pick her up; she parked, got out and that man hurried back inside his car and took off. My beautiful sister, 16 years at the time, could have been missing and even murdered. Even when I was walking, six months pregnant, these men were following me." This young author, Jodie Woodward, finishes by suggesting that "it would be great if every person in Regina would help out when we see a situation that doesn't look right."[8]

Dr. Shauneen Pete, who at the time of the conference was academic dean and vice-president at First Nations University, reflects: "I don't know any First Nations women who haven't experienced childhood sexual abuse or family violence, and violence directed towards them because of their gender. . . . The fact that I'm 43 this year in some ways is almost miraculous, because of the wide range of forms of oppression that exist."[9] Within these profoundly disturbing accounts, we see the interplay between sexism and racism within the context of a country traumatized by practices of assimilation, residential schools, and cultural genocide. A country cannot be considered healthy if any of us are comfortable with that reality.

This topic demands solidarity among women and calls for an end to divisions along lines of race. Reflections such as those of Woodward and Pete need to be heard by the comfortable Canadian majority. Yet the question remains as to what role non-Aboriginal women, and in particular those of white settler descent, should play in this solidarity. How do we as women connect with our multiple identities of sex, gender, and race? Earlier feminists argued that all women experience similar experiences because of their sex; later, the theoretical spectrum broadened to consider multiple layers of differing oppressions, including those of race, economics, sexual orientation, and so on. Aboriginal and non-Aboriginal women share certain experiences, yet most certainly have different experiences as well. Thus, the question in my mind throughout the process of planning the conference and various classes has been: how do I adequately prepare a space for the variety of Aboriginal women's voices without imposing my agenda, however altruistic it may be?

This question was in part answered for me just prior to the conference. During a pipe ceremony, an Elder reminded me that it is not useful to appropriate the pain of others, that that is not my role as a white woman. Tears certainly still flow as I hear the stories of another's pain, and I do identify with the pain of marginalization insofar as I have had these experiences as a woman in a patriarchal society. Yet, I appreciate this Elder's wisdom because he saw that grief can immobilize, even destroy. I can only speak for myself, that throughout this work I endeavour to provide as much support as I possibly can to those in pain—because I am a woman, because I am human, because I can. Perhaps making space for things to happen is a discourse we can begin with, and that is what the conference, and this book, offer.

The racial divide is but one of our social locations. The third question of why women are conceptualized so frequently as victims of violent crime requires examination. Feminist scholar bell hooks writes that sexism is the first prejudice people encounter.[10] We are immediately categorized and identified at birth based on our sexual organs. The question of whether the baby is a girl or a boy is followed by cascading notions of correct colours to wear, toys to play with, behaviours to encourage or modify. What are our notions of masculinity and femininity, and what assumed roles, duties, characteristics are socially enforced that may contribute in any way to our desensitization concerning violence against women? If masculinity is equated with dominance, and femininity with submissiveness or passiveness, then is it much of a stretch to understand why women are tiresomely cast as victims in mainstream media, in everyday films, video games, music videos, commercials? What ferocious nightmares are we playing out, for adults and children alike, to feed upon as "our daily bread"?

Some argue that, just as this mythology of dominance is enacted upon women, so there is another mythology that pushes back at that, a mythology of feminine power. The female need not be a victim, but indeed is a warrior. It is not coincidence that Elders in Mexico and Canada and Guatemala, three countries known for their statistics of missing and murdered women, speak of the need to honour the feminine. Many Indigenous cultures, in fact, teach that the health of the society is based upon the health of their young girls. If they are violated, it is understood that all of society suffers. Author and conference speaker Morningstar Mercredi challenges women to find that power of the warrior, to be able to tell our stories as she came to be able to tell hers after a life filled with trauma and violence, and to emerge in full community again.

Like racism, the discourse of sexual domination through violence is dependent upon creating borders, upon categorizing and excluding or destroying "others." Thus, the process of theoretically understanding how these borders or lines of race and sex have historically been imposed, and imagining ways to resist assimilative processes of colonialism (whether of race or gender), is an activist stand.

Just as the conference included Aboriginal and non-Aboriginal people, it also provided an opportunity for men to join women in this struggle, and many did. However, it was sadly evident to participants that women far outnumbered men; as a result, public calls to men, in particular Aboriginal male leaders, were made from the floor. Since the time of the conference, a group called Brothers in Spirit[11] has been initiated as a group supportive to Sisters in Spirit. Troy Westwood of Winnipeg in particular has spoken and sung eloquently of the need for Aboriginal men to recognize their own deep sexism and to stand up as men against all forms of violence against women.[12]

Understanding the context and background of racialized, sexualized violence is but the first step. From there, concrete strategies and solutions emerge. *Voices of Our Sisters in Spirit: A Research and Policy Report to Families and Communities,* a report commissioned by the Native Women's Association of Canada with federal funding and released in November 2008, recommends that much higher levels of resources go into educating young Aboriginal girls on safety issues, that children whose mothers have become missing or were murdered be actively supported, and that access to justice for Aboriginal women be guaranteed. The latter includes an end to discriminatory practices and policies, sensitization training, and more resources for investigations as well as support for traumatized families. Poverty, homelessness, and issues of affordable housing are mentioned as root factors leading to women's vulnerability to violence, and leaders are called on to improve not only the economic but also the social well-being of Aboriginal women and girls.[13] Are these not what all citizens should expect of their governments?

Mapping a Conference: Approach and Process

Critiquing social systems while simultaneously building a supportive, ongoing network is a challenging endeavour. Where we locate ourselves in our society and where others locate us may differ. For instance, those involved in church might be viewed as part of the problem, while they themselves might feel they are working at reconciliation and new beginnings. Issues of safety might be another concern; why would Aboriginal women entrust their stories to white settler women who still benefit from the privilege of being white?

Negotiating the variety of feminist approaches and the differing Aboriginal understandings and organizations, overcoming stereotypes of ivory-tower academia versus grassroots activists, bringing together those who represent the justice system and those who feel the justice system has failed them, using the media to raise awareness about the conference while yet recognizing that often media has been at the root of destructive stereotypes, encouraging men as well as women to be present—there were *many* potential pitfalls for the conference organizers. Yet, reflecting back on the conference one year later, and particularly after reading the submissions for this book, I am struck by the overarching discourse of kindness that permeated this experience. At the root of all who were involved, whether they were organizers, financial donors, or participants, there was a deep desire to connect. More than 300 participants came because they wished to be heard, to listen, to learn, to weep, to share, to find out what they could do to bring international awareness to the topic so that lives might be saved, and justice and healing could begin.

The conference was organized by faculty and students, Aboriginal Elders and leaders in Christian churches, community activists and, very importantly, family members with missing or murdered loved ones. The process was intentionally designed to incorporate as many voices and opinions as possible from all who have been impacted by this issue, and it is our contention that all in Canada, and indeed the world, are impacted whenever a woman is violated. However, we recognize that specific voices have often been silenced or ignored, and thus we looked to these voices, particularly the voices of family members, as our main guides in determining what would be most helpful and useful to include in this conference.

The core planning group felt that our approach of "making space for things to happen" was unique in that we attempted to include a range of voices. Participants included police, media, policy-makers, and justice workers, members of faith communities, academics, activists, and youth workers, those from Aboriginal, immigrant or white settler descent, young and old—

whatever their perspective, we asked that all come to this issue and this conference with both hearts and minds fully engaged. We realized we needed to provide a space where we could hear one another, where we could hear about the restrictions or goals in journalism, police resources, governmental policy-making, and how these problems or improvements impact on families and the general public.

During the conference, we strove to understand the interlocking parts of these systems, to understand that there is no single group or person to blame. While that would be easy, it would not be accurate, and the project would fail. We were challenging people to understand the systems that we ourselves might be complicit in, that we might benefit from, and we did so while recognizing that that kind of self-evaluation is never easy. At the conference, all seemed to rise to this challenge, and I was frequently moved by the willingness of participants to speak of very personal hardships and experiences.

Part of that safety came from our conviction that we needed to seek the advice of Elders. As part of our core planning group and our sacred space committees, several Elders provided us with insight into spiritual practices and the need for an holistic approach. It was important to us to have their prayers and support as we journeyed through some difficult waters and dealt with our own emotional responses to this heavy sadness. It was important to many of us that this conference not use solely an academic or theoretical approach. As feminists, we all recognized the importance of the motto "the personal is political," and we were determined first and foremost to "do no harm." That meant that as much thought and insight as possible needed to go into framing our discussions within a safe environment—one without judgment or repercussions—and that, while our minds would be challenged, our spirits would be cared for throughout our time and space together. A partnership including Elder Betty McKenna, Elder Norma-Jean Byrd, Luther College Chaplain Reverend Cheryl Toth, and students Alexis Johnson and Mahaila Scott conceptualized and implemented a "Sacred Space" for the duration of the conference. This large room served as a retreat for all to come to, incorporating the four elements of earth, wind, fire, and water, beauty to stimulate the senses, such as wind chimes, rocks, and crystals, and comforting teddy bears, quilts, and rocking chairs. Separate rooms were made available for counselling with Elders, Chaplains and secular therapists. Pipe ceremonies were held, smudgings performed, and prayers offered, and conference participants had the opportunity each evening to travel to the nearby Piapot reserve for a powwow. For some, this meant bringing their fancy dresses and dancing; for others, both local and from Mexico, this meant experiencing the drum for the first time. As well, an all-women local drumming group provided spiritual healing and guidance one evening, bringing the gift of the drum from women to all who could join. Tending to the spirit, and in particular honouring Aboriginal ceremonies, was a learning opportunity and was, in fact, a means of decolonizing all our spirits.

So, the mind and heart and body were all engaged in this space we shared together. We were then confronted with the dilemma of how to take these experiences and this knowledge back home, to our own spaces. The last day of the conference was committed to specific time for networking and strategizing in mapping out paths to justice from our diverse areas of involvement as journalists, police, artists, activists, youth workers, and so on. Participants were asked at the time of registration to specify what groups they wished to make contact with, and, by the colour of beads on their name tags, were encouraged to connect with those people throughout the conference. On the last day, these groups met to answer specific questions designed to encourage "the next step."

One of our goals for this book is that it might function partially as a guideline for anyone considering a similar conference. To that end, the conference programme and agenda is included on the accompanying DVD as a pdf file. Also on the DVD are a five-minute "trailer" with highlights of the conference and a slideshow of photographs from the conference—we hope that these faces and voices will help to "bring life" to the written words on the pages of this book. For those in the teaching profession, the DVD also includes a pdf file of the syllabus for my 2009 class, "Missing Indigenous Women: A Global Perspective," offered at a third- and fourth-year level in Women's and Gender Studies at the University of Regina. Appendix A is a summary of the recommendations of the Provincial Partnership Committee on Missing Persons, a document which was made available at the conference. Appendix B is a brief bibliography of useful books, articles, websites, and documentaries on the topic of missing and murdered Aboriginal women. We hope that future conferences will continue to refine and improve upon our holistic process of listening, integrating, and acting upon.

The Book

The structure of the book follows the same guidelines as the conference. The authors have all been asked to respond to the question, "What do you think people need to hear, or what do you feel you need to say about this issue from your own location." A variety of styles in their responses has been encouraged, so in many ways this book reflects the eclectic nature of the conference. Some direct transcriptions have been provided. Throughout these pages you will find theoretical and academic analyses, public policy reports, and very poignant, personal reflections. Just as the conference was a bridging moment, an attempt to hear and clarify the multitude of voices wishing to be heard, so this book attempts to provide another forum for those voices to be heard. It is the hope of the editors that this book will be accessible to all, that it will represent the discourse of kindness that framed the conference, and that it will facilitate opening up the more difficult questions of where we go from here.

The remainder of this introductory section includes three reflective pieces on the significance of the conference, the first by conference coordinator Brittany Matthews, the second by Pastor Cheryl Toth, and the third by Chelsea Millman in response to interviews with Elder Norma-Jean Byrd and Pastor Cheryl Toth on the significance of sacred space.

The second section pays tribute to the amazing courage of families willing to tell their stories. Knowing what is in the hearts of Canadian and Mexican women and men is an important place to begin. It is an activist stand to put your personal story within the analysis, and it is an activist stand to apply the theoretical to your personal location. We are indebted to Eva Arce, Paula Flores, Pauline and Herb Muskego, and Gwenda Yuzicappi for sharing their stories with us. The theory and activism cannot be done without the input of families who understand what needs to be done.

Some historical and global context is crucial. Section Three, entitled "The Violent Erasure of Women," points readers to the acknowledgement that the process of colonization is a legacy still lived. Systems of governance and economics continue to disenfranchise. Gordon Barnes from Amnesty International contextualizes the disappearances of women across the globe. Reverend Kim Erno from Mexico discusses how neo-liberal politics creates a world that values money above all else, and places that money in the hands of the very few, straight out of the hands of the many. Erno connects the abuses of the *maquiladoras* along the Mexican-u.s. border to this fundamental, unchecked greed of our modern market system. Similarly, journalist Leonzo Barreno relates his personal story of growing up in Guatemala, a country whose misogynist history collides with such corporate greed and governmental corruption that thousands of women have died horrifically.

Dr. Carrie Bourassa, from First Nations University of Canada, continues to connect the dots between the historical and present day. Bourassa describes how the Canadian government's policies of assimilation destroy Aboriginal and Métis women's identities, leaving them vulnerable to violence. Dr. Kiera Ladner, Canada research chair at the University of

Manitoba, and Ian Peach, special advisor to the Office of the Federal Interlocutor for Métis and Non-Status Indians, continue this conversation
by asking what Aboriginal women miss out on, and what institutional systems stand in the way of their full Canadian citizenship. To complete this
chapter, Betty Ann Pottruff, co-chair of the Provincial Partnership Committee on Missing Persons of Saskatchewan, provides an overview of that
committee's work in contextualizing, understanding, and addressing the
issue of missing Aboriginal women.

Part of active resistance comes in the form of artistry, and the conference
was full of powerful images and artwork. In Section Four, "Resisting with
all the Senses: Art and Activism," independent curator Dr. Elizabeth Matheson discusses how filmmaking, specifically the work of Lourdes Portillo,
brought world attention to the situation in Ciudad Juárez. The section
continues with artist Adrian Stimson's description of his living memorial,
Bison Sentinels, which was unveiled at the conference opening ceremonies.
This compelling piece continues to draw people to "The Healing Garden,"
located near First Nations University on the University of Regina campus.
Following this are numerous personal reflections by students and participants who shared their leadership and care through artistic expressions.
Jessica Greyeyes tells about her activism through the creation of a conference quilt, Charlotte Hauk describes an exhibit at the conference that
highlighted the journals and artwork of students who travelled to Mexico
to research grassroots resistance to violence against women, and Alexis J.
Johnson describes "The Healing Walk" and the significance of the pink
banners used during the conference. In Senator Lillian Dyck's poignant
reflection of her personal response to these banners, or prayer cloths (as
she relates to them), we come to understand how these artistic expressions
simultaneously heal us and move us forward to action.

Section Five, entitled "Organizational Resistance: Action from Within,"
profiles the work of individuals from varied professions who describe how
change can operate from within institutions. The first five contributions
discuss the crucial role media plays in either disseminating or deconstructing the stereotypes of Aboriginal women. One distressing and common
problem family members encounter upon the disappearance of a loved
one is the manner in which their case is discussed in the public media. Dr.
Carol Schick, professor of anti-oppressive pedagogy, draws parallels between discourses in public education systems and media. Holly A. McKenzie, a recent graduate of Women's and Gender Studies at the University
of Regina, discusses the shift in media representations in the case of
Daleen Kay Bosse (Muskego). Darla Read, a journalist from northern
Saskatchewan, relates her personal struggle in reporting on murder trials

in an accountable way. Doctoral candidate Amber Dean discusses media responses to the murders of women from Eastside Vancouver in her article "Inheriting What Lives On: The 'Terrible Gift' of Sarah de Vries's Poetry." Lourdes Portillo, the Academy-nominated filmmaker who first shed light on the murders of women working in the *maquiladoras* in Ciudad Juárez in her film *Señorita Extraviada,* speaks about her decision to become a documentary filmmaker in order to tell the stories that were not being told and to work for justice for those who are marginalized.

It was important to the conference planning committee to include the voice of law enforcement. Family members frequently relate stories about the lack of response from investigators, yet these stories are also accompanied by accounts of compassionate, tireless officers. Constable Michelle Solomon discusses the challenges, accomplishments, and needs of Regina Police Service's Missing Persons Department.

The chapter continues by illustrating the ways in which academics are involved in justice work. Dr. Cynthia Bejarano charts her personal story as an academic at the University of New Mexico and her ability to use that privileged position actively to support family members of missing women in Ciudad Juárez, including journeying with Eva Arce and Paula Flores to our conference amidst some danger to all. This is followed by the conference presentation by Judy Hughes, president of the Saskatchewan Aboriginal Women's Circle Corporation. This piece speaks of the necessity for continued funding for research and policy development work in the case of Sisters in Spirit and the Native Women's Association of Canada. These authors and their dedicated work illustrate both current critiques and actions to resolve the issue of missing and murdered Aboriginal women in Canada and Mexico.

How do we heal from such trauma? Is healing possible? Section Six shows the need for "Self-Care and the Healing Journey," and specifically describes a project by that name that was researched by RESOLVE (Research and Education for Solutions to Violence and Abuse). This article includes statistics, analysis, and solutions regarding Aboriginal women and intimate partner violence in Canada. A personal reflection by Lori Campbell relates the significance of the drum and Mother Earth in her healing journey. In "Kamāmakos: The Woman Who Wouldn't Fly Away," Chelsea Millman, recent graduate of the University of Regina, shares a portion of her psychology honours paper that tells about the significance of finding and claiming her Métis roots as part of her healing. This piece integrating personal story and theoretical positioning illustrates a new wave of feminist, activist academia. And finally, Ernesta Vileitaite-Wright, another recent graduate at the University of Regina, relates how a group of students who were involved in the conference later formed the group People Before Profit to enable them to assist women both locally and globally. The importance of taking care of self amidst the flurry of activism, and in the midst of such pain as this topic raises, is clear from all of these brave contributors.

The final section of the book begins to move us back to our worlds, our own locations as journalists, police, family members, the general public. Dr. Wendee Kubik, conference planner and program chair of Women's and Gender Studies at the University of Regina, organizes the themes of the discussions within the conference affinity groups. The richness of personal insights is encouraging, and yet we see how difficult it is to move the stories from the conference into concrete action plans. Far from being disheartening, however, the pieces are laid out for us and it remains the burning task for all of us to respond in our own ways.

Some stories cannot be transcribed. The conference was positively brimming with strong, powerful women leaders. The deep, heavy sadness of the topic could only be addressed by including story after story of resistance and activism. Three women in particular brought compelling leadership to this conference.

Maria Campbell, Order of Canada recipient and keynote speaker at the opening ceremonies of the conference, began with stories—stories from the perspective of a little Métis girl growing up in Canada, stories of an Elder who is dismayed at the violence she sees around her, stories about herself. Those of us who have not experienced such a depth of marginalization and brutality are brought to that place by Maria's story, so we can all understand, at least partially, what this part of Canada is like.

Marta Perez took us to Mexico with her story of how rape is used as an institutional, governmental weapon. The injustices at San Salvador Attenco burned in our ears, as did her call for justice during our demonstration walk.

And finally, author Morningstar Mercredi brought us hope. She told us of the worst and of the best in humanity. Morningstar challenged us to spread the symbol of the pink banner across South, Central, and North America, to represent each and every woman and girl who has been torn from our midst.

We include the stories of these three women on the DVD in the hope that their voices will continue to direct more of us to action, and to hope.

And Beyond . . .

More than a year has gone by between the conference and the writing of this book. Have things changed since the conference? Has there been a difference in the way police have handled cases, in how media has reported on trials of missing persons, in the general public awareness of the issue? That is a difficult question, and one that I can only answer from my own personal location. I understand the conference to be but one step amongst many, benefiting from previous efforts and hopefully encouraging and promoting further steps. Since the conference, a posthumous education degree was given to Daleen Bosse by the University of Saskatchewan; more journalistic articles are beginning to give more time and space to examining the multiple layers of complexity within this issue. I have watched young women form a group called People Before Profit, whose express purpose has been to empower women in the community, which is identified as both local and global. I have read excellent academic papers by young students who are dedicating their time to understanding this issue in order to help change the world. I have listened to the passionate goals of students, some Aboriginal and some non-Aboriginal, making plans for another public use of the pink banners. I believe that others who were involved in the conference have likely had similar experiences since our time together. There is a momentum that cannot be stopped now.

I have been frequently dismayed at the number of phone calls I now receive from media or other groups asking me to give an opinion on this matter. I typically decline to do this, which seems to surprise many. *"Aren't you the expert?"* they ask, and I am astonished at the ease with which one is asked to appropriate the power of others, perhaps especially when one is part of academia. *"No,"* I reply, *"for if I declare myself an expert in this, then I am stating I know more about this than you do, and that is not acceptable to me. If you live in Canada, if you live in Mexico, if you live on this globe, then you should also be an expert on this issue."* I cannot give a sound bite. The stories belong first and foremost to the families, but it is too easy for us to look to the experts to solve this, and that is not a correct position to hold. We can counsel one another, support one another, but the responsibility rests with *all* of us to know the details, to understand the systems, to be able to comment about our own countries and the justice or injustice for all people. Do not look in this book for expertise alone; look in this book to find your heart, your voice, and your path of action.

ENDNOTES

1   Amnesty International, *Stolen sisters: a human rights response to discrimination and violence against indigenous women in Canada,* October 2004, http://www.amnesty.ca/campaigns/resources/amr2000304.pdf (accessed 20 March 2009).

2   "Canada must probe cases of slain, missing aboriginal women: UN," CBCNews, The Canadian Press, http://www.cbc.ca/canada/story/2008/11/24/missing-women.html (accessed 22 June 2009).

3   Sisters in Spirit, *Voices of our sisters in spirit: A research and policy report to families and communities,* November 2008, http://www.nwac-hq.org/en/sisresearch.html (accessed 22 June 2009), 51.

4   Anita Nevill home page, http://www.anitaneville.ca/HofC.html (accessed 20 June 2009).

5   Liberal Party of Canada, "Harper Conservatives forget missing and murdered Aboriginal women," 13 May 2009, https://www.liberal.ca/en/newsroom/media-releases/15800_harper-conservatives-forget-missing-and-murdered-aboriginal-women (accessed 20 June 2009).

6   Amnesty International, "Stop the killing of women in Guatemala," http://takeaction.amnestyusa.org/siteapps/advocacy/index.aspx?c=jhKPIXPCIoE&b=2590179&template=x.ascx&action=7119 (accessed 20 June 2009).

7   Amnesty International, *Mexico: Killings and abductions of women in Ciudad Juárez and the City of Chihuahua—the struggle for justice goes on,* http://www.amnestyusa.org/document.php?id=engamr410122006&lang=e (accessed 20 June 2009).

8   Jodie Woodward, "A place where women are stalked," *Leader Post,* 8 June 2009.

9   Marie Powell, "Our missing mothers, sisters and daughters," *Degrees: The University of Regina magazine* vol. 20, no. 2 (Fall 2008): 19.

10 K.A. Foss, S.K. Foss, and C.L. Griffin, "bell hooks," *Feminist rhetorical theories* (Thousand Oaks, CA: Sage Publishing), 69.

11 Native Women's Association of Canada, "Brothers in Spirit," http://www.nwac-hq.org/en/brothers.html (accessed 20 June 2009).

12 Troy Westwood, "Little Hawk music," http://www.myspace.com/littlehawkmusic (accessed 20 June 2009).

13 Sisters in Spirit, *Voices of our sisters in spirit,* 55.

Hands

BRITTANY MATTHEWS

It was my honour to serve as one of the many concerned citizens who contributed to the conference, "Missing Women: Decolonization, Third Wave Feminisms, and Indigenous People of Canada and Mexico," in August 2008. I would like to share my reflections on what I believe was central to my experience as one of the conference coordinators—that is, the presence of many hands.

When I met Marta Perez, she and I stood beside the glass tipi at First Nations University of Canada and shook hands. Though eager to welcome her, I struggled to bridge the distance between her Spanish and my English. When I showed Marta a copy of the freshly published conference programme, she began speaking to me spiritedly in her indigenous language, a smile blazing across her beautiful face. She spread her strong hand across the cover of the programme, showing me how her own hand fit perfectly within the drawn hand featured on the programme cover. Marta understood the power of the names and the words *ni una mas* written inside the hand, just as I understood, in my own language. As the two of us spoke to

---

BRITTANY MATTHEWS is a young teacher dedicated to activating responsible citizenship among young people in Regina. She is grateful to have had the opportunity to learn from the many strong, inspiring women and men involved in the "Missing Women" conference.

each other with our hands, Marta prompted me to remember that the time and the space we called the "Missing Women" conference had been built by many hands. I saw the hands of those who prayed and the hands of those who smudged. I saw the passing of broadcloth and tobacco into the hands of the Elders. I witnessed the exchange of respect through the shaking of hands. I saw families holding in their hands the photographs of missing loved ones. I marvelled at the many hands that painted words and symbols of resistance on fabric and those same hands that carried messages of hope into our communities. I stood among those who raised their hands to ask questions, to demand answers, and to declare themselves warrior women and men in the struggle against violence and exploitation. I participated in the joining of hands at the round dance, illustrating our interconnectedness. Many hands presented many gifts to our collective endeavour to draw attention to and stop violence against Indigenous women, and many hands continue to lend themselves to this essential work.

I remain grateful for the contributions made by these many hands. In particular, I extend my appreciation for the devoted leadership demonstrated to me by the guiding members of the conference planning committee, and in particular, to the guiding Elders and Elders' helper, all of whom welcomed me into their wisdom and ceremonies. May our common visions of strong, peaceful communities become clearer realities through our efforts each day.

Women Missing, Missing Women

PASTOR CHERYL TOTH

The conference in August 2008 to consider the issue of missing women in Canada and Mexico was a gathering primarily of women: women missing/missing women. As someone involved in the conference as an organizer and spiritual care provider, I have wondered about what it meant for us to gather as women for women who are missing. The question that intrigued me throughout my pondering was the question of female bodies—the bodies that are missing and the bodies of those who are missing them. We are embodied beings. Elaine Graham suggests that "our bodies are microcosms of the macrocosm of society, and can be read as metaphors for our social and political concerns and fears."[1] In what way, then, did our bodied selves reflect the issues of missing and violated women, and in what ways did our body care resist or augment that violence?

Each of us who came to the conference came carrying our history as women. The stories of our lives include the joys of love, the passion of intimacy, the ecstasy of childbirth; they also include the sorrow of broken

CHERYL TOTH is the chaplain at Luther College, University of Regina, and was a member of the Core Planning Group for the "Missing Women" conference. Cheryl has worked for many years on issues of justice and inclusion, including those affecting First Nations and Métis people.

relationships, the pain of emotional distance, and the grief of emotional or physical child loss. Interwoven with these events that have shaped our lives are the emotional and sometimes physical marks from them that we carry in our bodies. Scars from childhood falls, stretch marks from pregnancy, laugh lines around our eyes—all tell our stories. Many of us have also been violated—words, hands, and bodies used against us that left us with wounded bodies and wounded souls. These events caused us to lose an aspect of our original and whole selves, and we became women missing something of who we were. We came to this gathering on missing women knowing somewhere in our beings that we were embodying the very violations that we came to discuss.

The patriarchal mindset that buttresses the violence of racism and sexism and justifies a hierarchy of worth in society has scarred us body and soul. During the conference, when we discussed the ways in which that violence had victimized other women, those scars began to ache and we were awakened again to the pain of being women missing. We became more acutely aware of where we were wounded in our lives—what we were missing—as we listened to the painful stories of missing women. Our bodies became the sites that told of what is contested and molested in women's lives.

Unlike *our* bodies, which were physically present in the room as stories were told, the bodies of missing women were present by their absence. The sisters, mothers, aunts, and daughters who had disappeared were held present by their family members and friends. Their faces were on tee-shirts, their bodies embracing family or friends were illuminated onscreen, their smiles were frozen in snapshots on the honour wall. The telling of their taking was given voice by grieving mothers or nieces or sisters, and their voices whispered to us in the telling. We were acutely aware of their absent presence, space made for them in the body of women and men gathered to honour their stories.

We knew the end to some of the stories when we learned that a woman's body was found and a family was able to give her a place to rest. Others were suspended tales, waiting for some evidence of what had happened and where she was. Bodies found are lives found, endings able to be told. Bodies missing are lost, tales unfinished. In Christian tradition, as in others, a body is never just a body. Bodies are spirited, breathing. They hold life, and when breath is gone their spirit no longer lives in them. Where and how spirit/life moves on is understood differently in different spiritual traditions, but all have some way of honouring the body to honour the life it breathed. Prayers are said, rituals observed. We do not let a body go unnoticed to the grave, for to do so is to let someone's life slip away from the earth unnoticed. It would be a final violation of her life. That, I believe, is one of the reasons that having women missing is so painful. Without their bodies to honour, it is impossible to know how, or if, their life ended; their story is incomplete. And it is very difficult to grieve because placing bodies in the ground or scattering ashes (or however we choose to care for the body) helps us to mark a moment of finality. It frees us to begin to let the ones we love go. We, and they, can move on. It is much harder to do this when bodies are unfound and stories unfinished. Grief is suspended and we are not at rest. We need to remind ourselves that they are missing to us but not to the Creator. The One who birthed them to the earth knows where on the earth their bodies lay. Their spirits, too, have a home with the Holy One. It is we who cannot rest.

The fact that women are missing and bodies cannot be found is yet another act of violence in a violent story. During the conference the violence that we brought to the gathering in our bodied stories wound together with the violence done to the women whose bodies were violated. How we responded to that violence was also bodied. Whether we cried or were angry or were afraid, our bodies expressed it through harsh voices, weeping eyes, trembling hands, tense shoulders, aching backs and so on. In many ways we were in a constant state of grief. We grieved what we were missing, we grieved the women who were lost, and we grieved a society that lets it happen. Grief wears on the heart and mind; it frays the soul; it drains the body.

To resist the violence and the grief it engendered, the sacred space room was created. Envisioned by young adults and Elders of Aboriginal and Christian traditions, the sacred space focused on what we had in common—our spirited bodies. All the senses were engaged within the space we created. There was tea to be sipped and there were berries to be tasted. There was cedar to be smelt. There were chimes and running water to be heard. There were stones of varying hues to be seen and touched and taken. There were plants of varying sizes to breathe with us and cleanse the air. The overhead lights were dimmed; instead, candles and "firefly" lights rested the eyes. There were comfortable chairs and rockers in which to rest. There were cushions and stuffed animals and shawls from which to draw comfort. All of it was meant to create a gentle and sacred space. Attentiveness to the body was attentiveness to the spirit. It was also an act of resistance to violence. As we discussed missing women and bodies that had no final resting place, the sacred space gave our bodies a place to rest, our spirits a place to heal. In the sacred space, rather than being violated, bodies were honoured. There women met to sit together in silence, to tell stories, to protest, to weep, and to laugh. Body and soul were rewoven after the fraying of grief.

The conference came to a close with a traditional round dance. As we moved together in a circle, holding hands, we celebrated the women who were missing, we acknowledged what was missing in our lives, and we affirmed our determination to move beyond the violence. Our bodies danced and our spirits lifted. The laughter we shared as we ended our time together filled the space with hope. Violence may enter our lives and mark our bodies, but we will not allow it to determine our character or our world. We will dance together, shaping a future in which women of every colour and every land are honoured as the gifts of the Creator they are meant to be.

ENDNOTES

1. Elaine L. Graham, *Making the Difference: Gender, Personhood and Theology* (London: Mowbray, 1995), 131.

The Significance of Sacred Space:
Reflections upon Conversations with
Elder Norma-Jean Byrd and Pastor Cheryl Toth

CHELSEA MILLMAN

lthough the "Missing Women: Decolonization, Third Wave Feminism and Indigenous People of Canada and Mexico" conference included many academic voices and was sponsored by many academic institutions and organizations, it was unlike any academic conference most people have ever attended. This conference was not only a space to explore ideas situated in race theory, post-colonial theory and feminist theory, to share personal feelings and emotions, and to engage in intercultural dialogue; it was also a space where spiritual dialogue took place. It was a healing space. Situated in a dimly lit corner on the periphery of the conference space was a room that was named the "Sacred Space." The creation of this space was initiated by Pastor Cheryl Toth, Elder Norma-Jean Byrd, and Elder Betty McKenna.

The "Sacred Space" was not tradition-specific, in that it had symbols that could be seen as sacred symbols but that didn't *necessarily* have to be viewed as sacred. Pastor Cheryl Toth viewed the creation of such a space as naturally developing over the course of many conversations with people from differing faith communities. She said, "My intention was to be clear that we could have a space with elements that could be seen as sacred

A Métis woman who was raised in southern Saskatchewan, **CHELSEA MILLMAN** was a member of the Core Planning Group for the "Missing Women" conference. Chelsea began working on the issue of missing and murdered women in April 2007.

traditions without being tradition-specific. The most sensitive issue might have been if the symbols were predominantly Christian, because of the legacy of residential schools, racism, and colonialism." Throughout her interview it was very apparent that she was not only aware of, but also sensitive to and willing to accept, the need to be inclusive of Indigenous spirituality in an authentic way within the "Sacred Space."

When thinking about the space itself, all committee members believed that the most important factor in creating a safe and successful space would be to "really engage the senses" and to "engage the spirit by entering into the body" in every area of the space. Sound was engaged with the use of calming nature sounds, the stillness of the room, a water fountain, and wind chimes. Although the "Sacred Space" was housed in a room without wind, guests were encouraged to reach out and touch the wind chimes as they entered the room. Taste was engaged by providing guests with a selection of fruits and herbal teas. Dried roses, sage, cedar, and red willow were used to engage the sense of smell. Dim lighting, coloured cloth hanging in each direction, and small white lights on the ceiling to symbolize fireflies were used to engage sight. Touch was engaged with fabrics of differing textures and rocks that could be held and/or rubbed.

A sense of home was also created in the space, in that most of the furniture and objects in the room were brought by the Sacred Space committee members from their own homes. This was done not only for comfort but also to create a sense of security and safety. The need for such a space was evident throughout the conference, as conference volunteers entered the room to find conference attendees sleeping, holding teddy bears, and cuddling under warm blankets. Although used by many people, the "Sacred Space" was a very personal, private space.

This space would not have been possible without the contributions of these three amazing, open-minded, wise women. These women are proof that differing traditions can come together to create a safe, spiritual, and loving environment for all who participate. We thank you all for your brave spirits and open hearts.

FAMILY STORIES

PRESENTATION

"MISSING WOMEN" CONFERENCE, FRIDAY, AUGUST 15, 2008.

TRANSLATED INTO ENGLISH BY A VOLUNTEER AT THE CONFERENCE,

THEN TRANSCRIBED AND RETOLD IN THE THIRD PERSON BY CHELSEA MILLMAN.

The Story of the Disappearance of Sylvia Arce

EVA ARCE

Evanjalena (Eva) Arce spoke of her missing daughter, Sylvia Arce. Her daughter disappeared on March 11, 1998. Although it has been almost ten years since she disappeared, no one knows where she is or what happened to her. When Eva first realized that her daughter had gone missing, she did not share this information with anyone because she was afraid of retaliation from the authorities. Instead, Eva began to search for her daughter herself. After four days of searching she realized her daughter was not going to come home on her own.

On the day Sylvia went missing, she had gone to a bar to get paid by the dancers who worked there for the jewelry and cosmetics she sold them. Eva went to the bar to ask questions, but no one had seen Sylvia for days. Even though she was not getting any information from the people who owned and worked at the bar, Eva kept searching. After being told very contradictory and suspicious stories by the people at the bar, she finally went to the authorities. The authorities told her they couldn't do anything about it because it was Saturday and the police don't work on weekends. She was told to go back to the police station to file the report the following Monday. After a week had passed she went back to the police and they laughed at her. An attorney then told her that the police had done their investigation and they hadn't found anything. The attorney told her to go and speak to another officer, who laughed at her and said, "What on earth are you doing? Why are you here looking for your daughter when she is likely out partying, taking drugs, and drinking. Go home. The only thing I can tell you is to look for a youth centre for rehabilitation purposes for her when she does come home."

Because of the way she was treated, Eva, along with two of her co-workers, held a demonstration in front of the police station and continued to hold these demonstrations for almost a year. Soon, many, many people who had lost their loved ones came to support them during their protests. Rather than changing their investigative policies, the police responded by telling everyone to go home and never to hold another demonstration. The police threatened the mothers by telling them that if they didn't stop demonstrating, the police wouldn't help them find their daughters.

Eva explained that the chief of police was involved in many of the disappearances of young women. Many police officers were also in contact with the people who stole young women from the area. Many of the young women who were stolen were kept in a house that belonged to the chief of police. In the house there was a book that contained pictures of all of the women. Men could choose which woman they wanted by looking at a picture in the book. One young woman, a dancer, who was forced to stay in the house escaped. She did not want to go to the police or tell anyone what had happened because she had been drugged and beaten up. When the "guards" realized she had escaped, some of them searched for her and told her that if she told anyone what happened they would kill her, her family, and her children. Thankfully, she had the courage to make copies of the pictures from the book. Pictures of some of the police officers and even the chief of police were in the book. An organization gave Eva the funds to go to Barracruise in order to talk to the chief of police, to find out what had happened to her daughter. She knew he was implicated in the disappearance of her daughter in some way, because he was in jail for kidnapping the other women who were kept in his house. When she finally had everything ready to go to Barracruise, she was told it was useless to go because the chief of police was no longer in jail and, in fact, was no longer even in Mexico.

Eva continues her struggle to this day, even though she has faced so much frustration, anger, sadness, and corruption. Eva says, "I have become stronger, and I only ask God that he gives me strength to keep going because I'm not going to quit. I'm not going to take one step backwards, even if I am threatened or beaten. Finally, I want to thank the organizers of this event, because losing a daughter is not easy; it is painful. I just want to tell you that there are many of us. There are many like me who have daughters who have disappeared. It's very difficult to forgive those who have done so much damage to us. I am so sorry for those Canadian moms who have also lost their daughters, because when one of our daughters is taken from us, it causes a lot of pain. Let's hold hands. Let's keep working on this. Let's go on with the struggle."

PRESENTATION
"MISSING WOMEN" CONFERENCE, FRIDAY, AUGUST 15, 2008.
TRANSLATED INTO ENGLISH BY A VOLUNTEER AT THE CONFERENCE,
THEN TRANSCRIBED AND RETOLD IN THE THIRD PERSON BY CHELSEA MILLMAN.

The Story of the Disappearance of Maria Sagrario Flores

PAULA FLORES

Paula Flores's 17-year-old daughter, Sagrario, went missing in 1999 on her way home from the factory where she worked. Besides working in a factory, Sagrario also helped with catechism lessons in the Catholic school in her neighborhood. She was learning how to play the guitar and she loved to write poetry. Sagrario worked the same shift as her father at the factory, but for legal reasons the factory owners changed her shift. Two months after her shift was changed, Sagrario disappeared.

When her daughter didn't return home, Paula knew something bad had happened because her daughter never went anywhere after work without permission. Sagrario was missing for two weeks before the authorities found her body in a place called "The White Hill" in Juárez. Paula was not informed of this by the police; instead, a reporter told Paula that a woman's murdered and raped body had been found and that the body was likely Sagrario's.

Paula's son went to identify the body, but was unable to confirm that it was Sagrario because the coroner had already begun an autopsy. In September of 1999, a DNA test was performed and the test results indicated that the body was not Sagrario's. This gave Paula hope that her daughter was still alive. Suspicious events then took place and Paula's family asked if their daughter's body could be exhumed and another DNA test performed. The authorities exhumed a body, but it was the wrong body from the wrong gravesite. Eventually the authorities did exhume the correct body and confirmed that it was in fact Paula's daughter, Sagrario. To this day, however, Paula constantly wonders if that body was in fact her daughter's or if the authorities lied to her.

A man has been in jail for three years for Sagrario's murder, but he claims that there were two other people involved. This man said the other two people paid him $500 to take them to where Sagrario worked. He even gave the authorities the names, addresses, and pictures of the people who killed Sagrario, but to this day the police have not investigated these leads. Because of this, Paula believes that the authorities and even the governor are complicit in all of the murders and disappearances. The authorities, however, are not punished for their involvement, but are instead promoted. Paula says that "the only thing that seems to be important in Juárez to the authorities is that we quit messing up their city with our crosses. They want to kind of sideswipe the issue. All the news and all their concerns are on drug trafficking and all the drug issues that are happening, and they are trying to take away the limelight from the missing women. And so we are just being pushed aside."

Throughout all this tragedy, however, Paula says, "I ask God to help me to forgive. I want to have the same strength that Gwenda* has. I want to have her peace. And we are united, no matter what the distance is. We are united."

---

*Gwenda Yuzicappi, the mother of Amber Redman. Her story—"Wicanhpi Duta Win"/Red Star Woman—is found on page 40.

Sisters in Spirit

The Sisters in Spirit initiative is a multi-year research, education, and policy initiative of the Native Women's Association of Canada (NWAC), designed to address the disturbing numbers of missing and murdered Aboriginal women and girls in Canada.*

Voices of Our Sisters in Spirit: A Report to Families and Communities, now available for free download in its second edition at www.nwac-hq.org, summarizes information gained through storytelling (interviews) with families of missing and murdered Aboriginal women and girls. Using the life cycle as a guide, families are invited to share the life stories of their daughters, sisters, mothers, and grandmothers. The life stories are placed within the broader framework of other work conducted through the Sisters in Spirit initiative and serve to confirm conclusions based on other research, to illustrate common themes, to inform policy recommendations, and to identify future directions for further investigation.

This second edition includes new life stories of our missing or stolen sisters and messages from their families. Also included are an expanded research framework, updated research results, and reports on communications and education highlights. It concludes with interim Sisters in Spirit

---

* See "The Sisters in Spirit Initiative: Native Women's Association of Canada" by Judy Hughes on page 208 for a full description of the activities of Sisters in Spirit.

trends and recommendations developed to address the serious levels of violence against Aboriginal women and girls in Canada. Addressed to family and community members, this report represents the Native Women's Association of Canada's commitment to sharing our work with those most intimately concerned with this important issue.

The stories that follow—the story of Daleen Kay Bosse (Muskego) and the story of Amber Tara-Lynn Redman—are taken from *Voices of Our Sisters in Spirit.*

Daleen Kay Bosse and her daughter, Faith, when Faith was seven months old.

The Story of the Disappearance of Daleen Kay Bosse (Muskego), *March 25, 1979—May 19, 2004**

PAULINE AND HERB MUSKEGO

Daleen's story was written in the spring and early summer of 2008. In August 2008, she was found ten miles north of Saskatoon, near Martensville, Saskatchewan. Daleen's family has provided an update, which appears at the end of this story.

Daleen Kay Bosse (Muskego) was last seen on May 18, 2004, in Saskatoon, Saskatchewan. Her family has been looking for her since, organizing search parties and awareness walks, establishing a toll-free number, and financing trips across Canada to investigate tips. Her family and friends want answers; they want to know what has happened to the beautiful and outgoing woman who wants to be a teacher, who loves to make people laugh, who has a passion for drama and fine arts. They want to know what has happened to their beloved daughter, sister, mother, wife, and friend.

Daleen was born on March 25, 1979, in Saskatoon, Saskatchewan. Her parents, Herb and Pauline Muskego, were overjoyed by her arrival. Herb and Pauline would have two more children, and Daleen quickly matured

---

*Reprinted from *Voices of Our Sisters in Spirit: A Report to Families and Communities,* www.nwac-hq.org.

into a caring, devoted, and protective sister to her younger brothers, Dana and David. Pauline, both of her parents, and Herb's mother had attended residential school, and these experiences made the Muskegos absolutely determined to be good parents, to give their children a different experience than their own.

As a girl, Daleen spent time in both Saskatoon and in her home community of Onion Lake Cree Nation. Her extended family was very involved in her life. They taught her Cree greetings, beadwork, and how to make bannock. Daleen was particularly close to her grandmother, and Herb recalls how little "Daleen sko" (meaning Daleen Woman in Cree) loved to recount every detail of their time together. As an infant, Daleen was given a Cree name in a traditional ceremony and was later dedicated in the church.

As parents, Herb and Pauline wanted their children to see as much of the world as possible. They tried to broaden the children's horizons, taking them to fairs, on trips to Edmonton and the mountains, and bigger trips to Disneyland and Mexico. Herb and Pauline tried to include their children in everything they did. The family would often have a concession booth at powwows and Daleen would work alongside her siblings, parents, and grandparents. "Broadening horizons" also meant working to give Daleen and her brothers the opportunity to try different sports and activities. As a girl Daleen was incredibly active. She took ballet lessons, swimming lessons, skating, piano, gymnastics, acting; she tried a bit of everything!

Daleen was only 13 when she got her first job working in a restaurant. She was determined to start working and, although her parents did not push her to get a job, they were incredibly proud to see her do so. A few years later, in grade ten, she got a job in a Lloydminster bank as part of a high school work experience initiative.

In high school, Daleen became involved in drama and speech writing. She was a very good actress and quickly developed a love for drama and the arts. She was also involved in modelling and public speaking. Daleen would later act for the Saskatoon Native Theatre in one of its very first plays, the making of which was chronicled in the 2003 documentary *Circle of Voices*. In addition to her passion for the arts, Daleen was also academically inclined, earning excellent grades. An ambitious girl, she talked about becoming a doctor or a lawyer. Her parents encouraged her to follow her dreams, telling Daleen and her brothers that they had the potential to become whatever they wanted to be. Both Pauline and Herb are teachers, and Pauline believes that their work had an influence on Daleen, who would eventually decide to become a teacher as well.

Daleen's outgoing nature brought her many close friends. People were drawn to her caring personality and her positive outlook. She had a real impact on those around her. Shortly after she disappeared, Herb and Pauline received a concerned call from Daleen's eighth grade teacher. After inquiring about her whereabouts, he commented that Daleen was "one of his all-time excellent students." And months later, at one of the many searches organized to look for Daleen, another reminder of her compassionate nature came when a young man stepped forward, saying he had come to search because Daleen had helped him with his schoolwork when they were younger.

After graduating from high school Daleen considered applying for a theatre program in Toronto, but ultimately decided to stay in Saskatoon near her friends and family. She eventually settled on a course in business administration. It was here that Daleen met her future husband, Jeremiah. After six months of dating, Jeremiah proposed to Daleen on Valentine's Day. They were married in 1999 and their daughter Faith was born two years later. At the time of her disappearance, Daleen was beginning her fourth year as a student at the University of Saskatchewan where she was studying to become a teacher like her parents.

Daleen was last seen on May 18, 2004, outside a Saskatoon nightclub. She never came home. When Jeremiah woke up the next morning and realized that Daleen was missing, he immediately called the Saskatoon Police Service (SPS). An officer came to the house, asked two or three questions, and left. The family characterizes the police response as "being shrugged off and brushed to the side." It was Daleen's family who made the first missing person posters, plastering them all over Saskatoon. After eight desperate days of searching, the family hired a private investigator to assist them in finding Daleen.

In the 2007 documentary, *Stolen Sisters,* Sergeant Phil Farion attempts to explain the Saskatoon Police Service's response by saying, "Because right off the bat you would say, 'Well there's no reason for my family member to leave, so it has to be criminal. Someone has taken her. It has to be.' And yet, oftentimes it's not and sometimes people go away and come back." Daleen's family and friends are unmoved by this reasoning saying simply, but resolutely, that Daleen would never leave her daughter for so long; she would never not call.

On June 4, two weeks after Daleen went missing, a family friend spotted Daleen and Jeremiah's white Cavalier parked on a street off Central Avenue. He immediately called Jeremiah, then the police. A search revealed that the steering wheel cover, floor mats and seat covers had been removed from the vehicle and that Faith's car seat had been moved. In addition, several hundred kilometres had been put on the vehicle. To the surprise of Daleen's family and friends, police did not perform a forensic search of the vehicle. They did, however, dust the car for prints, but found none. Daleen's family, friends, and the private investigator hired by the Muskegos believe that the missing items are related to Daleen's disappearance, evidence of an obvious "clean-up." The police were unconvinced, saying that the items might have been stolen from the vehicle during the three week period it sat abandoned. Investigators did not hold the car for long; it was returned to Jeremiah two or three days after it was found.

Seven months after her car was found abandoned, Daleen was still missing. Her credit cards and bank account remained untouched. In January 2005, the SPS announced that Daleen's disappearance was "more serious than a missing person that doesn't want to be found." A press conference was held and police appealed to the public to help them in locating the items taken from Daleen's vehicle. Police also performed a complete forensic investigation of the vehicle, but found nothing. However, it is possible that forensic evidence *was* present at the time the car was recovered, but was lost (through wear or routine cleaning) during the seven months the car was in use. It is very difficult for Daleen's family to consider that valuable forensic evidence may have been lost due to police inaction. They are left to wonder if a more thorough investigation of the vehicle would have yielded a break in the case, a clue that might have led them to Daleen.

When asked about their relationship with the police in Saskatoon the Muskegos use words like "injustice," "anger," and "roadblocks" to describe their experiences. In the days after their daughter went missing it quickly became apparent that police believed Daleen was going to come home on her own. When Herb and Pauline filed a missing person report, police were quick to emphasize that most missing persons return home within 10 to 14 days. When weeks passed without any communication from Daleen, police replaced their initial assurances with new ones, telling Herb and Pauline that missing persons often return home for important family events like birthdays or Christmas and to wait a little longer.

Again and again the Muskegos were told to wait. When they pressed for action they were met with resistance, apathy, and in some instances, patronizing excuses. Pauline recalls one particular instance in which the sergeant responsible for the case responded to their concerns by saying that the files for missing persons in Saskatchewan were a foot high. He said, "These are the missing persons cases that are in Saskatchewan right now. And your daughter's is right here, down at the bottom." The Muskegos were told repeatedly that cases concerning missing children had priority, and while they respect this policy Herb and Pauline say *something* should have been done about their daughter's disappearance. Instead, they feel the police response amounted to saying, "Ok, she's missing. Stick her there on the pile. She's just a number." Many times they tried to see the sergeant responsible for missing persons only to be told he was not there. They came to feel as though no one was doing anything at all.

Frustrated by the lack of cooperation and the unwillingness of police to accept Daleen's disappearance as a serious case, Herb and Pauline made complaints. They voiced their anger and demanded action. The police responded by citing the numerous tips they had received about Daleen's whereabouts, that she had been seen here or there and not to worry—she was going to come home. The Muskegos felt, however, that the police were attaching too much weight to the supposed sightings, sightings that were in their opinion unsubstantiated. A few weeks after she went missing police received a tip that Daleen had been seen at a bank in Saskatoon, the same bank where she had worked after graduating from the business administration program. Newspaper reports suggest that police were fairly confident about the sighting since the tip came from a woman who had worked with Daleen. Herb and Pauline regarded the sighting with caution; they wanted proof. However, when asked to see the bank's surveillance footage they were told that the cameras were down on the day of the sighting. They then asked police to check Daleen's bank records as the woman had been seen waiting in line to access an ATM. They were told that there was no record of any transaction. In fact, the only evidence that Daleen had ever been in the bank rested with the word of a woman who had not seen Daleen for years.

Daleen was supposedly seen at several other Saskatoon locations: a mall, a 7-Eleven, a nightclub. In each instance Herb and Pauline asked to view surveillance tapes and in each instance they were told by police that it was not necessary for them to see the footage. Pauline considers the unwillingness of police to share surveillance footage one of the most frustrating roadblocks in their search for Daleen. The police wanted Herb and Pauline to accept that Daleen had disappeared willingly yet refused to provide them with any real proof that this was actually the case. And without proof Herb and Pauline say they had no choice but to continue looking. "Without proof, we'll continue to look forever until we find her," says Pauline.

When Christmas 2004 passed with no communication from Daleen, the Muskegos had had enough. They were very active in the month of January, increasing not only their search efforts but also their engagement with the media. In the months after Daleen went missing, Pauline made a point of avoiding the media. She says talking about Daleen's disappearance was too hard; she could not face being interviewed, and both she and Herb worried about how their family might be portrayed. It was the coverage surrounding the death of Neil Stonechild that eventually changed their minds about the media. The attention surrounding the case, as well as statements by family members crediting certain reporters for their coverage, showed them that the media could be used as tool, a tool to raise awareness about Daleen's disappearance and assist them in their search. Since then, they have been trying to use the media as much as possible. In addition to the support they have received from family, from their community, and from other organizations like the Federation of Saskatchewan Indian Nations (FSIN) and Child Find Canada, the Muskegos say that their engagement with the media has led to support from other groups and individuals that otherwise might not have known about Daleen's disappearance.

After months of frustration and no discernable police action, the Muskegos lodged a complaint with the FSIN Special Investigations Unit. Herb and Pauline believe it was this action that prompted the SPS finally to respond seriously to Daleen's disappearance. Herb goes on to note that something curious happened after Daleen's disappearance was declared a criminal investigation. Herb called to speak to the sergeant responsible for missing persons and was surprised to learn that he was no longer there, that he had retired. Pauline and Herb do not know if the sergeant's seemingly abrupt exit was merely coincidental, but they consider the timing suggestive.

In December 2006, Chief Clive Weighill of the SPS came to Onion Lake to speak to Daleen's family and the chief and council about the police response to Daleen's disappearance. The family had mixed feelings about the visit. While they appreciated the gesture, Daleen is still missing and they cannot help but feel that the case would have been handled differently if Daleen was not an Aboriginal woman. Herb says, "It is not from their goodwill that they decided they were going to look seriously at the case. It was because of our consistency. We were at their door . . . My family, my community." Daleen's family continues to search, continues to pray for their daughter, for their sister, for their mother, wife, and friend. For Daleen.

Update (October 2008)

AUGUST 10, 2008. *Chief Weighill, true to his word, requested a meeting in person to inform the family of new information they had received about Daleen.*

AUGUST 11, 2008. *The accused made his first court appearance in Saskatoon. He was charged with first-degree murder and indignity to a body. Daleen's family describes the second charge as "excruciatingly painful," as they did not know that Daleen's body had been burned.*

AUGUST 12, 2008. *The accused made his second court appearance in Saskatoon. And so on and so on. The preliminary hearing is scheduled to begin in April 2009.*

Amber Tara-Lynn Redman.

Wicanhpi Duta Win / Red Star Woman:
Amber Redman's Story*

GWENDA YUZICAPPI

mber Tara-Lynn Redman was born on January 30, 1986. Amber was from Standing Buffalo Dakota Nation; she was the middle child and only daughter of loving parents, Gwenda Yuzicappi and Art Redman, Sr. She was very close to her older brother, Bevin, and her younger brother, Dreyden. Amber went missing on July 15, 2005, and after almost three years of searching her remains were found on May 5, 2008.

Amber led a beautiful life filled with positive experiences. From the moment she was born at the General Hospital in Regina, Saskatchewan, Amber was loved by her mother and father. She brought joy into her family's life and made everyone happy. Amber was breastfed and this mother-daughter bond continued as she grew into a chubby baby. When relatives came to visit baby Amber, she would run to the door to greet them, her thick hair sticking out in all directions. Family members would constantly pick Amber up and place her on one of her favourite toys, a rocking horse. Amber was a "daddy's girl" who was very spoiled; her father would carry her around until she fell asleep in his arms.

*Reprinted from *Voices of Our Sisters in Spirit: A Report to Families and Communities*, www.nwac-hq.org.

As Amber transitioned from baby to toddler, she became adventurous and mischievous. Her mother, Gwenda, remembers that Amber loved to be outside and could often be found wandering around in the bushes or playing with the puppies. When she was indoors Amber would watch her favourite show, *The Flintstones,* with her teddy bear. An intelligent toddler, Amber knew exactly what time the show would play.

When she was three years old Amber's father, Art Sr., designed and beaded her first fancy dance outfit in her favourite colours, purple and pink, and her parents travelled with her on the powwow trail. Amber felt the pride of being a Dakota Winyan (woman), and dancing to the heartbeat of the drum inspired her Spirit to dance with All The Relatives. Amber danced to be a part of the Sacred Circle and to strengthen her Spirit; it was not about winning. Her spirit shone brightly as each step was a glimpse of what she was feeling. Amber enjoyed the inexplicable experience of being one with the Wannage (Spirit). Another inspiration for Amber was the Dakota language. This gift was taught by her great-grandmother, the late Agnes Yuzicappi (Wakan Win); Unchi (Grandma) would speak in Dakota to Amber. Amber listened with her heart and captured each teaching there. Unchi inspired Amber to receive her Dakota name and Amber was honoured with the gift of her name "Wicanhpi Duta Win" (Red Star Woman). She wanted to learn about the Star Teachings, which are a vital part of the Dakota history. The family would see "Wicanhpi Duta Win" as she shone brightly as a "Red Star" in the night sky.

As she entered childhood, Amber's parents ensured that she had a balance of traditional Dakota and western influences in her life. Gwenda and Art Sr. practiced the Dakota traditions. Amber's parents allowed their children to choose the paths they wanted to follow. When she was 14 years old, an Elder asked Amber if she would consider being the Sundance Mother. Amber was honoured to replay the history of the White Buffalo Calf Woman, who brought the teachings of the Sacred Pipe to the Lakota People. Amber witnessed and felt the power of prayer, sacrifice, being humble, and being close to Wakan Tanka (Great Spirit). At the end of this experience Amber left the Sacred Pipe for the People to continue to practice this teaching. She then exited on the same path that she began and turned four times with a wave to her Dakota Oyate (family). All the Helpers, Sundancers and Relatives felt in their Hearts the Love and Power of Prayer, which are the greatest gifts given by the Creator. Amber's mind, body, and spirit were in balance. Each story tells of Amber's life experiences; she was seen in the Stars, the Animals, the Trees, the Rocks. Everything on Mother Earth has a Spirit and a Teaching.

Amber's beauty was seen by a person who did not know her at all. This experience illustrates the teaching that some people have a gift that allows them to see the spirits of others. Here is a story told by Amber's cousin, Jessica:

Amber and Jessica attended a memorable powwow in Bismarck, North Dakota. There was a young man staying beside their campsite. When this young man saw Amber he fell in love with her beauty. He introduced himself to Amber and told her that she looked like a "princess." He then asked if she would do him a favour. Amber was shy and turned away, but Jessica encouraged her to listen to his request. The young man asked if she would take a picture with him coming out of the tipi. Amber began to laugh and walk away but the young man persisted, explaining that his fellow singers would not believe he had a picture of himself with this "princess." Jessica once again encouraged Amber and insisted that there would be no harm in having this picture taken. Finally, Amber agreed and they took the photograph. Amber felt embarrassed when she saw how happy this picture made him. When Amber went missing in 2005 and this young man saw her poster at a powwow, he asked Jessica, "Is this my princess?" When Jessica said yes, he turned and walked away from the powwow. Jessica felt his sorrow.

Amber shared in the joy of her family's accomplishments and made sure to support their dreams and aspirations. Her older brother, Bevin, competed in basketball at the North American Indigenous Games (NAIG) and he told Amber that he wanted her to watch his game. Amber had recently started a new job. When she asked for the time off work and was denied, Amber followed her heart and decided to quit. She explained to her employer that her brother was her priority and watching him play against New York was a once-in-a-lifetime experience. Amber was excited to watch Bevin play his best. The whole family was proud of Bevin. When the game was over, Gwenda took Amber and Dreyden to eat at a revolving restaurant at the top of a high-rise building (Bevin had to stay with his team). The three of them shared in the experience of tasting escargot. Dreyden said he was eating octopus, and Amber used her fork to pick it up so she could see, smell, and then taste it. She said it was gross. Gwenda enjoyed watching each of their reactions as these experiences are kept in a mother's heart. Gwenda strongly believes the greatest gift from the Creator is the gift of a child.

Amber saw gifts given by the Creator. Amber and her mom witnessed a gift being born and Amber named this baby girl after her late paternal grandfather and her late paternal great-grandmother. Amber became one with the baby and later encouraged her mom to bring the baby home. Amber asked if she could adopt the beautiful little girl and Gwenda agreed. Amber's heart pounded with excitement when she held her baby girl.

To this day, the young girl talks endlessly about Amber. When she sees Gwenda struggling, she sits down beside Gwenda and uses her healing hands to caress Gwenda's hair and wipe her tears. She tells stories of Amber. Only Amber knew of this young girl's gifts, and Gwenda will ensure she reaches her full potential.

Amber was athletic and enjoyed playing basketball and volleyball in high school. She and five friends from Standing Buffalo were on the basketball and volleyball teams, and Amber loved travelling with them to compete in tournaments. Amber's passion for sports and being with her team showed when she played. She smiled at her teammates, played her best, and used humour in each game.

After she disappeared Amber sent a message to her loving companion, Cody, when he went to NAIG in Denver, Colorado. Once a great athlete, Cody stopped playing sports after Amber went missing. When he decided to return, he tried out for the North American Indigenous Games and made the Saskatchewan athletics (track and field) team. The night before the competition began he dreamed of Amber. In his dream he felt Amber was real. He held her and continually told her, "Oh, my God, I can't believe I am with you!" Amber took Cody to the very top of the mountain where the clouds were below. In the dream he took off his jacket and put it on the ground so that Amber could sit down. Cody tickled and hugged her and watched every smile. He especially remembers her laughter echoing in the air. Amber asked Cody why he stopped playing sports until then. She knew of his potential. Amber pointed into the clouds and Cody saw his bedroom wall and on it were three medals. Cody was so happy to be with Amber that he did not think of the medals. All he wanted to do was hold her and keep her close. He was not going to let her go.

Cody woke up and realized it was a dream. He quickly called Gwenda and told her of his dream. Gwenda and Cody became emotional over the phone and Gwenda told Cody that no matter where he is, distance is not a factor. Her spirit travelled to his and this is where their spirits united as one. Gwenda explained to Cody that he would always be her only son-in-law; he would always be a part of her family. Gwenda said to Cody, "Amber brought you a message to be the best, the athlete she knows you to be. Cody, follow your heart and your dreams will come true." Cody came home with three medals, which are with Amber's medals.

Amber's childhood and youth were not without some hardship. Amber was unhappy when her parents separated. Additionally, as a teenager Amber was bullied by girls who were jealous of her relationship with her boyfriend. Because her teachings instructed her not to fight but to leave the situation, Amber endured the pain of verbal abuse without retaliating. She came home crying and the anger grew in her Mother's Heart as Amber told her mom of the experience. Her mom suggested they talk with the girls. Amber's response was, "No, Mom, I just want to forget this happened." Gwenda held her daughter close and told her everything would be all right. Amber fell asleep in her mother's arms. Gwenda thinks the moral of this story is forgiveness; in spite of the pain she endured, Amber forgave these three young girls for their verbal abuse and for keeping her cornered in a room. Gwenda has a message for Amber: "My girl, as your mother, I now understand why you chose not to confront these young girls but to forgive in your heart."

Amber was a very independent woman. She bought herself a car with her bingo winnings. Driving on a grid road through mud, slush, and snow was hard on the car; it needed a mirror, a muffler, and an oil change. Amber bought the parts and drove her car onto a ramp in her driveway where she herself changed the oil and replaced the muffler. Two of Bevin's friends came over while Amber was working on the car and asked Bevin what she was doing. Bevin told them that Amber had just given her car an oil change and was now changing her muffler. Bevin's friends laughed and insisted Amber did not know how to repair these things. When they realized that Amber really was fixing her car, they felt embarrassed and resorted to teasing one another. Amber's ability to accept and complete a challenge was evident on this day. Bevin was so proud of his sister and how she showed up his friends.

On July 15, 2005, Amber went to Trapper's Bar in Fort Qu'Appelle with Cody and her cousin Tommy. Earlier that day Amber had been paid for babysitting and had taken her aunt and cousins out for pizza and chicken. By the time Gwenda got home Amber was already gone. It was unlike Amber to go out to the bar on a Thursday night. When Gwenda asked the waitress about Amber, she said she served Amber only two drinks and was surprised when Amber fell and appeared intoxicated. Gwenda believes something was slipped into Amber's drink. Amber and Cody had an argument in the bar that night and Cody left. Tommy said he went to the bathroom and when he came out he could not find Amber. Amber had Tommy's car keys so he called his mom, who came to get him. This was the last time Amber was seen by those close to her.

Cody called Gwenda every day to see if Amber was home. When Gwenda asked what happened, Cody told her about the argument. Knowing this, Gwenda told Cody that Amber might need some time and advised him to call back the next day. On Monday morning, Cody filed a missing persons report, then called Gwenda to tell her. Gwenda was in shock. Six days after Amber was last seen, Gwenda, her family, and the community organized the first of a series of searches that lasted for three weeks. The neighbouring communities volunteered to help out. Gwenda's family and community continued to search endlessly. It took nine days before the media began to cover Amber's disappearance. Despite this delay, Gwenda felt that the media coverage of Amber as a missing woman was both helpful and respectful.

Gwenda does not believe that the police took immediate action to initiate a search. The police explained to the family that they were following a process where they had to contact and interview everyone in the bar, and Gwenda understood that this process was time-consuming. Gwenda asked to deal primarily with a female First Nations police officer and this request was honoured. As the days passed, police gave the family daily updates, offered support, and let them know that officers were only a phone call away. It is evident that the police's determination and dedication resulted in locating Amber's remains. The Yuzicappi and Redman families showed their gratitude towards the many law enforcement officers who participated in this process by shaking each one of their hands and thanking them for their efforts. As Amber's mother, Gwenda understands that although none of the officers knew Amber, seeing her picture spoke a thousand words. Gwenda believes in the prayers that were also sent to the police officers to assist in their efforts.

Amber and her family received strength from the Unchi Hanwi Oyate (Grandmother Nation). As each full moon passed, the Grandmother's face appeared in the moon and her lips whispered prayers onto the family. Gwenda has a message for the Grandmother: "Unchi, I know in my heart you are with me during this time of hardship. Unchi, you told my Tanke (younger sister) that when the family smells the scent of sweetgrass you are with us. Your strength is felt as each second passes and only you know the pain endured in this travesty. Unchi, I am starting to grasp the understanding that Wakan Tanka (Great Spirit) honoured me with the gift of Wicanhpi Duta Win. Through my Ancestral Teachings, I was sought out to be one of the Inas (Mothers) who is able to gain strength from these teachings with the power of prayer. I know, Unchi, that you were with Wicanhpi Duta Win along with All Our Relatives. As a mother, knowing this gives me so much comfort as I now understand Wicanhpi Duta Win was not alone."

Gwenda and Amber's family believe strongly in the power of prayer and hoped for Amber's safe return home. Her family continually asked the Grandmother Nation to help locate their loved one. The enduring pain of not knowing where Amber was and whether or not she was safe was excruciating for her mother, brothers, grandmother, sisters, her loving companion, aunts, uncles, cousins, and nieces, as well as for the loved ones who have journeyed to the Spirit World, including her father, uncles, aunts, and grandmother. The family's love for Amber was in the hands of the Creator. As each season passed, the family fed Amber's Dakota Spirit to keep her spirit alive. The family did not know where Amber was so they asked the Creator to keep her alive in their hearts.

On May 5, 2008, Amber's remains were located. The Yuzicappi and Redman families went to the site where she was found to offer prayers and sing the sacred songs. The ceremony was one of the many that the family held regarding Amber's journey to the Spirit World. The family felt and heard the presence of All Our Relatives and this confirmed that Amber was not alone on the day her life was taken so tragically from the physical world. Gwenda gave thanks to Amber's father, the late Art Redman Sr., for fulfilling his promise that, no matter what, he would find his "baby girl." Exactly seven months to the day before the day that Amber was found, her father journeyed to the Spirit World. Art knew the pain that the family was going through and he did everything he could to assist in bringing his daughter home.

Art told Gwenda that Amber came to him as he was driving. Amber asked her Dad to bring her home. Art was determined to fulfill his "baby girl's" request. Art showed his love for Amber when she was born and he held her in his arms until she fell asleep, when he designed her regalia of her first outfit, when he listened to her words "I Love You, Dad" as she gave him a hug each time she saw him. Amber said her heart would race with excitement when love was shared in their hugs. Art was proud of his daughter at her graduation. Amber asked her father if he would keep her Eagle Feather for her and he did. Art and Amber now share an everlasting life where there are Love, Peace, and Teachings. Gwenda believes Art and Amber are happy and that Art continues to be the best father he can be for Amber. She believes that if their family calls on both of them they will help guide us. Gwenda says, "I look forward to that beautiful day when I will see Wicanhpi Duta Win and All My Relatives."

On May 13, just over a week after Amber's remains were found, as Gwenda and her family sat outside, Amber's cousin Tanya whispered to Gwenda, "Look behind you." When Gwenda turned she saw two beautiful buffaloes walking up the pathway towards the fence. Gwenda offered a prayer then patiently watched each movement they made. The bigger buffalo looked at the women three times and proceeded to walk down the valley and then up the other side of the hill. When the buffalo reached the top of the hill she began to dance, turning around and around and kicking up both back legs. Tears filled both of their eyes as they watched this beautiful buffalo's graceful dance. In her heart Gwenda knew Amber had come back to let her know that she was alive in the Buffalo Spirit. Later that night, Gwenda received a call confirming that more of Amber's remains had been located. Gwenda believes that Amber came to bring strength to her family before they received this news, to encourage and help them to remain strong in prayer.

Amber sent another beautiful message to her family as they prepared for her final journey. The family was preparing for a ceremony offering food and prayers when Amber's nephew, Dallon, witnessed four deer dancing from each of the four directions. As each deer danced towards the centre of the circle, the flowers within the circle turned red, yellow, white, and black.

Gwenda forgot the bowls, cups, and utensils to feed the family, so she invited everyone to her home to eat. As each person entered her yard, he or she could see a big buffalo running towards the house. As the buffalo got closer to the house, she switched pace and began to walk. Gwenda offered prayers and thanks for experiencing Amber's message of thanks for her family's prayers and strength. As the Buffalo Spirit brought strength to the family, their prayers were answered.

Gwenda, as Amber's mother, was given the ability to prepare for her journey to the Spirit World. Gwenda also realizes that there are many families out there who take each step not knowing where their loved one is. Seconds and days pass, and families continue to live with excruciating pain, a pain that will not be forgotten. Gwenda's heart and prayers are with all the families who have loved ones who are still missing or who have been murdered. Gwenda will be there to support and offer her prayers for you.

Amber came back to her family in different forms of life to let them know that she was found, that she loves and misses them, but that she is happy to be with Our Relatives in a place where there is everlasting love and no harm can ever be brought upon her again. Gwenda continues to tell the story of her daughter's life and gives thanks to the Creator for allowing her to be Amber's mother and to experience the love and teachings Amber shared with those around her. Gwenda would like to dedicate these messages to four beautiful girls named after Amber: Patience Amber, Isabelle, Amber Rose, and Kanesha Amber. Gwenda believes that the Spirit of Amber will live strongly in each one of these beautiful young women. Gwenda, as Amber's mother, will be watchful of Amber's teachings and she will offer thanks as each is received by the young girls. Pidamiye! Wopida! Midakuye Owasin!

Update

A mber's remains were found on May 5, 2008, on Little Black Bear First Nation after a police sting operation. Two men, Albert Patrick Belle-garde, 29, and Gilbert Allan Bellegarde, 31, were charged with first-degree murder. On December 12, 2008, the Crown stayed the first-degree murder charge against Gilbert Bellegarde. On January 22, 2009, Albert Bellegarde pleaded guilty to second-degree murder and was sentenced to life in prison with no chance of parole for 15 years.

The family believes only one portion of the story was told by Albert Bellegarde's sentence. They feel that justice has been only partially served and that Gilbert Bellegarde should also be held responsible for his actions. Gwenda also firmly believes that some members of Little Black Bear First Nation knew what had happened to Amber and kept silent. She believes it is important for First Nations communities to speak out in order to en-sure that Aboriginal women and girls are safe.

A Message from Gwenda on behalf of Amber's Family

Amber will not be forgotten. I will continue to speak out regarding my daugh-ter's murder. I have written a poem for my daughter:
  I call to the Grandmothers in the West . . . hear my prayer . . .
  I call on the Grandmothers in the North . . . hear my prayer . . .
  I call on the Grandmothers in the East . . . hear my prayer . . .
  I call on the Grandmothers in the South . . . hear my prayer.
  Wicanhpi Duta Win I feel your presence . . . I listen to each message that you send . . . I see your beauty within the animals and the elements of Mother Earth . . . I am beginning to understand your purpose from which the Creator has given your spirit.
  Creator, I give thanks for allowing me to be her mother, as do her father, her brothers, her grandmothers, her niece, her uncle, her auntie, her cousin, her friends . . . for allowing me to learn from her teachings . . . for allowing me to understand each gift she inspired. Wicanhpi Duta Win, we are honoured to be a part of you.
  All my Relatives, I am pitiful, small, and weak. I ask for your guidance and understanding as each day passes.
  This journey that our family has endured taught us patience and enhanced our love as a family. When situations are difficult we think about the teachings they provide: Learn Life's Lessons, strengthen our Dakota Nation, and ensure Prayers are being heard from the Wakan Tanka.

It has been very difficult to comprehend all that has happened within the last few months. In January 2009, our family was called to the Fort Qu'Appelle detachment to hear the details and ask questions about Amber's murder. The very next day in the Court of Queen's Bench in Regina, we heard every detail of her tragedy. Amber's family felt the pain that she went through. It was very difficult to be in the same room as the person who murdered Amber and hear the story of how he disrespected a Dakota woman. The auntie asked Albert Bellegarde to look at her, but he did not have the strength to lift his head as we shared our stories of Amber's personality, of her family's love, of her many gifts. If only he had known who Amber was as a Dakota woman.

We do not believe that justice has been served. It was two years and ten months before arrests were made. One man remained in custody until sentencing, but the other was released in July 2008 and the charges against him have since been stayed. It is hard to understand. How is it that two men were charged with first-degree murder but eight months later one pleads guilty to second-degree murder and the other walks free?

It was very difficult to be in the same room as this person who took Amber's life and hear the story of how he murdered a Dakota woman. I have been told that Amber forgave these two men for what they did to her. Amber's purpose here on Earth was to bring this issue of the missing and murdered women to the forefront because society did not see this as a priority. Search deep within your hearts and listen to the teachings that the women bring to each family and let us not forget their role as women.

We, as women, are givers of life. We, as women, have rights. Where are the leaders? Why are our missing and murdered women not made a priority? I believe that if my daughter was a Caucasian woman her disappearance would have made the national headlines, that the search for her would have begun immediately, that the media would have continued to keep her story alive, and that people would have come from all walks of life to help in the search.

Leaders, help the many, many families who have missing loved ones. Too often the result is that our loved one is found murdered. We, as Canadians, tend to believe we live in a country that is rich in equality and rights. As one mother, I am challenging our leaders to initiate this change. Prioritize our women's rights, put aside your meetings and stand strong beside our women. Help us end the silence.

We need that balance to help find a solution as to why our women are going missing and being murdered. Our communities need to take responsibility for the safety of our women and girls. Wrongs must be made into rights. We must honour the teachings of respect, honesty, empathy, and compassion. I understand there is a Brothers in Spirit group who believe strongly that our women need the strength from the men, who believe this balance is a step in finding a solution to this issue.

I will be having a four-year memorial* for the late Amber Redman and I want to invite each one who reads this story to come and join in celebrating her life as a Dakota woman. There will be a Women's Volleyball Tournament and a Men's 3 on 3 Basketball Tournament. Amber enjoyed these sports and my family believes she will be there with us laughing, enjoying this time with all who attend. Lastly, Amber wanted me personally to thank all who contributed to solving this crime. Pidamiye! Wopida! (Thank you) Midakuye Owasin (All My Relatives)!

---

*The memorial was held July 15, 2009.

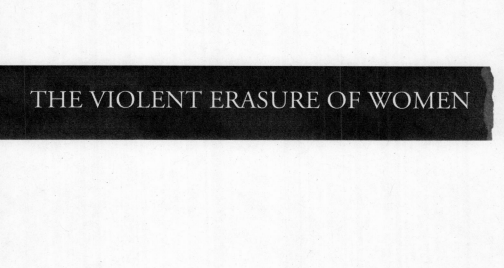

THE VIOLENT ERASURE OF WOMEN

A Message from Amnesty International

GORDON BARNES

In October 2004, Amnesty International released its research report entitled *Stolen Sisters: A Human Rights Response to Discrimination and Violence Against Indigenous Women,* which documents the incredibly large number of Indigenous women who have been murdered or are missing in Canada. The report links high levels of violence experienced by Indigenous women and girls across Canada to deeply rooted patterns of marginalization and discrimination. This discrimination has put large numbers of Indigenous women and girls in situations of heightened vulnerability to violence, has helped fuel violent acts of hatred against them, and has denied Indigenous women and girls adequate protection under the law and by society as a whole. The *Stolen Sisters* report also notes that similar concerns have been repeatedly brought to the attention of Canadian officials by Indigenous peoples' organizations and by official inquiries.

No one should suffer the grief of having a sister, mother, or daughter suddenly disappear, never to be seen again. No one should have to live in

---

GORDON BARNES has been active in Amnesty International for many years and is a volunteer Amnesty International fieldworker. In addition to participating in the "Missing Women" conference, Gordon has also been involved in the organization of other events related to this area of Amnesty International's human rights work.

fear that she will be the next woman or girl to go missing. Canadian officials have a clear and inescapable obligation to ensure the safety of Indigenous women, to bring those responsible for attacks against them to justice, and to address the deeper problems of marginalization, dispossession, and impoverishment that have placed so many Indigenous women in harm's way.

The following call for action is based on the recommendations made by the families of missing women, frontline organizations working for Indigenous women's welfare and safety, and official government inquiries and commissions, as well as standard interpretations of the human rights obligations of governments:

- acknowledge the seriousness of the problem;

- support research into the extent and causes of violence against Indigenous women;

- take immediate action to protect women at greatest risk;

- provide training and resources for police to make prevention of violence against Indigenous women a genuine priority;

- address the social and economic factors that lead to Indigenous women's extreme vulnerability to violence; and

- end the marginalization of Indigenous women in Canadian society.

In August 2003, Amnesty International published a report focusing on the ten-year cycle of abductions and murders of girls and women in the cities of Ciudad Juárez and Chihuahua in northern Mexico: *Intolerable Killings: 10 Years of Abductions and Murders of Women in Ciudad Juárez and Chihuahua*. The report documented more than 370 cases of women murdered in Ciudad Juárez and Chihuahua City. Of those cases, research indicated that at least 137 of the victims suffered some form of sexual violence and at least 70 of the total number of women murdered remained unidentified. At least 70 other women or girls also remained unaccounted for after having been officially reported missing.

Amnesty International called on the representatives of the Mexican federal and state authorities for an immediate and decisive intervention by the federal authorities to ensure justice in Ciudad Juárez and the city of Chihuahua and for the state and municipal authorities to cooperate fully with these steps. AI also called for an independent judicial review of the cases investigated by the Chihuahua Procuraduría General de Justicia del Estado (PGJE), State Public Prosecutor's Office, or brought before the courts, with the goals to:

*   correct miscarriages of justice;

*   investigate and punish any official responsible for abuses;

*   set in motion substantive reform of the system of administration and procuration of justice in the state of Chihuahua;

*   demonstrate respect for the dignity of relatives and the organizations working for women's rights;

*   prevent, investigate, and punish intimidation or harassment against relatives and the organizations working for women's rights; and

*   publicly recognize the legitimacy of their struggle.

One of the problems Amnesty International faced after the release of the reports regarding both Canada and Mexico (particularly in relation to Canada) was getting people, including the media, to realize how serious a human rights concern this is.

When we first heard of the plans of the University of Regina faculty and students to organize and host an international conference—"Missing Women: Decolonization, Third Wave Feminisms and Indigenous People of Canada and Mexico"—we were impressed with the vision, determination, and ambition of the faculty and students involved. The energy of the conference organization itself created incredible opportunities for learning and activism. The conference provided the opportunity to connect with people with a wide variety of experience and interests. The inclusion of the experience of Indigenous women in Mexico was very valuable.

The conference itself was very difficult to participate in. There was sharing of incredible personal pain. Family members and all participants found support in the conference itself and from each other. Strategies were developed to continue building upon relationships established at the conference. There is no doubt that since the conference there has been much more significant attention given to missing Indigenous women by our media. This is perhaps one of the most significant accomplishments of the conference.

In Regina, Amnesty International has always partnered with the Saskatchewan Sisters in Spirit group to organize an annual vigil in Victoria

Park on October 4. We will continue to do this, and the increased network of people that has developed as a result of the conference provides an opportunity to include more people from the university and the community in this kind of event.

Amnesty International is very appreciative of the initiative taken by Brenda Anderson and Reverend Carla Blakley, as well as all of the faculty and students who worked on the conference organization. We will continue to make this area of our human rights work a priority.

KEYNOTE ADDRESS
"MISSING WOMEN" CONFERENCE, FRIDAY, AUGUST 15, 2008.
TRANSCRIBED AND EDITED BY CHELSEA MILLMAN.

Political Realities:
The Effect of Globalization on Indigenous Women

KIM ERNO

I want to begin by expressing my deep appreciation for the privilege of gathering and being present with you to share this time and this space—to give my thanks to the Elders, to the grandmothers, to the grandfathers, to Carla, to Brenda, the coordinators, to this institution, and to all of you who have gathered here with this theme of missing and murdered Indigenous women. If we have gathered here because there are missing and murdered Indigenous women, it is because we are also in a world that has lost its way. And so part of our search, part of our reason for this gathering, is trying to recover that way, to pick up the lost stitches, to re-weave the torn fabric, and to struggle and hope for a world that is not only *possible,* as we say in Latin America, but a new world that is also *necessary.* So I thank you very, very deeply for the privilege of being in this time and this space with all of you.

As I was reviewing the agenda for today with my colleague, Marta Perez, who will be sharing this podium in a short while, Marta said, "Look, Kim. They are all women in the presentations." And I said, "Well, Marta, not quite." And so I asked myself, "What is my particular role, my presence,

KIM ERNO is an ordained Evangelical Lutheran Church in America (ELCA) pastor and the program director of the Transformational Immersion Programs at the ELCA's Lutheran Center in Mexico City.

here; what is my contribution?" In Latin America we like to dance and I am looking forward to—we are going to have a chance here, too, I understand—to dance together, to sing together, to move together. The dances that we have are salsa and merengue and cumbia. They have a lot of rhythm and a lot of movement. They say that a good male partner realizes that he is simply the frame; that the woman knows the moves and knows the steps. So a good male dancer knows that he is a frame for the work of art who is the woman. So that's what I understand is my role, and what I will attempt to do here this morning is to set a frame. And I trust my sisters will bring the moves in the steps. And the frame that I have been asked to give is the theme of globalization.

The first step in addressing globalization is to locate ourselves, because part of what we are seeing in this globalization is an effort to erase who we are—our languages, our cultures, our origins, our roots. As I join you in this land, I am very, very conscious of my homeland. My homeland according to the original peoples is the Dawn Land. It is the land that stretches from the waters that lie in between the people of the Longhouse and the people of the Dawn Land that stretches to the sea and the rising sun. And so I bring readings from the Dawn Land. I am also very conscious of my new land to the South: the Cradle of Corn. There are as many varieties of corn as there are original peoples and languages, and for that reason the original peoples refer to the people as the Children of Corn. And so I bring readings from the land that is the Cradle of Corn. Also, to locate myself and my perspective on globalization, I need to say that I grew up on a border, on the Vermont/Quebec border. So I grew up moving back and forth between cultures and languages. I grew up on a border line. And while I most certainly can enjoy the privileges, the access, and the power that come with my white maleness, I am most comfortable on the margins and on the border lines. So I have a perspective that comes from being able to enter into those centres of power but also from being able to step back from them.

The second step after we have located ourselves in globalization is to imagine this beautiful globe, to imagine her spinning and moving and dancing through space, to imagine her with her multitude of colours, of browns and yellows and whites and blues and reds, to see her valleys and mountains and deserts and waters and rivers and oceans, to see her in all her beauty and realize that she is a living, breathing being and that she carries scars. She carries scars because she has been sliced and diced, cut into pieces by what we refer to as borders. These are barriers that are not natural divisions between peoples and lands, but rather, most often, they are the spoils of war. They are acts of violence that serve the interests of global profiteers.

The u.s./Mexico border is a case in point. The perspective from the south is much different than the perspective from the north. u.s. history textbooks about this particular period in history most often tell us to remember the Alamo—the holdout of the brave Texas rangers in that mission in Texas called the Alamo—with no mention of how those Texans got there in the first place, crossing illegally, breaking Mexican law that had already abolished slavery. So while American students are challenged to remember the Alamo, Mexicans never ever forget that almost half of the territory of Mexico was lost in what is considered an unjust war of aggression provoked by President Polk and justified by a white supremacist theology called "manifest destiny" that says that the white race has been ordained by God to rule from sea to shining sea. One more scar on the landscape.

And now we are in this new world order with the dominant economic model that is often referred to as neo-liberal economics—liberal, though not in a political sense, but rather in an economic sense, saying that economics and economic policies and practices are to be liberated; that there are not to be any restraints, particularly any restraints by the state. So if there are state enterprises, be they transportation, communication or banking, they are to be privatized, sold off to the highest bidder. It says that if there are any laws that could interfere with maximizing profits—even if those laws are designed to protect the environment or to set minimum wages—then they are to be relaxed. It says that if there are taxes that are designed to protect national regional economies by taxing imports—what are known as tariffs—they are to be eliminated.

Neo-liberal economics would tell us that those borders, those boundaries, are opening up so that we can enjoy this one globe all together as one people. There is both a truth and a lie to that, because there *is* an opening of borders, but it is a very selective opening. Again, an opening that is designed to benefit global profiteers—raw materials, finished products, capital investment, and speculation are free to cross borders in this new world order. But people who inhabit this globe and, for that matter, all beings who might want to move across the lands are restricted and so, in effect, what we have set up is competition in capital production between the labour markets. Factories, investments, materials are free to move anywhere in the planet based on what's called "maximizing your competitive advantage." So, if in Mexico our competitive advantage in the global marketplace is cheap labour, then we need to keep cheap labour cheap, which means that we weaken our unions, that we keep the daily minimum wage to 52 pesos (about five dollars). You'll find that the prices in Mexico compared to the United States and Canada are not that significantly different, and so imagine surviving on five dollars a day—but that is our global "competitive advantage."

As a result of these kinds of economic policies, we have achieved the highest concentration of wealth in human history, but some refer to this as the champagne glass economy. Some 20 percent who make up the wealthiest sector of this world now control 83 percent of the world's wealth and resources. As we enter into this new millennium there are 475 billionaires whose wealth was equal to the combined income of the poorest 50 percent of the world. So if we are on a planet with six billion inhabitants, we are talking about 475 individuals whose wealth is greater than three billion human beings. In theological terms, there are many sectors referring to this global system, this neo-liberal system, as idolatry, saying that idolatry has two primary characteristics: first, that it is unquestionable; it simply justifies itself; it is untouchable; the market exists because the market exists; it's like the law of gravity; it just is. The second characteristic is that it always, always demands human sacrifice.

And so that is where we begin to locate the missing. I would like to lift up four particular categories in which this sacrifice carries down. The first is through *exclusion*, the next through *exploitation*, the third, *expulsion*, the last, *extermination*. And I'd like to cite particular communities in Mexico that I've come to know. So we are going to do a little bit of a tour of Mexico, but I guarantee that these places are not the ones you'll find in your guidebooks; these are way off the tourist trails.

So the first stop we'll be going to is the state of Guerrero, one of the most southern states of Mexico, best known for the tourist city of Acapulco, where the cliff divers make their death-defying leaps into the waves below, and where young college students from the north come for their spring break. We don't even translate in Spanish, we just say "spring breakers." So they come to bathe in the sun and guzzle beer. But if we were to go way, way off the tourist path in the state of Guerrero and climb up into the mountains, we would come to an Indigenous village where the people still speak their native language, a language that predates the Spanish conquest and the conquest of the Aztecs.

The village was founded in 1523, two years after the Spanish conquest of 1521. People were afraid for their lives, so they were fleeing into the mountains to escape the onslaught of the Spanish conquest. It still remains a very, very isolated village. There's barely a road; it just winds and spirals around the mountain and, as you come to the outskirts of the village, as is common to many of the villages, you pass the village cemetery. And if you were feeling particularly brave that day, you might stop and wander through the tombs. I say "particularly brave" because in this village there are not enough resources for the living, so there is nothing left over for the dead. So in a country where there is so much respect and care for our ancestors, this village is unable to care for their ancestors. In this cemetery you will find that some of the tombs have broken open and suddenly you are face to face with human remains. The first time I was in the village was some twenty years ago and I met a grandmother who held her grandson Leonardo in her arms as he took his last breaths. Her major preoccupation was how she was going to feed the gravediggers (as payment) and have enough food left over for all the hungry mouths in her home.

Contaminated water continues to be a major health issue, so much so that cholera has been the major cause of death in that village. Some years ago when the North America Free Trade Agreement—one of the expressions of the neo-liberal economic policies of opening up borders—came into effect, the delegation visited the village and later had a meeting with an official responsible for economic policy. Very good questions were raised about how this new world order, how these trade agreements, would affect or benefit those who are part of the village. The official—incredibly cold, but perhaps, in his perspective, honest—said, "That's what cholera is for." Do you understand? If people cannot produce and cannot consume in this global economy, they count for nothing. They are zeros in this global economic equation. That's what cholera is for; we're better off without them. They are the *excluded* ones.

This village is a village where the major source of income comes from these beautiful baskets that women weave with quick fingers, moving quickly, weaving stories. Right now Mexico is being inundated with arts and crafts that are being made in China and sold much cheaper. Tourists cannot tell the difference or really don't care. So if these people in this village were to disappear off the face of the earth, who would miss these baskets? They really are not producers and consumers in the global economy and so they count for nothing. They are the excluded. And the women who care for their households, who wonder if there will be enough food to feed the hungry mouths, women in these Indigenous villages who bring in the water, who collect the firewood, who give birth to life, who breast-feed their babies—none of that shows in the gross national product. They carry out economic activities that are zeros; they are the excluded ones. But there is work. There is work that is paid, where you can earn a salary, where you can earn the daily minimum wage of 52 pesos, correct? So we move to the next category of *exploited.*

Detailed work, repetitive work: putting the tiny screws into the sunglasses—3,500 pair per day—until you start to squint to see more clearly; bending steel cables for seat belts to keep the drivers and passengers of Ford and GM vehicles safe and buckled up—3500 cables a day—until your hands are tired and so sore that you can't bend down to tie your shoes.

The blue wire goes here, and the yellow wire goes here, and the circuit board goes—God knows where. Stitch after stitch after stitch sewing Gap jeans, 13-,14-,15-,16-year-olds sewing Barbie costumes for Toys "R" Us, but they lock us up until we've made the quota for the Christmas sales. All of this requires nimble fingers, quick hands, keen vision, minute after minute, hour after hour, day after day until the fingers are too bruised, the wrists ache from carpal tunnel syndrome, and the vision is too weak, and your three-month contract is not renewed. You're out of work. You're not even 30 years old, and you feel like you've lived three lifetimes.

For neo-liberal profiteers, you exist for capital production, not for human reproduction. Each woman is given a medical exam, which includes a pregnancy test, before she is hired, and if the test is positive, the position is unavailable. During your term of employment, you receive regular checkups, part of the benefits, again including a pregnancy test, the results of which will determine your continued employment. Some factories decided to dispense with the façade of checkups and just demand to see the used sanitary napkins once a month. It saves time and money, and that's the bottom line. A women who was reproductive for human life is not considered productive enough for corporate life; she becomes part of the landscape of capital waste, thrown out with the factory's toxic waste.

In the community of Tijuana, there is an industrial park, although park is a misnomer—it's more like an industrial wasteland. The battery recycling factory is long gone, but the eighty-five hundred tons of toxic waste remains. And so it seeps into the ground, it runs into the streams, it collects in puddles where the children like to run, and so they develop skin blisters. Parents sleep with children because they're afraid that their children might drown in the pools of blood that come from spontaneous nose bleeding in the middle of the night. Women who work in the factories have high rates of miscarriages, birth defects, and have children born with no brain stems. The local school has set the record for the highest levels of lead in its students' blood.

If the women organize, if they demand rights, if they try to increase the wages or obtain better working conditions, then the factories like the battery factory in Mexico just (as we say) "sprout wings and fly away." But if factories can sprout wings and fly away, why can't the workers do the same? And so we go to the next category which is *expulsion*.

We go to a village somewhere in the desert. The name—Ultar—is derived from a rectangular stone. Some years ago in the eighteenth century there was a missionary who came across this rectangular stone and it reminded him of an altar, and so he would gather people and invite people to come and celebrate the Mass at it. Nobody knows where the stone is any more; it has been buried under the sand, the riverbed has been shifted, but the name sticks. And so it is now an altar of human sacrifice. In Spanish, we say that this is the *trampolina,* this is the trampoline, this is the staging ground for the migrants getting ready to make their risky crossing through the desert to go north. In the years of 2000, 2001, in the peak months of crossing, which are January through May, some 2,000 migrants per day gathered in Ultar, a village that in its immediate vicinity numbers 5,000 inhabitants. So in a village of 5,000, 2,000 arrive per day.

This was once a farming community, but it has also lost its way in this NAFTA, this free trade, this neo-liberal economics that allows the free flow of grains like corn coming in from the U.S., genetically altered corn that comes in with heavy subsidies so that companies like Cargill can set the prices and sell the low production cars in Mexico and rule the world economy. So Ultar is no longer a rural village. It is a village that has its entire economy revolving around human trafficking.

Around the plaza you'll find the prestos, you'll find the stands where you can buy your new tennis shoes, baseball caps, bottles of water that will never ever be enough to keep you from becoming dehydrated—you have to carry at least 20 to 30 pounds of water into the deserts. There are vans around the plaza that have had the back seats taken out, and replaced with benches so that you can crowd 20 to 25 migrants and make the race two hours up to the line. And then when there is the opening—that window of opportunity—the migrants, or the young men who are the guides, go off into the desert for two days, for three, four, or five days and nights to make the crossover.

So what we would say is that while we have these borders, they are open to some and closed to others and, in effect, we have filters. So the desert acts as a filter to select the labour market that the U.S. economy requires. According to U.S. labour statistics, 53 percent of all agricultural workers in the U.S. are undocumented. In California that goes up to 90 percent. So if you can make it three, four, five, six days and nights through the desert, then you've proved your worth and you can pick lettuce in California, apples in Washington, tomatoes in Michigan, blueberries in Maine, cucumbers in North Carolina, and oranges in Florida.

Why this area? When the free trade agreement came into effect in 1994, there was also another initiative called Operation Gatekeeper by the United States, to shut the border in the places that had been the traditional places of crossing, and Tijuana and the urban areas, and so that's where the barriers, that's where the walls went up. The walls are made with former helicopter landing pads from the Vietnam war and the first war in Iraq. Metallic walls become the first barrier. Stadium lighting, motion detectors, helicopters, all kinds of sophisticated surveillance technology now drive the migrants to the most hostile environment, which is the desert, to make that dangerous crossing, and it becomes the filter.

It once had been the flow back and forth primarily of men, going up for seasonal labour and then coming back to be with their families and their homes and their communities. Because of the risks, because of the costs, they now stay, so there are more undocumented in the u.s. after NAFTA, after 1994 and Operation Gatekeeper, than before. As a result, while males continue to be the higher percentage of those who are crossing, there has been a significant increase in women who are making that risky crossing with their children. Why? Because they want to be reunited with their families, with their husbands, for their children to know their fathers. And so, they are left with a choice to stay behind in the ghost towns or to make the dangerous trek north and to become part of this migrant trail of those who are the expelled in this lonely economy. But you could stay, right? And if you stay, you could fight for change, right? And so we go to the last category of *extermination*.

We go to the south of Mexico and to the southernmost state, which is the state of Chiapas, the state that ethnically and linguistically identifies with the Mayan peoples, where people still speak the traditional language. Mayan languages present a different worldview—there is no word for "I" or "me," only "we" and "us." There is no word in Mayan languages for "rich" or "poor" because they don't exist as social categories. For many, many centuries there was no word for "enemy." Chiapas is one of the richest states in terms of natural resources, of anything that you could imagine—from water to generate hydroelectric power, which generates over half of the electricity in Mexico, to uranium to timber to coffee to land. Whatever you want to imagine, Chiapas sets the record for the greatest wealth of resources in Mexico.

At the same time it has some of the poorest living standards in all of Mexico. Chiapas is "off the grid"; the land reform carried out in Mexico in the 1930s didn't quite make it all the way south, but the Indigenous peoples, the farmers, held onto the promise and the hope that someday that communal land would be theirs because it was protected by law in the Mexican constitution under article 27, which would not allow the purchase nor the sale of communal lands. But in anticipation of the North American Free Trade Agreement, under pressure from the United States to pave the way, the administration in 1992 amended its own constitution to allow for the purchase and sale of this communal land. For Indigenous families that was taken as a death sentence. On January 1, 1994, when NAFTA came into effect and when the power brokers in

Mexico City were celebrating and toasting their entry into this new world order, an Indigenous army of Mayan peoples occupied six municipalities in Chiapas as part of a protest. Mayan mathematicians had done some quick calculating and had determined that, based on the infant mortality rate, they had just a few generations left, and so they decided to go down in a fight.

Onto the scene appeared the Zapatista Army of National Liberation (*Ejército Zapatista de Liberación Nacional*). Twelve days of fighting ended in a ceasefire. Civil society in Mexico also rose up and called for negotiations and identified with the cause of the Zapatistas to defend communal lands, to defend cultures and traditions that are part of the Indigenous peoples. So there was a ceasefire, and the Zapatistas have respected that ceasefire since January 12, 1994, without having fired a shot. In the meantime, the Mexican government has continued to carry out a military strategy of counter-insurgency, sometimes described as "in order to kill the fish, you drain the ocean," which is to say that all life becomes a military target. And so counter-insurgency policies in the southern state of Chiapas have pushed people out, have cleared areas, only allowing those who agree to collaborate with the government to stay, as a way of trying to remove any popular base of support for the Zapatistas, and because of the concerns of the north, including a memo that once came from Chase Bank to the president saying "unless you eliminate those Zapatistas, we can no longer consider Mexico a secure environment for investment."

So in a little village in December 1997, people assembled, Indigenous peoples who were on the run because they understood that there was a military operation coming into the area. So they gathered and while they themselves were not Zapatistas—in fact, they had formed themselves into an organization called the Bees—they shared the causes of Indigenous rights, protection of culture and traditions, land reform, democracy, human rights, but they did not share the strategy of taking up arms. And so they gathered in the little village hearing rumours that there was a military operation on the way, and they gathered in the little wooden chapel to pray and to fast for peace.

In the morning of December 22, 1997, trucks started to arrive. Young men in uniforms got down armed with high-caliber rifles and they took positions around the chapel and on high ground, and at 11:00 in the morning they began to open fire. You can still see the bullet holes in the wooden panels. The people ran, they fled, they dove down the embankments, they gathered their children, they covered them up, they tried to hide in the vegetation. The shooting continued until 5:00 in the afternoon; at 2:00 it reached its peak.

In the end, 45 lives were lost, the majority women and children. The men had moved out of the area, assuming that they would be the ones targeted for violence, but they were dead wrong. In this strategy, the women were targets. It was gender-directed violence. Among the 19 women killed, four were pregnant; one died because her abdomen was cut open. Just 200 metres away from the killing spree were public security forces. They blocked the only potential escape route from the village. This is a military strategy called the hammer and the anvil. The anvil holds the escape route, and the hammer comes in to do its work.

The government, in an attempt to cover up its complicity, stated that it was just a dispute between Indigenous peoples—you know how they are. There was a sand pit and they were just fighting over that. The authorities tried to cover up the gender-specific brutality. Cultural anthropologists who have investigated the case say that this kind of heinous violence has absolutely nothing to do with Indigenous cultures, but has everything to do with a culture of military counter-insurgency training. And so in this globalized world, this new world order that promises profits and trickle-down economics, there is a system that demands human sacrifice through exclusion, exploitation, expulsion, and extermination.

But the global profiteers do not have the last word. They do not get the last say. There is a cosmic shift that we also feel; our solar calendar shows two serpents coming together head to head. One is the serpent of light; the other is the serpent of shadows. The Elders in Mexico tell us that we are now in the shifting of the pendulum, that the serpent of the shadows is now being pushed aside, and the serpent of light is coming into force and power. In Spanish, the way we say "to give birth" is "to give light." And so this Earth Mother of ours is not only crying out because of the pain of her lost, murdered, and missing sisters; she is also crying out in labour pain. She is giving birth to a new creation, and what some refer to as an eco-feminist creation that places food sovereignty above food as a commodity; that places worker cooperation above maximizing our competitive advantage; that places meeting basic human needs above maximizing corporate greed.

And so we are awaiting the birth of a new order, and as those who are here as midwives, we participate by sowing seeds—we start small because we want to concentrate the life force—seeds that are cultivated, that become plots, that thicken, that write a new history and a new story. We start thin with many threads of many colours to weave a new tapestry. And we start slowly because we are in it for the long haul. We are in this marathon of life and hope and we will not be stopped. And we are not alone.

Who has called us here? I would say that our missing and murdered sisters have also called us. You can feel them, their presence; they are here. Yesterday when Maria Campbell shared her powerful, moving, eloquent words, and she talked about walking through the cemetery and remembering her sisters who had died such violent deaths, outside the window I saw in the clouds a kite flying. In Guatemala, on the day of the dead, people fly kites in the graveyards to remind them of the spirits that soar and lift them up. We are not alone. Our sisters lift us up and they have called us and they have convened us in this marathon of hope.

So I want to close with the words of a sister from Guatemala who reminds us of this marathon of hope in a poem that she wrote, called "They have threatened us with resurrection."*

They have threatened us with Resurrection
Because we have felt their inert bodies,
and their souls penetrated ours
doubly fortified,
because in this marathon of Hope,
there are always others to relieve us
who carry the strength
to reach the finish line
which lies beyond death.
They have threatened us with Resurrection
because they will not be able to take away from us
their bodies,
their souls,
their strength,
their spirit,
nor even their death
and least of all their life.
Because they live
today, tomorrow, and always
in the streets baptized with their blood,
in the air that absorbed their cry,
in the jungle that hid their shadows,
in the river that gathered up their laughter,
in the ocean that holds their secrets,

---

* excerpt from Julia Esquivel, They Have Threatened Us With Resurrection / Nos han amenazado de Resurrección, *Spiritus* 3 (2003): 96–101. © 2003 by The Johns Hopkins University Press.

in the craters of the volcanoes,
Pyramids of the New Day,
which swallowed up their ashes.
They have threatened us with Resurrection
because they are more alive than ever before,
because they transform our agonies
and fertilize our struggle,
because they pick us up when we fall,
because they loom like giants
before the crazed gorillas' fear.
They have threatened us with Resurrection

From Genocide to Femicide:
An Ongoing History of Terror, Hate, and Apathy

LEONZO BARRENO

Genocide[1]

In the late 1970s and early 1980s one of the largest genocides in the western hemisphere was taking place: genocide in Guatemala[2] that the world knew little about. Only after survivors told their stories to those who dared to listen and to write about them did we learn the extent of a campaign carried out by "an army blinded by ignorance, hatred [towards the Mayan people], and fear."[3] What this campaign of state terrorism created and left in Guatemala was a culture of violence and fear amongst the general population, impunity for those who committed crimes against humanity and apathy among the select few who continue to govern that Central American country.

Growing up in an urban town in Guatemala in the early 1980s, I recall the news—from clandestine radio stations, from urban *foci* informants, or from secret discussions at high school and university students' gatherings—of the daily rural *matazones* (massacres). Official news on radio and television minimized the extent of the massacres by telling people that the national army was fighting against the "evil of communism." One president, General Efrain Rios Montt, even told Guatemalans in his Sunday

LEONZO BARRENO is a Mayan from Guatemala. He came to Saskatchewan in 1989 and is currently the provincial coordinator of the Saskatchewan Association of Immigration Settlement and Integration Agencies (SAISIA).

speeches that God had chosen him to rule Guatemala and that killing rebels was part of his sacred duty.[4] He was in fact ordering the massacres of ten of thousands of Mayan people.

Speaking publicly against the massacres in the urban areas was uncommon due to the fear caused by the several terrorist instruments used by the Guatemalan state: neighbours (*orejas*) spying on neighbours; selective disappearances and mass killings of university professors and students, unionists, and Catholic leaders; assassination of youth suspected of being *guerrillas* (rebels); and military surveillance of collective gatherings. In short, the country became a militarized state where dead bodies were left on the streets for the purpose of causing fear within the urban population. There were no political prisoners in Guatemala, and no single high-ranking officer ever faced justice for all these crimes.

The rural areas of northern and western Guatemala, highly populated by Mayan people, suffered the worst of state terrorism. Entire rural zones were difficult, even "illegal," to visit. Guatemala became divided not only along social and cultural lines but also into geographic zones. Those in power ruled with an iron fist, and with contempt for and "devaluation" of the rural Mayan population. Army generals, since the 1954 CIA-orchestrated invasion of Guatemala, had taken turns as "Presidents" of the country. Generals such as Schell Laugerud, Romeo Lucas, Efrain Rios Montt, and Hector Gramajo, as presidents, were the masterminds of the genocide of more than 200,000 people, mostly Mayan people.

Under the Rios Montt government (March 1982–August 1983) the army destroyed "some 400 towns and villages, drove 20,000 rural people out of their homes and into [concentration] camps, killed between 50,000 and 75,000 mostly unarmed indigenous farmers and their families, and violently displaced over a million people."[5] In the Guatemalan army rhetoric the rural Mayan people were the water keeping the fish (*guerrillas*) alive; "in order to kill the fish," they said, it was necessary "to get rid of the water," literally. Very few people escaped from the massacres and it was their personal stories documented by Jesuit priest and anthropologist Ricardo Falla in his book *Massacres in the Jungle* (1994) that helped the world first, and the rest of Guatemalans years later (since Falla's book was considered a "subversive book"[6] and illegal to read), to know about the effectiveness of these military regimes. *Massacres in the Jungle* documented some of the massacres in one single region (*Ixcan*).

Falla says that although racism was not the main motive for the genocide it became a characteristic of it. Foot soldiers in the field and army generals stationed in Guatemala City were influenced by the racism and hate they felt for the Maya, whom they only referred to as *Indios* (Indians)—

"a despicable being, whose life is worth less than a normal person's and whom one can therefore exterminate without scruples to save the country from a great evil such as communism."[7] Non-Maya (in the Guatemalan lexicon referred to as *Ladino,* or people of mixed Spanish and Indigenous blood) killed in the massacres were treated so because they looked like Indians and were "infected" by the Indian way of doing things.[8]

By 1996, when a "peace agreement" was signed between the Guatemalan government and the rebel forces grouped under the URNG (Union of Guatemala's Revolutionary Forces), the war was supposed to be over. *Guatemala: Never Again* was the title of a 1998 report written by the Catholic Church that documented the atrocities of both army and rebel forces during the 36 years of fighting. The report estimated that "150,000 people had been killed and another 50,000 had disappeared. Eighty percent of the casualties, it asserted, were inflicted by government forces."[9] The Catholic Church took on this project after learning that the Historical Clarification Commission, a commission agreed to by the rebels and the government, had agreed to impunity for the two sides: nobody was going to be prosecuted for the crimes committed in 36 years of "war." Notwithstanding its limitations, the Commission's 1999 report concluded that "the conflict had caused more than 200,000 deaths, and blamed the military for 93 percent of them."[10]

The URNG became an insignificant political party and Rios Montt became President of Congress. Other generals became politicians or rich entrepreneurs. Nobody paid for the crimes against humanity. Terror, hate, and apathy, despite the peace agreement, were far from over. In his final report, the head of the Historical Clarification Commission, Christian Tomuschat, emphasized the "special brutality directed against Mayan women, who were tortured, raped and murdered."[11] This was one of the few occasions in which violence against women began to be acknowledged. However, despite early hopes for a better society, terror and violence continue to be rampant in Guatemala. The killing of women did not stop; it continues even more now.

Femicide[12]

Killing females or "woman killing," femicide has become so common in Guatemala's daily violence that in April 2009 the national newspaper *Prensa Libre* posed the question: is the Guatemalan society sick?[13] The response to the question was found in the lack of values, such as solidarity, and lack of respect for human life. Added to this was the lack of programs to educate people about those values. According to journalists C. Bonillo, S. Valdez, and M. Marroquin, their sources concluded that "the war against corruption, violence, and organized crime is lost if such war in not accompanied by programs to teach social values to youth and families."

Every year thousands of people are killed in Guatemala. In 2008 alone, more than six thousand people were killed violently; 12 percent of them, or 722, were women.[14] According to Guatemalan Women's Group (GGM), from 2000 to 2008, more than 4,300 women and girls were killed in the country; 1,110, the GGM says, are considered femicide.[15]

Who is killing women and young girls and why? Is it organized crime killing women and young girls who disobey their commands to commit illegal acts, or who refuse to be sexually exploited? Or is it some police officers, as some gang leaders say, who are in a campaign of social cleansing and thus show their bosses that they are doing "something" against crime? Or is it the direct apathy and inaction of the social, economic, and political elites whose women are not victims of femicide? There is no single answer.[16]

Chilean photojournalist Carlos Reyes Manzo told a group of journalism students at the School of Journalism, University of Regina,[17] that gang leaders told him during his visit to Guatemala that it was the National Police killing their women to send them—gang leaders and their "groupies" —a message.

In one of the few public confessions about femicide and killing for money, gang leader Axel Danilo Ramirez (a.k.a. Smiley) told *Prensa Libre* journalists that killing gives him pleasure: "Yes, I kill, especially killing opposing gang members and their nosy women," he said. When asked what he feels when killing, he responded: "I feel nothing, what would I feel." Then he said, "I am accused of a lot of things . . . But the Police also kill for money, just like me."[18] Whether it is organized crime (drug cartels and gangs or the police, or all), the killings continue amid the apathy of national authorities.

Apathy from Guatemalan authorities is shown in the fact that of the thousands of cases involving femicide, only two have made it to the courts. There are several reasons for that, the GGM claims; the first is that, even though the evidence for femicide is clear and unequivocal, the courts treat these murders as domestic violence which, though illegal, carries a minor penalty; furthermore, there is a lack of knowledge among judges about femicide; and, finally, there is a lack of financial resources, said Judge Beatriz De Leon.[19] The apathy is also demonstrated in the fact that despite horrific crimes against women the law against femicide was just passed in May 2008.

Femicide even caused concerns in the U.S. House of Representatives, which in April of 2007, through Resolution 100, was attempting to bring an end to femicide in Guatemala and other Central American countries.[20] Enacting resolutions on foreign soil may or may not have effects on the political elites of Guatemala.

Conclusion

The root causes of the 36-year war and the causes of the Mayan genocide are very much alive. Poverty and racism are endemic in Guatemala. The Maya, the majority of the population, and the poor non-Maya, or *Ladinos,* are mostly remembered every national election with lots of promises and little change to the "corruption, violence and organized crime," identified by *Prensa Libre,* that keeps the general population in a constant state of fear.

In this culture of violence and organized crime, femicide has found a fertile ground. Killing women and young girls is endemic in a society whose national authorities have never dealt with the crimes against humanity of the recent past (genocide) and which continues to show apathy to the thousands of femicide cases. If judges have no education about femicide, if no resources are provided to deal with these crimes and no political concern is shown for the lives of women, these crimes against humanity will continue.

ENDNOTES

1   "Acts committed with intent to destroy in whole or in part, a national, ethnical, racial or religious group." Ervin Staub, *The roots of evil: The origins of genocide and other group violence.* (New York: Cambridge University Press, 1993), 8.

2   Noam Chomsky, *Year 501: The conquest continues* (Montreal: Black Rose Books, 1993), 28; Ricardo Falla, *Massacres in the jungle* (Boulder, CO: Westview Press Inc., 1994), 4.

3   Stephen Schlesinger and Stephen Kinzer, *Bitter fruit: The story of the American coup in Guatemala* (Cambridge, MA: Harvard University David Rockefeller Center for Latin American Studies, 1999), 257.

4   Personal experience.

5   Schlesinger and Kinzer, x.

6   Beatriz Manz, foreword in Falla, *Massacres in the Jungle,* xv.

7   Falla, 185.

8   Ibid., 86.

9   Schlesinger and Kinzer, 264.

10 Ibid., 265. Despite the American ambassador's attempts to call the report a "Guatemalan internal conflict," in his visit to Guatemala, former American President

Bill Clinton said that the U.S. support "for military forces and intelligence units which engaged in violence and widespread repression was wrong, and the United States must not repeat that mistake."

11 Ibid., 265.

12 Other traits of femicide, according to Wikipedia, include deliberate abortion of female foetuses, deliberate killing of female babies, honour killing, trafficking of females and domestic violence. http://www.wikipedia.org/wiki/Femicide.

13 *Prensa Libre* (Guatemala), 19 April 2009: 2.

14 Guatemala has an approximate population of 13 million people. http://es.wikipedia. org/wiki/Guatemala.

15 *Prensa Libre*—Electronic edition—National, 28 April 2009. http://www.prensalibre.com.

16 According to Stephen Meiners, Guatemala has become a major passway for South American cocaine, which the American ambassador to Guatemala, Stephen McFarland, estimated at 300 to 400 tons per year. Mexican and Guatemalan cartels operate in Guatemala, employing former elite soldiers as well as local gangs. Stephen Meiners, "Centroamerica: Con un Nuevo papel En el trafico de drogas." *La Tribuna: Nacionales,* 30 March 2009. http://www.latribuna.hn/. Organized crime may be responsible for a large portion of the crimes against males and females in Guatemala (from the writer).

17 Meiners, "Centroamerica," *La Tribuna,* 30 March 2009.

18 *Prensa Libre,* 17 April 2009: 4.

19 *Prensa Libre,* 28 April 2009, www.prensalibre.com.

20 http://cgrs.uchastings.edu/campaigns/femicide.php (accessed 26 March 2010).

The Construction of Aboriginal Identity:
A Healing Journey

CARRIE BOURASSA

As a scholar, I write about the construction of Aboriginal identity and the effects on the health and wellness of Aboriginal people and, in particular, Aboriginal women. I was honoured to present at the "Missing Women" conference hosted by the University of Regina and First Nations University of Canada in August 2008. I was asked to provide a written submission for the conference report and I do so not only as a scholar, but also as a Métis woman who is on her own healing journey. I will speak first-hand about the effects that the social construction of my identity has had on me, with the hope that readers will understand that colonization still lingers in our country and that colonial legislation continues to affect the daily lives of Aboriginal people and, in particular, Aboriginal women.

I will begin with a quote from my kookum (grandmother), Elder Betty McKenna:

> *"We are like trees. Our roots are put down very deep. And we take things from the four directions and we take them into our lives. And*

CARRIE BOURASSA is an associate professor of Indigenous Health Studies at First Nations University of Canada. She is Métis, belonging to the Riel Métis Council of Regina Inc.

if you pull us up by the roots, we are lost. We have to go back and find those roots, find those beginnings that are strong so that we can live a good life."—Elder Betty McKenna, 2005.

I believe identity is something that many people take for granted. If you grew up secure in who you were with a strong value system and a sense of pride, then likely you haven't ever had to examine the concept of identity. However, for Aboriginal people and, indeed, for any people who have experienced colonization, identity becomes a very important issue and one that affects our health and well-being. There are reasons that Aboriginal people have the highest rates of chronic and infectious disease, the highest levels of poverty, the lowest levels of education and the highest incarceration rates in Canada (Royal Commission on Aboriginal Peoples 1996). The experience of colonization has contributed to the various maladies that we face. One central concept of colonization in Canada was the policy of assimilation. Assimilation was official government policy from 1876 to 1973 (Elias 2002) and the goal was to ensure that Aboriginal people and, more specifically, First Nations people would cease to exist. In essence, they would be stripped of their identities.

Canada is the only nation in the world formally to define, in legislation, Aboriginal people (Armitage 1995). The formal definition began originally by defining "Indian" in 1876 via the Indian Act. With its initial passage in 1876, the Indian Act would become the primary tool of assimilation used by the new Dominion government. The intent was to absorb Indian people into the body politic of Canada so that there would be no "Indian problem" and, in the words of Sir John A. Macdonald, " . . . to wean them by slow degrees from their nomadic habits, which have become almost an instinct, and by slow degrees absorb them on the land" (Wotherspoon and Satzewich 2000).

The Indian Act had three central goals. These were to:

1. define who Indians were and were not;

2. manage and protect Indian lands;

3. concentrate authority over Indian people (Indians were to be civilized and Christianized) (Wotherspoon and Satzewich 2000).

A central element of the Act was to advance the government's assimilation policy through the process of enfranchisement or losing one's Indian status under the Act. For example, under Section 12(1)(b) of the Act, an

Indian woman could lose her status if she married a non-Indian man. Women could not own property, and once a woman left the reserve to marry she could not return because non-Indians could not reside on the reserve. This also applied to her children. However, if an Indian man married a non-Indian woman, he not only retained his Indian status, but the non-Indian woman gained status under the Act and so would their children. This legislation stood until 1985, when revisions to the Act occurred as a result of the repatriated Constitution and the Charter of Rights and Freedoms, which prohibited discrimination on the basis of gender. There were other ways for Indian people to lose their status—for example, if they received a university or college education, became clergy or acquired any professional designation, lived outside of the country for five years or more, or wanted to vote (Bourassa, Hampton, and McKay-McNabb 2005).

Because of the sexist specification inherent in this legislation, ramifications of the Indian Act were more severe for Aboriginal women than men, ramifications that continue to have severe impacts on our life chances today. Bonita Lawrence (2000) notes that the Act ordered how Aboriginal people were to think of all things "Indian" and created classifications that have become normalized as "cultural differences." She argues that the differences between Métis (or mixed ancestry people), non-status Indians, Inuit, and status Indians were created by the Act, and those differences became accepted in Canada as cultural in nature when, in fact, they were social constructions imposed by legislation. It should be acknowledged that cultural distinctions did and do exist within and amongst Aboriginal people; however, those cultural distinctions were never categorized nor embedded in legislation prior to 1876 and did not have the same impact until commencement of the Act. Indigenous scholars agree that the Indian Act has controlled Aboriginal identity by creating legal and non-legal categories that have consequences for rights and privileges both within and beyond Aboriginal communities (Lawrence 2000; Mihesuah 1998).

One important consequence of the Indian Act is that status Indian women (hereafter referred to as Indian women) who married non-Indian men lost their Indian status and their band membership under this Act. Prior to 1869, the definition of Indian was fairly broad and generally referred to "all persons of Indian blood, their spouses and their descendents" (Voyageur 2000, 88) After 1869, Indian women who married non-Indians were banished from their communities, since non-Indians were not allowed on reserves; this was true even if a divorce occurred (McIvor 1995). From the government's perspective, these women had assimilated and had no use for their Indian status. The goal of assimilation was a central element of the Indian Act 1876 because it advanced the government's policy of genocide through the process of enfranchisement: the removal of Indian status from an individual. Further, Indian women could not own property, and once a woman left the reserve to marry she could not return to her reserve, so she lost all property rights. This legacy of disenfranchisement was passed on to her children (Wotherspoon and Satzewich 2000). In contrast, an Indian man who married a non-Indian woman not only retained his Indian status, but the non-Indian woman gained status under the Act, as would their children. Even upon divorce or the death of her husband, a non-Indian woman who gained status under the Act through marriage retained her status and band membership as did her children (Voyageur 2000). In contrast, an Indian woman's identity was defined by her husband and could be taken away. The imposition of this Eurocentric, sexist ideology on Aboriginal families was a direct disruption of traditional Aboriginal definitions of family. Under Indian Act legislation, enfranchised Indians were to become Canadian citizens and, as a result, they relinquished their collective ties to their Indian communities (Lawrence 1999). However, Indian women were not granted the benefit of full Canadian citizenship. Lawrence notes that, until 1884, Indian women who had lost their status could not inherit any portion of their husband's land or assets after his death. After 1884, a widow was allowed to inherit one-third of her husband's land(s) and assets if she "was living with her husband at his time of death and was determined by the Indian Agent to be 'of good moral character'" (Lawrence 1999, 56). Furthermore, if a woman married an Indian from another reserve, the Act stated that she must follow her husband and relinquish her band membership in order to become a member of his band. If her husband died or if she divorced him, she could not return to her reserve, as she was no longer a member. These policies governing marriage and divorce were just one of several ways that Aboriginal women were stripped of their rights and privileges. For example, from 1876 to 1951 women who married Indian men and remained on the reserve were denied the right to vote in band elections, to hold elected office, or to participate in public meetings. However, Indian men were eligible to take part in all of these activities (Voyageur 2000). Therefore, colonization was an instrument by which sexism and racism were created and reinforced on and off reserve lands, resulting in diminishing power and resources available to Aboriginal women in Canada.

The passage of the Charter of Rights and Freedoms made gender discrimination illegal and opened the door for Aboriginal women to challenge the Indian Act. In 1967, Aboriginal women lobbied both the federal government and Indian bands for an amendment to the Act. Sharon McIvor (1995) notes that in *Lavell v. Her Majesty* (1974) Aboriginal women challenged the government based on the argument that the government had been discriminating against Indian women for over 100 years via the Indian Act. The Supreme Court of Canada, however, ruled that since Canada had jurisdiction over Indians it could decide who was an Indian and that the Act was not discriminatory. Continual lobbying by Aboriginal women finally resulted in action, and the Act was amended in 1985 through passage of Bill C-31.

However, despite the amendment, long-standing implications of the Indian Act for Aboriginal women in Canada are still evident. As Lawrence notes, the government's "social engineering process" (1999, 58) via the Act ensured that between 1876 and 1985 over 25,000 women lost their status and were forced to leave their communities. Lawrence states: "Taking into account that for every woman who lost status and had to leave her community, all of her descendants also lost status and for the most part were permanently alienated from Native culture, the scale of cultural genocide caused by gender discrimination becomes massive" (Lawrence 1999, 59). She notes that when Bill C-31 was passed in 1985, there were only 350,000 female and male status Indians left in Canada. Bill C-31 allowed individuals who had lost status and their children to apply for reinstatement. Approximately 100,000 individuals had regained status by 1995, but many individuals were unable to regain status. Under Bill C-31, grandchildren and great-grandchildren were not recognized as having Indian status and, in many cases, no longer identified as Indian (Lawrence 1999; Voyageur 2000). In addition, legislative decision still blocked Aboriginal women from full participation in their communities. For example, the Corbiere decision in 1999 (*John Corbiere et al. v. the Batchewana Indian Band and Her Majesty the Queen*) specified that Indian women living off-reserve could not vote in band elections because the Indian Act stated that Indian members must "ordinarily live on reserve" in order to vote. Thus, reinstated Indian women and their children were still at a disadvantage despite having legal recognition under the Act. In the end, the amendments did not repair the damage of previous legislation. Kinship ties, cultural ties, and participation in governance were significantly disrupted. Long-term consequences for these women and their children include the erosion of connections and rights that might have enabled them to work collectively to address social disparities.

Lawrence's reference to social engineering is an important one. The construction of Aboriginal identity continues based on Bill C-31 and the revisions to the Indian Act. While blatant discrimination based on gender has been removed, identities are still shaped based on who one decides to have children with. Today, there are 6(1) and 6(2) status Indians: 6(1) Indians are those who had status before 1985 and 6(2) Indians are, for the most part, reinstated Indians. Consider the following chart:

6(1) + Non-status = 6(2) child
6(2) + Non-status = non-status child
6(1) + 6(2) = 6(1)
6(2) + 6(2) = 6(1)

Thus, once again, depending on who you have a child or children with, you may or may not retain status within the family. This "contemporary" legislation is clearly still racist and colonial in nature and continues to affect Aboriginal people's everyday lived experiences.

It is ironic that the only recourse Aboriginal women have is to appeal to the federal government and judicial system—the same government and system that instituted and upheld the sexist, discriminatory, and oppressive legislation for over 100 years. This government holds different principles of justice than traditional Aboriginal government, leaving women once again vulnerable to multiple oppressions. As Jan Langford writes, "If First Nations governments are built on the traditional Aboriginal way of governing where equity is built into the system, there wouldn't be a need for the 'white' ways of protecting rights" (1995, 35). However, band governing bodies are not working according to the traditional Aboriginal way, instead using legislation to exclude women and protect male privilege.

After fighting for the recognition of Aboriginal rights, Aboriginal women have found themselves at odds with some of their own community leaders. Indian women and their children have not been welcomed back to their communities. Since the 1980s, when the federal government began the process of devolution of control to Indian bands, band governments have been able to refuse band membership. It should be noted that there has been an influx of status Indians going to their bands to seek membership. However, the government has consistently refused to increase funding to those bands. Cora Voyageur notes that some bands have not given band membership to people given status by the federal government because they do not have the resources or the land base to do so. Most reserves are already overcrowded, and many feel that conditions will worsen if a rush of reinstated Indians want to return to the reserve. Some reinstated Indians are referred to as "C-31s," "paper Indians" or "new Indians" (Voyageur). In addition, many of these individuals may have previously been identifying with Métis or non-status Indian communities and were rejected not only by their Indian communities but also by the communities with which they had identified. As Lawrence (1999) reports, that resistance to acknowledging the renewed status of those reinstated under Bill C-31 has been expressed throughout the Native press.

Furthermore, women have been formally excluded from constitutional negotiations as a result of patriarchal legislation that was applied in the federal government's decision to exclude them. The Native Women's Association of Canada (NWAC) has argued that the interests of individual Aboriginal women should not be overshadowed by collective social values and operational mandates that may be enshrined in customary law (Jackson 2000). However, Aboriginal women find themselves caught between bands who appeal to traditional practices to avoid action and a federal government that avoids involvement in deference to self-government (Green 2001). In this way, government intrusion has succeeded in ensuring that divisions among Aboriginal people are maintained, if not more firmly entrenched.

Finally, as Lawrence (1999) argues, "Who am I?" and "Where do I belong?" are common questions among what she calls "people of mixed-race Native heritage." She examines the impact of the Indian Act and Bill C-31 on Métis people in addition to Indian people and argues that the Act has externalized mixed-race Native people from Indian-ness and that this has implications for Native empowerment. What this discussion reveals is that other Aboriginal peoples have also been affected by these policies, and this has likely had consequences for identity, empowerment, and quality of life of all Canada's Indigenous peoples. Indeed, S. 35.1 of the Canadian Constitution (1982) states that "Aboriginal" is defined as "Indian, Inuit and Métis people of Canada." The term "Aboriginal" might lead one to think that we are a homogenous group; however, we are very diverse and, as demonstrated above, the construction of our identities through colonial policy and legislation has led many to question their identity.

A review of the post-contact history of Indigenous people in Canada clearly demonstrates that direct practices of genocide have transformed into legislated control of Aboriginal identity and colonization-based economic, social, and political disadvantage that disproportionately affects Aboriginal women. The government's definition of who can be called Indian, who cannot, and who must exist in liminal spaces where they are outsiders both on and off reserve lands clearly has implications for citizenship, but it also has implications for access to health services and for the ability to maintain health and well-being. With this knowledge, we must re-examine data that suggests Aboriginal women are excessively vulnerable to cerebrovascular disease, coronary heart disease, diabetes, suicide, cancer, depression, substance use, HIV/AIDS, and violence/abuse in light of how colonization and post-colonial processes have conferred risks to the health of Aboriginal women, and barriers to accessing quality health care. These risks and barriers contribute to rates of morbidity and mortality that are well above those of the average Canadian woman.

At a fundamental level, we understand that the colonization processes that began many years ago and continue today have material and social consequences that diminish access to social determinants of health for both Aboriginal men and Aboriginal women. Yet, as we have discussed, women have been especially marginalized through these processes and their lower social status is reflected in diminished resources and poor health. Health consequences for women have been identified, but largely within a western model of equating health with the absence of disease or illness (Newbold 1998). The wounds that result from the cultural ambiguity imposed on Aboriginal women are harder to catalogue. They are perhaps demonstrated to us in the plight of the Aboriginal women of Vancouver's Downtown Eastside. This neighbourhood is home to thousands of Aboriginal women who have been displaced from their reserve communities and extended families (Benoit, Carroll, and Chaudhry 2003). They are socially and culturally isolated, living in poverty, and often driven to substance use, violent relationships, and the street sex trade to survive and provide for their children (Benoit, Carroll, and Chaudhry 2003). Their material circumstances force acts of desperation, but the damage that has been done to their cultural identities can leave them without the foundation to cultivate health and well-being in their lives. Recent initiatives that have arisen out of results from the First Nations and Inuit Regional Health Survey (National Steering Committee) may offer some hope for these women, but they are still disadvantaged in benefiting from them. First, the development of culturally appropriate services will not be useful for women who have been excluded from the definition of that culture and excluded from the decision-making structures that will determine how Aboriginal health resources are to be designed and distributed (Benoit, Carroll, and Chaudhry 2003; Grace 2003). Second, the research that serves as the foundation of these initiatives has not included many Aboriginal women, both because women and children have been overlooked in the work (Young 2003), and because women who do not fit into research-defined categories of "Indian" (derived from federal categories) have not been included in the data collections.

My Personal Healing Journey—Finding My Roots

I began this paper with a quote from my kookum, who tells us to find our roots, our beginnings, so we can live a good life . . . so that we can be well. I have been on that journey since I was a child. The colonial policies and legislation stripped my family of our identity, all because my great-grandmother fell in love with a non-Indian. It has taken me many years to find my roots and, I must admit, I am still on my healing journey. I would like to share what has assisted me to reclaim my identity . . . an identity that was taken, not given willingly. It began in earnest with the beat of a drum . . . *ba boom, ba boom, ba boom* . . .

Some time ago, my kookum began talking about different traditional methods of facilitating healing. So many Indigenous people experience ongoing loss and trauma and do not know how to grieve. They don't know how to heal. I can relate to that. Loss of identity through an assimilation policy (a nice term for cultural genocide) remains one of the most difficult issues facing Indigenous populations. Like many other families, my family suffered identity loss and dealt with intergenerational pain, trauma, and grief through addictions that often led to violence . . . which caused more pain, trauma and grief . . . and so the cycle goes. I have been trying to find a way deal with trauma I experienced as a child for many years. Although I am proud to say I have reclaimed my identity and my culture, I have not been able to let go of the trauma. I decided that Kookum was right . . . if I didn't know how to heal, then I had to at least try to learn how, and since what I had been doing wasn't working, I began to embark on a healing journey with her help. I started to attend sweats and received my traditional name, Morningstar Bear. I earned my first feather and would go out on Mother Earth and pick medicines. One day I was out with Kookum, my daughter, and my friend on the medicine wheel. We were having a great day just observing nature and picking medicine. We were walking up a hill when I heard singing and the beat of a drum. I was excited! I turned to the others and said, "Do you hear that? Where is it coming from?" I was sure that Kookum would lead us over the hill to see people singing at a drum. However, no one else heard it. I stopped and could hear the song—"way hi oh way oh way way oh . . ."—and the drumbeat was strong . . . ba boom ba boom ba boom ba boom—I looked at Kookum in bewilderment. "My girl," she said, "those are your ancestors calling to you." It was one of the most profound moments of my life, yet I still didn't fully understand her meaning . . . though it would become clear in time.

Ba boom ba boom ba boom ba boom . . . you will be a strong child! Kicking your mama so hard . . . I was musing to myself as I let myself feel the vibrations of the drum. I closed my eyes to feel my baby kicking . . . not just kicking randomly but methodically to the beat of the drum. The first song ended . . . my baby stopped kicking. I laughed to myself . . . must be a coincidence . . . the second honour song starts . . . ba boom ba boom ba boom ba boom . . . My unborn child kicking to the beat of the drum . . .

It was a good day . . . a day of celebration. We had just finished a sweat with Kookum, and many of my students were there. Some were graduating and others were just starting out, but it was a good sweat and a beautiful night. My daughter, who had received her name a year before, sweated with us and she sat on my knee as we feasted and visited with our friends and extended family. Then four of the women got out their hand drums and stood in front of the fire. One of them, a wonderful, strong Métis woman, said that they were singing a song in honour of my recent accomplishment . . . obtaining my Ph.D. They sang "Strong Woman" and, although I hadn't heard it before, when they started singing to their drums it was like I had known it my whole life. I sang it with them, as did my daughter. I felt energy as I had never felt course through my body. My daughter held Kookum's drum and beat in rhythm with the women as if it were the most natural thing in the world . . . and perhaps it was. She asked if I wanted to drum . . . "no, my girl, you drum."

Thinking back, I have been called to the drum many times yet was unaware of it . . . or maybe I was. Perhaps I wasn't ready to let go of the pain. Maybe I was too comfortable with it. When you carry pain around with you your entire life it sometimes becomes so familiar that you wonder how you will feel if it's gone. So either consciously or unconsciously I avoided the repeated calls to the drum until one day not long ago when my kookum introduced the drum to a group of grieving women. We gather in friendship and we lay our burdens down. I've never felt such energy as I do when I am at the drum. This group of women, wounded warriors, gathers often, and although we've never shared our hurts and loss in words, we share it at the drum as we lay down our burdens. I know that I cannot change history, and I also know that I cannot stay in a place of anger and resentment. No one can heal for me . . . it is my responsibility. So I am thankful for my women warriors, my sisters, and for Kookum and for the strength I get from that drum. The drum is a gift from God and it has allowed me to move forward. I am learning to grieve and that is the first step to being whole.

Meegwetch Kookum and all my warrior sisters.

REFERENCES

Armitage, Andrew. 1995. *Comparing the policy of Aboriginal assimilation: Australia, Canada and New Zealand.* Vancouver: University of British Columbia Press.

Benoit, C., D. Carroll, and M. Chaudhry. 2003. "In search of a healing place: Aboriginal women in Vancouver's Downtown Eastside." *Social Science and Medicine* 56: 821–33.

Bourassa, Carrie, Mary Hampton, and Kim McKay-McNabb. 2006. "Racism, sexism and colonialism: The impact on the health of Aboriginal women." In *Canadian woman studies: An introductory reader,* ed. Andrea Medovarski and Brenda Cranney, 540–51. 2nd ed. Toronto: Inana Publications.

Corbiere v. Canada (Minister of Indian and Northern Affairs), [1999] 2 S.C.R. 203.

Elias, Peter Douglas. 2002. *The Dakota of the Canadian Northwest: Lessons for survival.* Regina: Canadian Plains Research Center.

Grace, Sherryl L. 2003. "A review of Aboriginal women's physical and mental health status in Ontario." *Canadian Journal of Public Health* 94 (3): 173–5.

Green, J. A. 2001. "Canaries in the mines of citizenship: Indian women in Canada." *Canadian Journal of Political Science/Revue Canadienne de Science Politique* 34 (4): 715–38.

Jackson, Margaret. 2000. "Aboriginal women and self-government." In *Expressions in Canadian Native Studies,* ed. R. F. Laliberte et al., 355–73.

Laliberte, R. F., P. Settee, J. B. Waldram, R. Innes, B. Macdougall, L. McBain, and F. L. Barron, eds. 2000. *Expressions in Canadian Native Studies.* Saskatoon: University of Saskatchewan Extension Press.

Langford, Jan. 1995. "First Nations women: Leaders in community development." *Canadian Woman Studies* 14 (4): 34–36.

Lawrence, B. 2000. "Mixed-race urban Native people: Surviving a legacy of policies of genocide." In *Expressions in Canadian Native Studies,* ed. R. F. Laliberte et al., 69–94.

McIvor, S. D. 1995. "Aboriginal women's rights as existing rights." *Canadian Woman Studies/les cahiers de al femme* 14 (4): 34–38.

Mihesuah, D. A., ed. 1998. *Natives and academics: Researching and writing about American Indians.* Lincoln: University of Nebraska Press.

Newbold, K. B. 1998. "Problems in search of solutions: Health and Canadian Aboriginals." *Journal of Community Health* 23 (1): 59–73.

Royal Commission on Aboriginal Peoples. 1996. *Report of the Royal Commission on Aboriginal peoples.* Ottawa: Supply and Services Canada.

Voyageur, C. 2000. "Contemporary Aboriginal women in Canada." In *Visions of the heart: Canadian Aboriginal Issues,* ed. David Long and Olive P. Dickason, 81–106. Toronto: Harcourt Canada.

Wotherspoon, Terry, and Vic Satzewich. 2000. *First Nations: Race, Class, and Gender Relations.* Regina: Canadian Plains Research Center.

Young, T. K. 2003. "Review of research on Aboriginal populations in Canada: Relevance to their health needs." *British Medical Journal* 327: 419–22.

Missing Out and Missing:

Connecting the Economic and Political Marginalization of Women to the Phenomenon of Disappearance

IAN PEACH[1] AND KIERA LADNER

I t is often argued that feminism is an Indigenous tradition that has been co-opted by the whitestream/mainstream feminist movement.[2] Indigenous women exist at the centre of their cultures, and their place in society (politically, economically, and spiritually) and status as women was (and is) honoured in Indigenous traditions. Travels in "Indian Country" lead one to conclude that subjugation, oppression and violence against women are not Indigenous traditions, as neither was tolerated traditionally. Instead, teachings about the ideal of "living the good life" speak of harmony, respect, kindness, non-judgement, responsibility, and non-violence. According to Devon Mihesuah, it was a world quite apart from our own today, where women were at very least the economic, political, and spiritual equals of men.[3]

IAN PEACH is a special advisor to the Office of the Federal Interlocutor for Métis and Non-Status Indians. In his twenty years of public service, Ian has been involved in numerous intergovernmental negotiations and policy development exercises, many focused on issues of constitutional law, federalism, Aboriginal self-government, and the socio-economic equality of Aboriginal peoples.

KIERA LADNER is associate professor and Canada Research Chair in Indigenous Politics and Governance in the Department of Political Studies at the University of Manitoba.

For the most part, this is history. While the centrality of women and inclusivity may still exist as discourses in Indigenous communities and may be viewed as grounding Indigenous cultures, traditions, and world views, reality paints a much different picture than the ideals of traditionalism. While gender violence was not tolerated traditionally within Indigenous communities, violence has become an epidemic within these communities today—thus creating a situation whereby victimization in Canada is a racialized (as well as a gendered) phenomenon.

Canadian criminal justice statistics make this reality clear. According to the 2004 General Social Survey, Aboriginal people[4] are three times more likely than non-Aboriginal people to be victims of violence.[5] As well, the General Social Survey indicates that Aboriginal women are not only 3.5 times as likely to be victims of violent crimes than non-Aboriginal women, but they are more likely to be victims of violence than Aboriginal men (at 343 incidents per 1,000 population 15 years old and older, compared to 292 incidents per 1,000 population for men), while non-Aboriginal women are actually less likely to be victims of violence than non-Aboriginal men.[6]

The 2004 General Social Survey also indicates that Aboriginal people are over three times more likely to have experienced physical or sexual violence from a spouse, partner, or ex-partner.[7] Unsurprisingly, Aboriginal women are particularly vulnerable, with nearly one-quarter of Aboriginal women reporting being the victims of spousal violence, compared to 18 percent of Aboriginal men.[8] Aboriginal victims of spousal violence were also more likely to sustain injuries than non-Aboriginal people and were much more likely than non-Aboriginal people to suffer the most severe forms of violence, such as being beaten, choked, threatened with a knife or gun, having a knife or gun used against them, or being sexually assaulted. Forty-one percent of Aboriginal victims of spousal violence reported that they were subjected to these sorts of violence, compared to 27 percent of non-Aboriginal victims.[9] This gap is even larger when only female victims are considered, with 54 percent of Aboriginal women who were victims of spousal violence reporting being subjected to the most serious forms of spousal violence, compared to 37 percent of non-Aboriginal women.[10] What is the source for this epidemic of violence against Indigenous women? Its roots lie in the experience of colonialism that so profoundly affects Indigenous people and communities to this day.

How is it that Indigenous nations went from being societies against power, subjugation and oppression, where violence was not tolerated, to a situation where violence has become normalized within Indigenous communities and violence against women has been described as an epidemic?[11]

Accounting for this discrepancy enables us to begin to understand the context within which women are vulnerable to violence (and other determining factors or conditions of vulnerability) and the context within which Indigenous women are missing and murdered.

Colonialism was and continues to be, as Andrea Smith has suggested, a gendered enterprise.[12] Colonialism has not simply resulted in a re-gendering of Indigenous society modelled after gender constructs and norms in western, Eurocentric society. Rather, colonialism is a gendered enterprise, which has been advanced by racialized sexual violence perpetrated and perpetuated by the church and the state as a means of securing control over Indigenous nations and their lands.[13] This re-gendering of society through state-sanctioned violence, oppression, and disempowerment affected both men and women, as both lost their autonomy and independence under the Indian Act, and all lost economic, social and political power as the state aggressively engaged in the destruction of these societies. But women were affected differently.

Colonialism was a gendered process that "maligned and devalued" women, while male privilege was "normalized and legitimized."[14] Colonialism was pursued as a gendered enterprise by most actors in the process, including missionaries (the introduction of spiritual beliefs and practices that have historically maligned and devalued women), the church (residential schools), and the state (contributing to the re-gendering of Indigenous society by engaging patriarchal policies and practices, such as its practice of addressing, and negotiating with, only the men of a nation). As a gendered enterprise that devalued women, normalized male privilege, and re-gendered Indigenous society, colonialism is most widely attributed to the state. This was achieved by the state through the patriarchal provisions of the Indian Act, which excluded women from formally participating in band governance until 1951, denied women property rights (property was originally allocated to male heads of households—a practice that continues and is reinforced by the lack of matrimonial property law), and were denied equal membership rights until 1985 (arguably, for the descendants of those who were reinstated as status Indians, equal membership is still denied).

The residential school system has proven to be a particularly powerful tool of colonialism, and of the gendered violence that accompanies it. Sexual, physical, and mental abuse became institutions in the Indigenous community through the residential school experience. Skyrocketing rates of substance abuse have often been linked to the traumas of residential school (both for parents who had their children taken from them and for the survivors) and gendered violence, domination, and oppression have roots in this experience and can be linked to state policies that disempowered and demoralized Indigenous people. While not all Aboriginal people went to residential school, most have suffered the effects and trauma of residential school (including a loss of language and culture, a lack of parenting skills among survivors, the cycle of abuse), and all have suffered the effects and trauma of colonization. But while all Indigenous people have been affected by colonialism and have endured its violence, oppression and disempowerment, women have been doubly affected by colonialism as a result of both gender and race. Suggesting that women have been doubly or disproportionately affected by colonialism should be construed as a statement of difference rather than as a diminution of the experience of men, as they, too, have suffered the effects and legacies of colonialism and continue to do so.

In explaining the discrepancy between traditional and contemporary Indigenous societies, it is important to understand that, while the state and the church have lessened their direct role in perpetrating and perpetuating gendered violence, devaluation, oppression, and disempowerment, the sexist policies and attitudes of both church and state have infiltrated Indigenous communities. According to Verna St. Denis,

> Some would argue that colonialism affected Aboriginal peoples in varying degree and scope, and therefore in some places Aboriginal cultural traditions and practices have remained more or less intact. I argue that the overwhelming majority of Aboriginal people have gone through some degree of socialization into Christianity as well as incorporation into the patriarchic capitalist political economy and education system, and are therefore subject to western ideologies of gender identities and relationships.[15]

All Indigenous people are forced to confront the legacies of colonialism on a daily basis. Yet while men had their roles, autonomy, and territory removed and have been privy to the same history of colonialism as a project of oppression, violence, and dispossession, women have been doubly subjected, as colonialism has become imbedded in Indigenous societies and is now perpetuated from within—resulting in a change from state-based perpetration of violence to one where communities themselves also engage in its perpetration and perpetuation. The widespread (yet incomplete) internalization of sexism and heteronormativity and the normalization of gendered violence, oppression, dispossession, and devaluation have led to the current state of Aboriginal communities.

Differentiating the experiences of Indigenous women from the experiences of women from the dominant culture (those with whom the women's movement and feminism has been most concerned), Mihesuah states, "In regard to Indian women, because of their varied economic situations, social values, appearances and gender roles, they have been oppressed by men and women—both non-Indians *and,* interestingly enough, other Indians."[16] That is to say, beyond the sexualized and racialized context of vulnerability that has been created by the state within Indigenous communities, there has developed a "trickle-down patriarchy" where women now have to contend with male domination and increasing marginalization.[17]

Of course, marginalization and victimization are closely tied together. The risk of victimization is elevated by a number of factors, many of which are also indicators of socio-economic marginalization. These include having low educational attainment, being unemployed, having a low income, being a member of a lone-parent family, living in crowded conditions, and having high residential mobility.[18] As the 2006 Census data reveals, Aboriginal people are more likely to live with all of these factors than are non-Aboriginal people. For example, 29 percent of Aboriginal children aged 14 and under, and 31 percent of First Nations children lived in a household headed by a lone mother (more than twice the percentage among non-Aboriginal children). When this data for First Nations children is broken down by residency, 26 percent of those living on reserves lived with a lone mother, compared to 35 percent of those living off reserves.[19] While detailed census tables with gender breakdowns are not yet available in many cases, it is well understood that Aboriginal women experience several of these risk factors even more than Aboriginal men. Yet the 2006 Census also reveals the efforts that Indigenous women are making to overcome their disempowerment and continuing economic marginalization, primarily through education.[20]

While a significant educational gap between Aboriginal and non-Aboriginal Canadians continues to exist according to the 2006 Census data on highest level of education (certificate, diploma, or degree earned), breaking down the Aboriginal data by gender reveals that Indigenous women in Canada are obtaining an education at a higher rate (and in some cases, significantly higher) than Indigenous men. For example, 46.3 percent of Aboriginal men 15 years old and older have no certificate of any sort, while 41.2 percent of Aboriginal women in the same age categories have none.[21] Similar gaps exist for university educations (with 5.2 percent of Aboriginal women having a bachelor's degree as their highest level of education compared to 3.0 percent of Aboriginal men), college or CEGEP educations (with 17.2 percent of Aboriginal women having college or CEGEP certificates or diplomas compared to 11.6 percent of men), and high school completion (with 22.9 percent of Aboriginal women having achieved high school completion as their highest level of education compared to 20.6 percent of men).[22] Indeed, other than in the "no certificate" category, the only category in which Aboriginal men are represented at a higher rate than Aboriginal women is in the trades.[23]

This educational attainment gap between Indigenous women and men exists whether they live in urban areas or on reserves. There is a significant gap, however, between educational achievement of urban Aboriginal people and Aboriginal people who reside on reserves, whether they are male or female. For example, the percentage of Aboriginal residents on reserves without any certificates, both male and female, is more than 1.5 times the percentage of those resident in urban areas, while the percentage of Aboriginal men residing in urban areas who have bachelor's degrees is over 3 times the percentage for Aboriginal men residing on reserves.[24] Aboriginal women are more than twice as likely to have a bachelor's degree if they are urban residents than if they reside on reserves.[25] If we accept that education is the key to economic empowerment in the modern economy, Indigenous women who live on reserves are more likely to be economically marginalized, and therefore vulnerable to exploitation, than those who live in urban areas.

As these statistics on economic and educational marginalization demonstrate, both the state and Indigenous communities create and perpetuate marginalization and, thus, conditions of vulnerability. Such conditions of vulnerability are direct corollaries to the urban migration of women, which, in turn, creates the conditions for women to go missing and be murdered. As Nancy Janovicek notes,

> While most scholars agree that Aboriginal people have been more likely to leave the reserve because they were pushed away, there is a consensus that more men than women chose to leave the reserve seeking employment or educational opportunities. Many women who left the reserve were compelled to do so because they had lost their status and housing. Despite the disparity between men's and women's migration patterns, gender has not been central to the analysis of the urban experience.[26]

While loss of status as a contributing factor to urbanization is no longer a factor, many women are compelled to leave their communities because of the lack of adequate housing on-reserve and because of the lack of matrimonial property law (meaning property ownership is typically male-dominated). According to the 2006 Census, 26 percent of First Nations people on reserves live in crowded conditions (though this is down from the 33 percent recorded in the 1996 Census).[27] First Nations people were four times more likely than non-Aboriginal people to live in homes in need of major repairs.[28] Poor housing conditions were especially common on reserves, with about 44 percent living in a house in need of major repairs, compared to 17 percent of First Nations people living off reserves.[29]

Also contributing to female marginalization (and related to housing) is the abject poverty that faces Indigenous peoples living on most reserves in Canada—as Lynne and Farley note, "given the brutal poverty that has been documented on Canadian reserves, migration is also critical for First Nations women's economic survival."[30] Other contributing factors, such as the epidemic of violence that besieges Indigenous communities[31] and the lack of services (counselling, health, treatment and other) available on reserve, also cause many women to seek refuge in cities. Thus, while the majority of First Nations people[32] are women (51.6 percent, according to the 2006 Census), they are actually a minority (49.3 percent) of the on-reserve population.[33] Looking beyond women, many youth also seek to escape reserve life and find refuge in urban areas. Because "prostitution is intimately related to homelessness, . . . First Nations youth who leave their communities for urban areas are particularly vulnerable to sexual exploitation in that they are both homeless and in an unfamiliar cultural environment."[34]

Though the government has been attempting to ease the transition of urbanization using a variety of program and policy mechanisms (such as the domestic work placement program of the 1960s) and funding programs and services through Friendship Centres and Aboriginal housing projects (these have been established by provincial governments), many Aboriginal people are negatively affected by the transition process due in large part to the same reasons for which they left reserves—lack of services, lack of adequate and affordable housing, and lack of employment.[35] Lack of adequate housing is by no means just a reserve problem; eleven percent of Aboriginal people lived in crowded homes, compared to three percent of the non-Aboriginal population, and nearly one-quarter of Aboriginal people lived in homes in need of major repairs, compared to seven percent of the non-Aboriginal population.[36] Partly as a consequence of the lack of adequate housing, Aboriginal people are slightly more likely to have moved within a year than non-Aboriginal people. Twelve percent of Aboriginal people moved within the same census subdivision in the year prior to the census, compared to eight percent of the non-Aboriginal population, and eight percent of the Aboriginal population moved between communities, compared to five percent of the non-Aboriginal population.[37] While they move seeking greater opportunities and better circumstances, many Indigenous people find themselves living in the same situation that they were seeking to flee—but without the support of family, community, and a familiar culture. Many find themselves living in so-called urban reserves such as Vancouver's Downtown Eastside or Winnipeg's North End, where they face new challenges—high crime rates, street gangs (and the accompanying violence), prostitution, homelessness, and increased rates of substance abuse.

For recent arrivals as well as long-term residents, the urban environment holds many of the same challenges that are faced on reserves—only there are far fewer services available and far fewer resources (especially for Métis and non-status people). That this environment creates and perpetuates the marginalization and context of vulnerability that contributes to the types of statistics that characterize "urban reserves" and the experiences of many urban Aboriginal people (though there are many stories of "success" among urban Aboriginal people) is a direct corollary to colonization and living with the legacies of colonization.

Even if one steps beyond seeing colonialism as the historical relationship between the state and the conditions of vulnerability which sometimes manifest as murdered and missing women, there remains a connection between the state and missing and murdered women that is readily articulated by Lynne and Farley. Their study of prostitution in Vancouver's Downtown Eastside, where 52 percent of prostitutes are Aboriginal, readily identifies a link between prostitution and the lack of policies, supports, and services. As Lynne and Farley comment, "Just as wife beating was historically viewed as having been provoked by the victim, prostitution is still viewed by some as a job choice in which the victim consents."[38] Their work, however, makes it clear that this myth is nothing more than that— a myth. Of those involved in the survey research conducted by Lynne and Farley, 95 percent articulated a desire to leave prostitution, but 82 percent specified that they needed drug and alcohol treatment, 67 percent needed job training, 66 percent needed a safe place to live, and 58 percent needed counselling.[39] Such services are not readily accessible, making it extremely difficult for women to address the core issues of their vulnerability.

So what are the answers to this situation? One needs to consider not only policy responses to address the particular causes of vulnerability and disempowerment, but also a structural transformation of the relationship between Indigenous women and the structures of the communities of which they are a part, whether through membership and heritage or residency. As well, action will require a variety of policy responses and will require the coordinated effort of the Government of Canada, provincial and territorial governments, First Nations and Métis organizations, and municipal governments.

In addition to a stronger response from those within the criminal justice field to the disappearance and murder of Indigenous women, four areas seem ripe for further action. The first area of opportunity is education, given the high economic returns to education for Indigenous women. Though labour market participation and employment rates for Indigenous women are almost always lower than for Indigenous men with equivalent education, and labour market participation and employment rates for Indigenous people of both genders are lower than for the non-Aboriginal population, the gender gap narrows as Indigenous people receive more education. For example, there is a labour force participation gap of nearly 17 percentage points between urban First Nations men and women with no educational certificates, but this gap narrows to just over 13 percentage points for those who have completed high school and only two percentage points for those who have university degrees.[40] Similarly, for those who reside on reserves, the gap narrows from nearly 11.5 percentage points between First Nations men and women with no educational certificates to slightly less than nine percentage points for those who have completed high school and less than one half of a percentage point for those with university degrees.[41]

The trend is the same if one compares employment rates for First Nations men and women. For those who reside in urban areas, the gender gap in employment rates goes from nearly 15 percentage points for those people who lack any educational certificates to slightly less than 13 percentage points for those who have completed high school and two percentage points for those who have university degrees.[42] The value of a university degree to First Nations women is even more obvious when one looks at employment rates for reserve residents. The gap between employment rates for male and female reserve residents who have no educational certificates.is nearly six percentage points (on very low employment rates of 28.2 percent for men and 22.5 percent for women) and four percentage points for those who have completed high school (at 51.1 percent for men and 47.2 percent for women).[43] The gender gap actually reverses, however, for those with university degrees. First Nations women who reside on reserves and have university degrees have an employment rate more than three percentage points *higher* than that of men with an equivalent education, with women having an employment rate of 74.8 percent and men a rate of 71.5 percent.[44] It is hard to imagine anyone arguing against making efforts to close the educational gap between Indigenous and non-Aboriginal women in the face of this data.[45] A number of responses, more or less radical, are worthy of consideration.

First of all, schools need to undertake better monitoring of student achievement and, most of all, better reporting, including reporting by ethnicity and gender. Some, such as John Richards, have long argued that good measurement and reporting lead to better results, particularly if incentives are provided to encourage improvement.[46] Certainly, good reporting will help to empower the parents of students by putting information at their disposal. This leads to the second point—innovative school governance that will increase parental involvement and control over their children's education. Various provinces have already experimented with changes to school governance; the role of Indigenous parents (and Elders) needs to be promoted and supported as part of these innovations.

Reform of school governance also needs to be part of the agenda on reserves. The stand-alone schoolhouse model, in which education is treated as another service provided by Chief and Council, cannot take advantage of the types of specialized programming available to students off reserves. Thus, First Nations should seriously consider establishing school boards at the regional level and use those board structures both to pool resources for services none could provide on their own and to create innovative school governance models.

The educational experience also needs reform, especially for Indigenous people who live in urban areas. Some efforts have been made by school boards in some provinces to create Aboriginal-focused (or at least Aboriginal-positive) schools, but the educational environment for Aboriginal students needs more. There need to be opportunities for the education of Aboriginal students to be transformative, to be part of the process of decolonizing the mind, so that Indigenous women are empowered and both Indigenous men and women re-establish valued social roles. Such decolonizing can be built on a return to, and evolution of, Indigenous traditions, but is likely to require schools governed and managed by Indigenous people themselves.

We recognize the concerns that such a proposal will raise about segregation and damage to already tenuous inter-societal relations, but Indigenous-run schools should be part of a diversified educational environment in which every student can find a satisfying, affirming, and challenging educational experience. If we can choose what we most prefer from a hundred brands of toothpaste, why should we not have a choice in something as important as the education of ourselves and our children? This is not segregation, because at the heart of this idea is both a legal and a practical opportunity for individuals and families to make meaningful choices. Even really radical ideas, such as using tuition vouchers to support parental and student choices about which schools they attend, need to be debated, and governments, both federal and provincial, need to be ready to provide financial support and expertise to innovative programming

designed to improve the performance of Indigenous students, and especially Indigenous girls and women.

As the work of Lynne and Farley points out, counselling and addictions
treatment should also be a high priority. By this we do not mean simply
more counselling and treatment, though more is clearly necessary, but also
more culturally relevant counselling and treatment. Helping Indigenous
women in need of counselling and those who are addicted to harmful substances to renew their cultural connections, as part of the counselling
process, can be an important part of renewing their self-worth and can
have benefits for the renewal of their communities if these women can
find a role for themselves in their communities. In some cases, this may
require some radical strategies, but radical ideas need to be taken seriously
if we are to bring an end to the disappearance and murder of Indigenous
women. Some women may need intensive, one-on-one mentoring from
other Indigenous people. Those suffering from addictions and mental
health issues and others, such as those suffering from Fetal Alcohol Spectrum Disorder, may need access to housing models in which counsellors,
teachers, and service providers are available right on-site. Governments
provide "assisted living" to the elderly and physically infirm; should governments not also be providing this form of housing to those suffering the
effects of addiction and mental health issues?

These comments lead to the third critical area—that of adequate housing.
We have already pointed out the potential value of an "assisted living"
model of housing, but governments also need to take their housing standards and their responsibility for the renewal of the affordable housing
stock seriously. Slumlords, crack houses, and gang headquarters do not
make neighbourhoods in which Indigenous women and their children can
feel safe from exploitation and violence. In Regina, a central component
of the Regina Inner-City Community Partnership has been the more effective enforcement of housing standards and the renewal of housing stock,
and it has been undertaken in conjunction with the community association
and residents. It is not reinventing the world in one great reform; yet, slowly
but surely, Reginans and their governments are improving the housing
stock in North Central Regina. This is a practical effort worth emulating.

We also know, of course, that reserves also need more housing, as often
a lack of housing forces Indigenous women and their families to leave their
reserve communities for urban centres. Whether for housing on reserves
or off, however, it is worth considering getting people involved in the construction of their own housing, thereby building "sweat equity" in their
homes and building their skills. Imagine, if you will, an Indigenous
Women's Housing Co-op in which Indigenous women not only have

access to adequate, affordable housing, but in which those women also have had a hand in building the co-op's homes. Such an arrangement would be one route to empowerment and self-respect.

Access to housing in a market economy will always, however, require access to funds. To ensure that Indigenous women from reserves have access to funds that will provide them with independence and security in the event of the dissolution of a relationship, it is also vital that these women have the benefit of a matrimonial property regime, just as women who live off reserves do. The current federal government has decided that this issue must be tackled, as it must, because property is economic power and the disempowerment of First Nations women who leave their partners cannot be allowed to continue. We recognize the challenges in creating such a regime in the context of a regime of collective property-holding by First Nations on behalf of all of their members, but such challenges cannot be used as an excuse for disempowering Indigenous women and denying them access to the funds necessary to start a new life for themselves and their children when they decide to leave a relationship.

Possibly the most important policy response is ensuring that Indigenous women have a voice in political processes, whether in the governments of their First Nations or Métis communities or in the governments of the dominant society where they reside, at the municipal, provincial, and federal levels. As Stout and Kipling state:

> Of course, . . . it can be argued that . . . real improvement is unlikely until Aboriginal women possess the political power necessary to force the pace and direction of change. . . . [T]here is growing evidence to suggest that Aboriginal women's struggle to obtain equitable representation within the administrative structures of their communities is achieving results, both within Aboriginal communities themselves and in the eyes of outside researchers and policy makers.[47]

Decolonization is, thus, an essential part of the equation, but this decolonization must be genuine. Negotiating self-government arrangements that simply transfer Indian Act governance and administrative structures to First Nations in the guise of decolonization will not suffice. Self-administration is neither self-government nor decolonization. The powers, jurisdictional authority and autonomy (or semblance thereof) of Indigenous nations (Métis, Inuit, and First Nations) need to be restored. That said, empowering these communities needs to go beyond creating political capacity and policy responsiveness.

Beyond securing recognition of the right to self-government and affirming existing and/or negotiated jurisdiction, there must be a commitment to reconfiguring the contemporary structures of Indigenous government (those that were created by and/or are now recognized by the state) to re-establish the central place of women in the communities, as existed prior to the imposition of colonialism. This is not such an easy task. While scholars, politicians, and community leaders have spent the better part of the last 30 years dreaming self-government and decolonization, the same cannot be said about gender. As Joyce Green has noted, decolonization has not been attentive to considerations of gender, but has instead framed gender as a secondary consideration that is to be dealt with after self-governance has been secured and nationhood (some semblance of Indigenous sovereignty and jurisdiction) re-established.[48]

As Cora Voyageur's work demonstrates, this is not simply a matter of "opening the door" or enabling the inclusion of women in government.[49] At very least, attitudes and structures need to be transformed fully to enable inclusion in existing processes. Including gender in policy considerations is another matter all together. Thus, decolonizing governance without decolonizing gender and making gender a primary concern in the process of political decolonization is unlikely to result in the structural, cultural, and policy changes that are necessary to end the colonial mentality (gendered violence, oppression, and domination) that has besieged Indigenous communities and which Indigenous governments commonly perpetrate and perpetuate. This is extremely important, for it is only by making gender a focus in the transformation of Indigenous governance and community that we will see the conditions of vulnerability (conditions that can sometimes lead to missing and murdered women) ameliorated.

Non-Aboriginal governments, too, must seek to find a place for the Indigenous minorities, and Indigenous women in particular, in their government structures. After all, Indigenous women live in cities and towns in provinces and territories of Canada and thus should have real opportunities to exercise their right to participate in the governance of those communities, too—if they so choose. Though many individuals and their nations oppose participation in the politics of the dominant society, having framed such activity as participating in the political processes of a foreign nation, many people choose to participate in Canadian politics and do not see it as detracting from the nation-to-nation relationship or the status of Indigenous peoples as nations. For those who choose to participate, it is important for Canadian governments to make every effort to facilitate the inclusion of Indigenous peoples and voices in government and in creating policies that effectively respond to the conditions that result in vulnerability. These governments might also discover that the influence of Indigenous women and the decision-making processes they traditionally used may lead to better government that makes better decisions and is more legitimate in the eyes of all of their constituents.

In an article examining the root causes of Indigenous prostitution, Farley and Lynne conclude that, "a lack of co-existence between [Indigenous] nations and states is at the root of social and political crises."[50] Thus, beyond transforming community governance (recognizing self-government) and encouraging the participation of Indigenous women in their own governments and/or those of the dominant society, co-existence needs to be addressed. As the Royal Commission on Aboriginal Peoples argued, co-existence or the relation between the colonizer and the colonized (and their respective nations) has to be addressed and reframed as a solid relationship upon which we can build a new future—one in which all peoples are included and respected as partners in Confederation. As such, to ensure that Indigenous peoples (particularly Indigenous women) have a voice in the political and policy processes that affect them (and in turn cause the conditions of vulnerability outlined in this paper), it may be necessary to move beyond a discussion of facilitating Indigenous participation through "normal" means of electoral participation, party politics, and lobbying, and to consider the formalization of the nation-to-nation relationship (but that is a whole other paper).

We are reminded of Thomas King's 2003 CBC Massey Lecture[51] about the stories of his life, and of colonialism, the state and of Aboriginal oral traditions. Though his stories do not speak directly to the gendered and racialized violence and conditions of vulnerability that we have drawn attention to, they do speak to the legacies of colonialism. More importantly, by asking his audience the poignant question "Now that you have heard the story, what are you going to do with it" at the end of his lecture, he also speaks to the responsibilities that all peoples have for the perpetuation of colonialism and its legacies. Thus, we ask, "Now that you have heard this story, what are you going to do about it?"

There are many ways in which we can respond to this situation so as to ensure that we drastically reduce the conditions of vulnerability that lead to missing and murdered women. Remember, prostitution is not a career choice. Young girls do not aspire to live a life dominated by violence or to be prostituted. Statistics show that most people engaged in prostitution would rather not—but lack the supports that they see as necessary to make other choices possible for them. The reality is that something can be done and something needs to be done. We have to make sure that we do not have yet another generation of girls and young women living in conditions where violence is an epidemic and vulnerability is normalized.

To this end, we have outlined four key areas in which policy responses are desperately needed. Beyond this, however, societal change is also needed to respond to the disjuncture between Indigenous traditions and the present-day reality in which violence has been termed an epidemic and vulnerability is normalized. The gendered and racialized violence that has defined colonialism and its legacies needs to be challenged—through both public policy and individual action. In so doing, however, one must not just look towards the lofty goal of decolonization. Instead, one must take action on issues such as this, and understand that true decolonization means renewing our understanding of gender, ending violence and conditions of vulnerability. Thus, now that you know this story, we must move to (re)gender Indigenous policy, and to (re)gender decolonization and we must work quickly so as to ensure a different life for that next generation.

ENDNOTES

1   While Mr. Peach was employed with the Office of the Federal Interlocutor at the time of writing, this paper is based on his experience as a scholar, as an official with provincial governments as well as the federal government, and as a former Director of the Saskatchewan Institute of Public Policy. The paper reflects his views and those of his co-author and do not necessarily reflect the policy of the Government of Canada.

2   Wagner, "The root of oppression," 11–13; Smith, "Indigenous feminism."

3   Mihesuah, "Commonality of difference," 20.

4   "Aboriginal people" means anyone who identified him or herself as North American Indian, Métis, or Inuit, a Treaty Indian or Registered Indian or a member of an Indian Band or First Nation. As "Aboriginal" remains more common in government documents than "Indigenous," we use the term "Aboriginal" when referring to government surveys and reports that also use this term.

5   Brzozowski et al., "Victimization," 5.

6   Ibid.

7   Ibid, 6. Twenty-one percent of Aboriginal people reported having experienced some form of physical or sexual violence by a spouse in the five years preceding the 2004 survey, compared to six percent of non-Aboriginal people.

8   Ibid.

9   Ibid.

10 Ibid, 7.

11 Farley and Lynne, "Prostitution of Indigenous women," 8.

12 Smith, *Conquest.*

13 Ibid.

14 Barker, "Gender, sovereignty and the discourse of rights," 133.

15 St. Denis, "Feminism is for everybody," 41.

16 Mihesuah, 20.

17 Guerrero, "Patriarchal colonialism and Indigenism," 58.

18 Brzozowski et al., 3.

19 Statistics Canada, *Aboriginal peoples in Canada*, 15, 44.

20 Unfortunately, 2006 Census data on the incomes of Aboriginal peoples was not available at the time of writing.

21 Statistics Canada, *Aboriginal identity (8), highest certificate, diploma or degree (14), major field of study—classification of instructional programs, 2000 (14), area of residence (6), age groups (10A) and sex (3)*. Of course, only 23.1 percent of the non-Aboriginal population in Canada has no certificate and only part of this gap can be accounted for by the fact that those aged 15 to 19 make up a larger proportion of the Aboriginal population than the non-Aboriginal population.

22 Ibid.

23 Ibid. While 14.9 percent of Aboriginal men have a trades certification, only 8.2 percent of Aboriginal women do.

24 Ibid.

25 Ibid.

26 Janovicek, "Assisting our own," 548.

27 Statistics Canada, *Aboriginal peoples in Canada*, 45.

28 Ibid., 46.

29 Ibid.

30 Farley and Lynne, 7.

31 Nahanee, "Dancing with a gorilla."

32 References to "First Nations people" mean people who provided a North American Indian identity single response on the Census, unless otherwise noted.

33 Statistics Canada, *Aboriginal identity (8), area of residence (6), age groups (12) and sex (3)*.

34 Farley and Lynne, 7.

35 McCallum, "Labour, modernity and the Canadian state."

36 Statistics Canada, *Aboriginal peoples in Canada*, 16.

37 Ibid., 17.

38 Farley and Lynne, 12.

39 Ibid, 6.

40 Statistics Canada, *Labour force activity (8), Aboriginal identity (8), highest certificate, diploma or degree (14), area of residence (6), age groups (12A) and sex (3)*.

41 Ibid.

42 Ibid.

43 Ibid.

44 Ibid.

45 This is not to suggest that there is an argument against greater efforts to improve the educational attainment of Indigenous men, considering that their educational attainment

rates are lower than for Indigenous women, but the data makes it clear that the economic returns to education for Indigenous women are higher than for Indigenous men.

46 See, for example, Richards, *Creating choices*, 77–78, 99–100.
47 Stout and Kipling, *Aboriginal women in Canada*, 31.
48 Green, "Taking account of Aboriginal feminism."
49 See, for example, Voyageur, *First Nations women in leadership*.
50 Farley and Lynne, 11.
51 King, *The truth about stories*.

REFERENCES

Barker, Joanne. 2006. "Gender, sovereignty and the discourse of rights in Native women's activism." *Meridians* 7 (1): 127–61.

Brzozowski, Jodi-Anne, Andrea Taylor-Butts, and Sara Johnson. 2006. "Victimization and offending among the Aboriginal population in Canada." *Juristat* 26 (3): 1–30.

Farley, Melissa, and Jacqueline Lynne. 2002. "Prostitution of Indigenous women: Sex inequality and the colonization of Canada's First Nations women." *Fourth World Journal* 6 (1): 1–29.

Green, Joyce. 2007. "Taking account of Aboriginal feminism." In *Making space for Indigenous feminism,* ed. Joyce Green, 20–32. Halifax: Fernwood Publishing.

Guerrero, J.A. 2003. "Patriarchal colonialism and Indigenism: Implications for Native feminist spirituality and Native womanism." *Hypatia* 18 (2): 58–69.

Janovicek, Nancy. 2003. "Assisting our own: Urban migration, self-governance and Native women's organizing in Thunder Bay, Ontario, 1972–1989." *American Indian Quarterly* 27 (3–4): 548–65.

King, Thomas. 2003. *The truth about stories: a native narrative.* Toronto: House of Anansi Press.

McCallum, Mary Jane. 2008. "Labour, modernity and the Canadian state: A history of Aboriginal women and work in the mid-twentieth century." Ph.D. diss., University of Manitoba.

Mihesuah, Devon A. 1996. "Commonality of difference: American Indian women and history." *American Indian Quarterly* 20 (1): 15–28.

Nahanee, Teresa. 1993. "Dancing with a gorilla: Aboriginal women, justice and the Charter." In *Aboriginal peoples and the justice system: Report of the National Round Table on Aboriginal Justice Issues.* Ottawa: Minister of Supply and Services.

Richards, John. 2006. *Creating choices: Rethinking Aboriginal policy.* Toronto: C.D. Howe Institute.

Smith, Andrea. 2005. *Conquest: Sexual violence and American Indian genocide.* Cambridge, MA: South End Press.

Smith, Andrea. 2006. "Indigenous feminism without apology." *New Socialist* 58. http://newsocialist.org/newsite/index.php?id=1013.

Statistics Canada. *Aboriginal identity (8), area of residence (6), age groups (12) and sex (3) for the population of Canada, provinces and territories, 2006 Census—20% sample data—Statistics Canada, 2006 Census*, Statistics Canada catalogue no. 97–558-XCB2006006.

Statistics Canada. *Aboriginal identity (8), highest certificate, diploma or degree (14), major field of study—classification of instructional programs, 2000 (14), area of residence (6), age groups (10A) and sex (3) for the population 15 years and over of Canada, provinces and territories, 2006 Census—20% sample data—Statistics Canada, 2006 Census*, Statistics Canada catalogue no. 97–560-XCB2006028.

Statistics Canada. *Aboriginal Peoples in Canada in 2006: Inuit, Métis and First Nations, 2006 Census*, Statistics Canada catalogue no. 97–558-XIE (Ottawa: Minister of Industry, 2008), 15, 44.

Statistics Canada. *Labour force activity (8), Aboriginal identity (8), highest certificate, diploma or degree (14), area of residence (6), age groups (12A) and sex (3) for the population 15 years and over of Canada, provinces and territories, 2006 Census—20% sample data—Statistics Canada, 2006 Census*, Statistics Canada catalogue no. 97–560-XCB2006031.

St. Denis, Verna. 2007. "Feminism is for everybody: Aboriginal women, feminism and diversity." In *Making space for Indigenous feminism*, ed. Joyce Green, 33–52. Halifax: Fernwood Publishing.

Stout, Madeleine Dion, and Gregory D. Kipling. 1998. *Aboriginal women in Canada: Strategic research directions for policy development*. Ottawa: Status of Women Canada.

Voyageur, Cora. 2003. *First Nations women in leadership in Canada*. Calgary: University of Calgary Press.

Wagner, Sally Roesch. 1989. "The root of oppression is the loss of memory: The Iroquois and the early feminist vision." *Akwesasne Notes*, 11–42.

Presentation of the Provincial Partnership Committee on Missing Persons

BETTY ANN POTTRUFF, Q.C.

Introduction

This material provides an overview of the work that the Government of Saskatchewan has done, with partners, to try to better understand and respond to missing person cases. I also want to acknowledge the work being done by other organizations such as the Native Women's Association of Canada on the issue of missing and murdered Aboriginal women through the Sisters in Spirit Campaign.[1] The issue of missing persons, including the specific concerns about missing Aboriginal women, is something the Government of Saskatchewan takes seriously.

Saskatchewan—some contextual facts

* Saskatchewan has a population of approximately one million.

* 14.9 percent of that population is Aboriginal [First Nations, Métis, non-status], roughly equally male and female.

* Research shows that Aboriginal women and children, particularly in Saskatchewan, are at substantial risk of being victims of violence.

BETTY ANN POTTRUFF spoke as the co-chair of the Provincial Partnership Committee on Missing Persons, Ministry of Justice and Attorney General, Saskatchewan.

- Two in three victims of violence know their assailant as friend, family, or acquaintance; stranger violence occurs in only 30 percent of cases.

What does this mean in relation to missing Aboriginal women in Saskatchewan?

- There are approximately 4,500 initial reports of missing persons in Saskatchewan annually, 100,000 nationally, as recorded by police.

- People go missing for a variety of reasons:
  —running away—64 percent of missing person reports relate to children and the majority are runaways (who face significant physical and sexual risks);
  —health reasons (dementia, suicide);
  —accidents (14 percent);
  —violence.

- Most cases are resolved in 24 to 48 hours. Those which are unresolved become long-term missing persons cases.

- In 2005, it was estimated that there were about 4,800 long-term missing persons in Canada, with about 270 new cases a year.

- Of the approximately 100 missing persons in Saskatchewan, roughly two-thirds are men and one-third are women.[2] There are about as many Aboriginal and non-Aboriginal people missing, but it seems that the majority of recently reported missing women are Aboriginal women. At the time of our report, about 60 percent of missing women were Aboriginal, and many of those are suspected to be missing as a result of foul play.

- Unfortunately, too often, the cases of missing Aboriginal women have been solved recently with a tragic result for their families, friends, and communities.

What is Saskatchewan doing to respond to the issue of missing persons?

Since 2006, Saskatchewan has dedicated resources towards improving the response to missing person cases by

- adding six police investigator positions dedicated to investigating historical cases and two crime analyst positions;

- conducting research on the number of missing persons cases reported in Saskatchewan and how the police respond (approximately 4,500 reports annually of approximately 3,000 individuals);

- establishing the Provincial Partnership Committee on Missing Persons in January 2006.

The Provincial Partnership Committee on Missing Persons

Organizations with interest and expertise or province-wide experience in dealing with missing person issues were invited to participate on a committee to improve collaboration and support provided to families and communities of missing persons. The committee had representatives from 14 organizations—police, search and rescue, Child Find and other community organizations, First Nations Women's Secretariat, Metis Family and Community Justice Services Inc. (MFCJS), Saskatchewan Aboriginal Women's Circle Corporation (SAWC), and provincial government. The Coroner's office has now been added, as it deals with the issue of unidentified human remains. The Partnership Committee is a process unique to Saskatchewan.

Mandate, Vision and Principles

The mandate and a summary of the work of the Committee and its recommendations are available today.[3] The full report (issued October 2007) is available on the Justice website.[4] The vision of the Partnership Committee is: *To work towards a future that ensures that when people go missing there is a full response that mobilizes all necessary participants and that recognizes the equal value of every life.* Our partnership work is based on the following principles:

- People go missing for a variety of reasons and so we will work to respond specifically to each of these reasons, as brought forward by the members of the Partnership Committee, while addressing the needs of all missing persons.

- While we need to try to respond to the different reasons people go missing, we also need to recognize that every family and community that has someone go missing experiences a similar trauma.

The work of the Partnership Committee has involved meeting with and listening to families of long-term missing persons and making recommendations to government, police, community agencies and individuals.

Meeting with families of long-term missing persons

We built on experiences with family gatherings with Aboriginal families here in Saskatchewan to hold three get-togethers with over 40 families of long-term missing persons in Saskatchewan in spring 2007. We learned a lot from these meetings and we are very grateful to the families for agreeing to meet with us and share their experiences. We hope to hold similar meetings in the future to help ensure we are addressing concerns.

Recommendations

The Committee made recommendations in three broad areas: how to prevent people from going missing; how to support families; and how to respond better to missing person cases. The recommendations require action from government, bodies such as the Saskatchewan Police Commission, other governments, community agencies, and individuals. The Committee is working on implementing some recommendations and monitoring implementation of others.

PREVENTION

o Governments, school authorities, etc., need better to understand why youth run away and what can be done to protect youth in these situations—research will be done on this issue and on the role and responses of various agencies to runaways.

o The public and at-risk communities—youth, etc.—need better information about:
—missing person situations (they can happen to any family);
—how to reduce risk (safety planning);
—what the police or other agencies can do when someone goes missing.

Justice is working with Child Find to improve information for children/youth runaways. The Partnership Committee will be developing an inventory of partner agencies and looking at information and collaboration needs.

SUPPORTING FAMILIES

o Families need supports such as checklists and media kits—the Partnership Committee is working on this.

o Families may need updated legislation to be able to manage the estate of a missing person—the Minister of Justice tabled Bill 50⁵ in the Legislature in Fall 2008 to address this.

o Families need support networks and also recognition of their loss through a memorial or otherwise—the Partnership Committee wants to work with families on these ideas.

o There needs to be improved communication between families and police at all stages of the investigation.

o Victims Services funded by Justice should support families of missing people—Justice agrees, and victims services are available to help families of missing persons.

RESPONDING TO MISSING PERSONS REPORTS AND CASES

o A provincial standard protocol to guide all police in dealing with missing person cases is needed—for uniformity and to ensure that all cases are responded to appropriately. Work has commenced on this.

o Police should immediately take down standard types of information when someone is reported missing, use a common tool to assess priority and risk, and immediately start investigations of missing persons in suspicious circumstances.

o Better linked or national websites are needed to profile information about missing persons—Justice Ministries agreed in September 2008 that this was an area to look at and the Canadian Association of Chiefs of Police made a similar recommendation in fall 2008; police and justice officials are now reviewing this issue.

o Search and rescue capacities across the province need to be improved, including building capacity in First Nations communities—government and voluntary agencies are working with First Nations and other communities to improve capacity in this area.

What else is Saskatchewan doing?

Saskatchewan raised the issue of missing persons with federal, provincial, and territorial ministers of Justice in September 2008 to start a national Justice dialogue on how to improve responses, and officials are participating in national forums on a range of recommendations.

Final comments

I appreciate that often it feels as though government response takes too long and involves too much process. However, developing an adequate and comprehensive response requires working collaboratively with a range of partners—from families of missing persons, to community organizations, First Nations, Métis, and federal agencies/governments, police, and other provincial government agencies. Collaborative processes take time but often result in better and more sustainable solutions. Government has a role in responding to the issue of missing persons, but so do families, communities, and other agencies, and we need to respect these other roles and the expertise of the partners in developing solutions. The responsibility to act to prevent people going missing and to respond when they do is a responsibility we all share.

ENDNOTES

1 See "Sisters in Spirit Initiative: Native Women's Association of Canada" by Judy Hughes on page 208 for a full description of the activities of Sisters in Spirit.

2 Statistics from the Saskatchewan Association of Chiefs of Police—www.sacp.ca/missing —as of 25 November 2008. The numbers continually change as new cases are added and other are deleted as resolved.

3 See Appendix A, page 257.

4 http://www.justice.gov.sk.ca/missing-persons-report.

5 The Absentee Act, Bill 50, 29 October 2008.

RESISTING WITH ALL THE SENSES:
Art and Activism

Missing and Taken

ELIZABETH MATHESON

In 2006, I initiated *Missing and Taken: A Symposium* as a way to begin a dialogue about the issue of missing women in Canada and Mexico. The inspiration for this project came from a single photograph entitled *Nada que Ver* (Nothing to See) by photographer Jaime Bailleres published in a *Harper's Magazine* article (December 1996) that told the story of the more than six hundred women who are missing and murdered in the northern Mexico state of Chihuahua. Bailleres' photograph of a young murdered girl whose remains were found a few metres from the American border is a haunting image, all the more so for being one of so many *aesinatos*/murders and *desaparecidas*/disappearances in this place and in my own country, Canada. When I began researching the global economic, social, and cultural impact of missing women for the symposium at the Dunlop Art Gallery (in association with the Department of Women's Studies at the University of Regina), I had little idea how encompassing such an issue could become, how fully and oppressively it devours community and life. My own interest in bridging between

ELIZABETH MATHESON is an independent curator, lecturer, and writer of Canadian and international contemporary art and culture. She is currently researching an international exhibition on the role of video in contested spaces within Latin America, entitled *Occupy, Resist and Produce*.

communities, crossing borders (between countries and disciplines) by bringing together families and community organizations with artists, writers, and filmmakers was soon swamped by ethical and theoretical considerations that, in time, I realized could be dealt with only in the most oblique and cursory manner. Yet, it became immediately and equally clear just how powerfully violence against women shapes our world, our attitudes, our bodies, and our lives.

The idea of artists speaking back to the violence against women across borders is by no means new. Almost a decade ago, documentary filmmaker Lourdes Portillo created *Señorita Extraviada* (2001), a compelling investigation into the circumstances surrounding missing girls and women in Ciudad Juárez and the dynamics of the various systems (nationalism, transnational capitalism, patriarchy) that bear down on this border town. But though the work's meaning originates in the specific politics of Ciudad Juárez, the sorrow and loss it evokes were recognizable across all borders. As part of the symposium Lourdes Portillo was invited to screen the film and speak about the current situation. Lourdes Portillo's presence at the symposium was also significant in that *Señorita Extraviada* had spurred projects by artists in Canada, including another invited speaker, Vancouver-based artist Deborah Koenker. Like other prominent Canadian artists such as Rebecca Belmore (Vancouver) and Claudia Bernal (Montreal) who invoke absence and loss in addressing missing women, Koenker is interested in redirecting traditional mediums of art, moving away from more formal orientated approaches towards social and emotional gestures. Koenker has an extended Mexican family, with strong connections to Tapalpa, a village in the mountains of Jalisco. Working in Tapalpa with three social activists—Cuca Flores, Guadalupe Ahumada, and Rebeca Rosas—Koenker initiated a three-year textile project—"Missing/Las Desaparecidas" (2005–08)—in collaboration with eighty-five artisans to embroider much-enlarged images of their fingerprints onto white cotton banners as a protest against the crimes against women in the border *maquiladoras* and to demonstrate their solidarity with the victims' families.

Bringing us subtly closer to violence, creative gestures such as this one have the possibility of restoring the human element to a part of twenty-first-century life that is often depersonalized. Victims of violence are frequently left unnamed or are described through statistics, as if to assert the distance between the places and people we are not familiar with. By contrast, artists, filmmakers, poets, musicians, and playwrights focus on the *people*—reminding us of the tragedy fallen on them. As such, artists' representations of murdered women and girls become invitations to share, partake, and empathize rather than attempts to reassure or disturb. At the conference "Missing Women: Decolonization, Third Wave Feminisms, and Indigenous People of Canada and Mexico," one did not need to look far to find creative gestures that also resisted voyeuristic or sensationalized evocations of disappearances and murders; artists preferred instead to position their work as transformative in an increasingly uncertain world. From the small crosses placed on trees along the Healing Walk to the *Bison Sentinels* created by Blackfoot artist Adrian Stimson in the Healing Garden at First Nations University, artists brought to the conference works that were statements of hope, in which the struggle to find meaning in tragedies makes for a shared experience that binds people together with imagination, courage, and integrity.

Carla Blakley, Shauneen Pete, and Brenda Anderson with *Bison Sentinels* by Adrian Stimson.
The four bronze bison sculptures, each measuring 5.25" x 7" x 9.5", are mounted in the Healing
Gardens at the First Nations University of Canada. *Bison Sentinels*—described as a "living memorial"
because of the Russian Larch (*Larix sibirica*) planted to grow up through the centre
of the installation—was unveiled on August 14, 2008, as part of the opening
ceremonies of the "Missing Women" conference.

Bison Sentinels:
A Living Memorial to Murdered and Missing Aboriginal Women

ADRIAN STIMSON

The symbol of the Bison holds many meanings for different groups, yet its being has come to symbolize Wisdom, Patience, Gratitude, Sacrifice, Prosperity, Abundance and Sacredness. Its teachings can include: the importance of being grounded; providing abundance for others; finding the strength to carry on our path; harmony with Mother Earth; giving selflessly from the heart; sacrifice; and the sacredness of life.

A living memorial is a way to preserve memories of a loved one and to transform an ending into a beginning. It is a memorial that, once created, has a life of its own. It transforms over time, being added to by visitors.

A sentinel is someone or something that keeps a lookout, watches for something to happen. It is a guard or sentry.

Bison Sentinels was made possible by generous funding provided by Casino Regina.

ADRIAN STIMSON was born and raised in Sault St. Marie, Ontario, and lived on a number of First Nations across Canada, including his home reserve, Siksika Nation (Blackfoot). His formative years were spent in Saskatchewan, on the Gordon First Nation and in Lebret. Adrian has been researching and experimenting with his personal blend of environmental art and activism, Indigenous knowledge, and sustainable communities.

The conference quilt incorporated First Nations and Mexican motifs, one of the conference logos, and felt hands inscribed with messages from conference participants.

Patching our Stories Together:
The Conference Quilt

JESSICA GREYEYES

B eing asked to make the conference quilt was a great honour for me. I believe it is a visual representation of the solidarity among not only our sisters but our brothers, too. Joylynn, Sadie, and I partnered in this endeavour. We had many conversations about our vision and what the quilt was to look like, and together we made it happen. The design was simple, but each part was as significant as the next. One of our conference logos was placed at the center, a woman's face with the hair covering one eye and a tear enclosing the female symbol falling from the other. Surrounding this were alternating colours of white, yellow, red, black, and purple. The first four colours represent the different directions in First Nations culture, and the purple represents healing, as directed by the Elders. The four colours were again mirrored in each corner of the quilt, one miniature star blanket design in each colour, again signifying the different directions. In the centre of each side were black and white swirls to incorporate the Mexican culture. Participants at the conference were then given the opportunity to write messages on hands cut from felt in the four colours. These hands, which were the other symbol of our conference,

JESSICA GREYEYES is a student at First Nations University of Regina working towards a Bachelor of Administration degree and a Bachelor of Arts degree majoring in Indigenous Studies and Women and Gender Studies.

were then attached to the blanket and woven into the hair of the woman. These signified to us the hands that support us as we grow and the hands that continue to show solidarity and support for one another.

The conference and the lead-up to it were very significant in my life. One way or another, directly or indirectly, we are all impacted by the effects of colonization on humanity and especially by what it does to our Aboriginal women. Prior to being a part of this conference, ignorance was bliss to me, but the more involved I became the more I realized that we have all been affected. I have since become more proactive in educating people who have the mindset that I once had.

If I could educate at least one person to become more aware and less bigoted, then I would be a happy woman. By not doing anything we are silently perpetuating the violence. With what we know now, how can we stay silent? Topics like this have not been generally talked about and have been brushed under the carpet, or, worse, the victim has been blamed. In my research and readings, I found that media reports often put a spin on situations and blame the victim, depending on her race, socio-economic status, or lifestyle. What about the families and the impact it has on them, those who have lost sisters, daughters, mothers, and grandmothers? This has been ignored for far too long, and for me, by participating in the making of the blanket, I was able to offer a visual representation that we are no longer going to be silent. The girl with the tear is held gently by the hands of a community that stretches across Canada and Mexico.

One of the conference participants from Mexico asked if she could write her message in Spanish. She herself could not speak English and it surprised me that she felt she needed to ask if she could say what she needed to say in her own language. It showed me how much colonization has affected us and makes us all transform ourselves into who society thinks we should be. Of course she wrote her message in her own language, and this was the first hand that I put on the blanket. I could not read the message, but she was a mother with a missing daughter, and I knew that it was a special one.

When I presented the blanket at the closing ceremonies, it was not yet finished. I was so disappointed in myself that I had let down this community of people with whom I had worked and those whom I had just met. A wonderful woman named Brenda Anderson reminded me that it was again a representation that our work was not yet done. I strongly believe this, because our work and education has to continue to whoever will listen with a respectful ear.

Prior to the conference I had the opportunity to participate in a class where we ventured to Mexico to study the effects of colonization on

Aboriginal women. Then, too, I was asked to make a star blanket as a gift from our class to the Evangelical Lutheran Church of America (ELCA) Centre. Because of Gwenda Yuzicappi's strength and struggles with having a daughter who at the time was missing, we decided to make a red star blanket. Her daughter, Amber Redman, was also known by her Indian name, Red Star Woman, and I made the blanket to honour her. The day we were leaving for Mexico we found out her remains had been found. I did not know Amber personally, but through working on the blanket I thought about her and the strength of her mother to share her story. I felt like I was starting to know this woman whom I never had the opportunity to meet. I believed that it was imperative that I incorporate some of the material that I had used on Amber's blanket on the conference blanket. The red mini star in the corner is the same material used in the blanket that went to Mexico in honour of Amber Redman. Unfortunately, I do not yet have the words to capture how this makes me feel; it was more than just coincidental, and I feel it has a higher meaning that has not yet been shared with me. When Kim Erno received the blanket, he said that this red star was now his northern star, his guide to the work for justice to connect the stories and lives across borders.

Generally, the products that I make I call mine. Each is made with much thought and love, but even though I had a part in making *these* blankets, they are not mine. They belong to all of us. Whether we were at the conference or not, the quilt represents that we are all together in this struggle and that we stand together. Even if we feel alone, we are not. I am very thankful for the opportunity to work on this and would like to thank all who were involved in showing society that we are together and that we are not going to let this continue to happen to our strong, beautiful brothers and sisters.

The quilt continues to travel across Canada with Sisters in Spirit, gaining support with "felt" hands that hold messages of love and calls for justice. When the time is right, the blanket will come to First Nations University to hang in the foyer—a witness to the work that continues to grow.

Art pieces and photos, contributed by a number of students who had travelled to Mexico in May 2008, were displayed throughout the conference. These dresses, imprinted with words from the stories of missing women, symbolize the vulnerability of women in Mexico and Canada.

Missing Women Art Exhibit

CHARLOTTE HAUK

n exhibition on missing women was created by students from various disciplines who travelled to Mexico City in May 2008 for a Women's Studies course entitled "Studies on Violence and Women in Mexico," which was taught by Professor Brenda Anderson. The course examined the underpinnings of violence against Indigenous women in Mexico, including displacement and dispossession of land, cultural genocide, and sexual violence as a strategy of domination. As part of the class, students were expected to create journals that reflected their experience in Mexico. The students studied at the Evangelical Lutheran Church in America (ELCA) in the "Transformational Immersion Program." The ELCA's program methodology is popular education and liberation theology with guest lectures, tours, and visits to impoverished Indigenous communities. Some of the topics covered were: sexual violence and femicide against Indigenous women; feminization of poverty; Indigenous women's resistance and leadership; globalization and global economics;

CHARLOTTE HAUK is a third-year Fine Arts student, majoring in ceramics, at the University of Regina. Charlotte curated an art exhibit at the "Missing Women" conference that showcased the work of students who had travelled with Brenda Anderson to Mexico City for nine days to study and visit the Indigenous communities where women were resisting violence against women.

Mexican history—revolution and social movements and solidarity economics; Indigenous diaspora and loss of culture; collective organizing and co-operatives; the Zapatista resistance; colonization; Indigenous ceremony; and environmental racism. The stories of rape and genocide from activists reflect a global strategy of conquest, severing cultural ties and relationships with the land. Our journals and art from the class trip reflect the fact that the experiences we shared alongside the hearts and minds of the marginalized communities raised our awareness of the interconnectedness of the people in a global context and of how our actions affect Indigenous livelihood. The class was also a healing journey for students because we had talking circles and time for reflection. We developed a strong sense of unity and strength between us. The exhibit at the conference was an act of resistance and a way for us to express visually our concern about this global problem.

She Is Not Forgotten:
The Healing Walk

ALEXIS J. JOHNSON

There was an abundance of spirit that came together to create the Healing Walk for the conference. A kilometre-long stretch of trees in Wascana Park was marked with over one hundred banners, representing missing and murdered women in Canada and Mexico. In order to reflect the fact that this is a global issue, the traditions in the awareness art were adapted from the Indigenous cultures of both countries. The pink fabric banners with black equal-sided crosses represent only a handful of the women who have been violently stolen from their families, communities, and Mother Earth. Their journeys were abruptly abandoned, but their stories are never forgotten.

There is a Mexican tradition called *Descansos.* From my understanding, this means "resting place." It is common in Mexico to mark the spot of a person's sudden death with a decorated cross, to be remembered and blessed. This information came to me while watching Lourdes Portillo's documentary, filmed in Mexico and entitled *Señorita Extraviada.* The moment it showed mothers of missing women painting telephone poles pink with black crosses, I was motionless with grief, anger, and disgust. It seemed

ALEXIS J. JOHNSON completed her B.A. Honours (Psychology) at the University of Regina in 2009. She currently resides in Victoria, BC, and shares healing through a women's circle and mentoring group.

Alexis Johnson ties one of the pink banners that marked the Healing Walk through Wascana Park during the conference.

as though these women were creating a path of *Descansos* for the many women they have loved and lost. They are grieving, they are angry, and they are terrified in their own neighbourhoods. The brutal imagery of the missing women, their families' emotional journeys through the corrupt system, and the pain that showed on faces in the film and in the classroom were disheartening. One does not escape these images easily; they stay with one, and because of this, an outlet is needed. *She is not forgotten.*

Fabric is an important tool in society and history. Women hold the fabric of society together, the woven fibres creating and maintaining children, families, and community. If a thread is loose, pulled, or snagged, the fabric will begin to unravel. What has been made is no longer. A loose thread is an injustice to the fabric—it is less durable, less secure, and less valuable. Much like a loose thread, an abused woman can bring an entire community to disarray. Mother, sister, grandmother, friend. Our beloved women, in the thousands across Canada and Mexico, are missing threads in our society's fabric. Fabric was used for this reason, to bind our sisters together once again. *She is not forgotten.*

The black equal-sided cross was adapted from First Nations culture. A medicine wheel is divided into four equal parts. Among the many sacred meanings, each part can represent a significant season, direction, or colour. The result is an interactive message of peace, harmony, and balance. The medicine wheel can also represent the colours of Mother Earth's children. Black, yellow, red, and white, we are all sisters.

At first, banners were gradually hung every few days after sunset. The intent was to have all 100 or more ready for the healing walk that would take place during the conference. By the end of week two, only two of the thirty banners remained. Concern about the missing banners echoed the very issue they were symbolizing. They were being silently stolen. The irony highlighted the carelessness and disrespect of a symbol, of a memorial meant to honour and mourn missing and murdered women. The missing banners themselves were not important; their meaning was created through community reaction. People often stopped to ask what they were for, and I imagine very few were able to leave the park without questions, a sense of sadness, anger, and most importantly, strength and awareness to contribute to the cause. *She is not forgotten.*

The rest of the banners were hung shortly before the conference began. People were invited to use the area for prayer and meditation and to use the surrounding nature as a source of healing. A demonstration walk marched past the trees adorned with the pink fabric. The walk began with a silent vigil to honour our sisters, and it ended with the large crowd chanting "Ni una mas!" (Not one more) and "Break the Silence, Stop the Violence." Elation for justice continued throughout the weekend, our voices heard throughout the streets.

The remaining banners were given to guests of the conference. The journey the banners will make is a demonstration of the commitment to spread awareness, hope, and ultimately, the need to repair society's unravelling fabric. *She is not forgotten.*

Thank you to Paula Flores and Eva Arce for being the first women to brave the injustice of these heinous crimes by painting the first pole in honour of their beloved daughters. Please, join us in this cause. Paint a pole. Blanket your trees, your clothes, your community in pink fabric. Questions will arise; strength will be gathered. *She is not forgotten.*

Carrying the Messages from the Missing Women

SENATOR LILLIAN EVA (QUAN) DYCK

The "Missing Women" conference in Regina is a thing of the past; much of what happened there, however, remains in my spirit, in my heart, and in my mind. It's hard to imagine that a conference on a topic so horrific could make one feel optimistic and proud of being an Aboriginal woman, but that's what happened to me. There were so many inspiring speakers who spoke about their trials and tribulations, about the losses of their daughters, about how they had overcome huge barriers in their own lives, about the societal and political underpinnings that allow violence against Aboriginal women to continue. The stories are not pretty, but the strength and resilience of the family members was awesome. Personally, I was so proud of the speakers, such as Maria Campbell, Joyce Green, Tori Lynn Wanotch, Shauneen Pete, and the incredible Marta Perez. Though Canadian and Mexican societies may view their Indigenous women as second-class citizens, we are not second-class. The Indigenous women who spoke at this conference were beautiful, first-class speakers, academics, and activists.

LILLIAN DYCK is a member of the Gordon First Nation, Saskatchewan. A neurochemist, Senator Dyck was the associate dean of programs in the College of Graduate Studies and full professor in the Neuropsychiatry Research Unit, Department of Psychiatry, University of Saskatchewan, before she was called to the Senate in 2005.

Conference participants follow the path of the "healing walk" along the route through Wascana Park marked by pink banners.

A black cross on a pink background is used to represent the spirits of the missing and murdered Indigenous Mexican women. At the "Missing Women" conference in Regina, pink cloth banners painted with black crosses were tied around the trees between Luther College and the Conexus Arts Centre. This marked the route that conference attendees followed on a protest march. I didn't march, but instead I took photographs of the marchers as they entered the University of Regina campus. The next day, I awoke early in the morning and decided to retrace the march going from the campus back to the Conexus Arts Centre. I decided to try to run part of the way, in a manner similar to what I knew Shannon Loutitt had done to bring Daleen Bosse's spirit back from where her body had been found. I started out running and looking at the pink banners on the trees, and as I ran up to one pink banner, I saw the next one further down the path. And somehow each of the pink banners gave me the strength to run to the next one, on and on, until I reached the Conexus Arts Centre. I am not a runner, but I had run about 1.5 kilometres! The spirits of the missing women gave me the strength and stamina to do that. Incredibly, I was also able to run another 1.5 kilometres back to the campus, drawn again by the pink banners. The spirits of the missing women were strong.

The pink banners reminded me of the prayer cloths that we tie around trees and hang in the sweat lodge. I collected some of the pink banners the next day, and took them to a sweat lodge to be smudged and blessed.

We tied these around trees and gave some to the speakers at the Sisters in Spirit vigil held in Saskatoon on October 4, 2008. The spirits of our missing sisters give us guidance and strength to work to end the violence directed against women, and Aboriginal women in particular. One of the pink banners is tied around a tree in my backyard, and as I sit at my desk I can look out and see it and remind myself of how lucky I am to be where I am and to do whatever I can to find ways to end the disappearance and murder of Aboriginal women.

ORGANIZATIONAL RESISTANCE:
Action from Within

Media:
A Canadian Response

CAROL SCHICK

I want to thank the organizing committee for inviting me to speak today and to greet all who are here, the international travellers, the Elders, and all people who are moved to be present at this very important event. It is an honour and a sincere pleasure to speak at the same conference with so many fine people. The activist stories of the two women we have just heard, Isabel Arvides and Lourdes Portillo, are indeed extraordinary examples among many other remarkable stories.

It is impossible to overstate the importance of being together to witness to the enormity of what has happened to hundreds and perhaps thousands of women whose deaths and disappearances have been treated as if the women were somehow outside the law and not deserving of respect, dignity, and human rights. A theme of this conference has been the importance of testimony and bearing witness to what is taking place locally, nationally, and internationally. This witnessing takes courage because there are always risks involved, for some more than others, in speaking of these things. Isabel reminded us of the importance of speaking out, and the

CAROL SCHICK is associate professor in the Faculty of Education at the University of Regina. She is involved in anti-oppressive education in teacher preparation programs and uses feminist theories, critical race theories, and whiteness studies to live and work through tensions of post-colonial education at all levels of schooling as found on the Canadian Prairies.

difference between doing so on the part of two groups: people who *must* speak—because their lives depend on it; and people who *may* speak—because other lives depend on it.

I wish to acknowledge that whereas anyone may be the unfortunate victim of violence, what we are talking about today is nothing less than a violation of the human rights of Indigenous women. The disappearance of these women is not only a criminal matter or a social issue, although it is these things, too. In a sexist, racist, and class-based society, the vulnerability of Indigenous women is based on the fact that they *are* women, Indigenous, and often living in poverty. Their human rights are violated *because* of who they are.[1]

I have been asked to speak on this media panel because of my own work as a researcher, professor, and teacher educator in the area of anti-oppressive education. My teaching focuses on the ways sexism, racism, class discrimination, homophobia, and other forms of marginalization are made to seem normal in everyday situations in a white settler society. This is my main area of study, and I am continually learning about this topic from many others, including these brilliant women here present who refuse to look away.

Although not specifically a media analyst, I recognize many parallels between public education systems and media in Western society. My research examines the way discourses of schooling and the nation produce social identifications such as whose story is worth telling and under what circumstances. Media treatment of public discourses reflects the society of which it is a part. It both reflects and produces public opinion by creating and repeating popular stories and lasting images. This reflection of popular opinion that supports the interests of some people and not others is not a monolithic project or the work of conspirators. On the contrary, in a white-dominated settler society, the media—like public schooling—has sufficient flexibility to look as if it is offering many sides of any issue while maintaining and guarding the hegemony of the dominant interests. Media can even lend a certain sophistication to the dominant culture by featuring mild forms of controversy and questionable behaviour before returning to regular programming.

Social systems of schooling, law, media, and government can be explicitly and overtly repressive or they can be a silent by-product and producer of residual prejudice in a liberal society. Even well-intentioned practices of a liberal press or social services such as education, the law, health care—even if they are justice-oriented—will invariably reflect the biases and tensions of a racist society that they serve. Like schooling, media reproduce discourses that their listeners will allow; I do not separate the notion of media from the racist society of which it is a part.

Media representations are not simply outlets for biased news reporting against First Nations women, sexual minorities, immigrants, and racial minorities. The power of media resides in the act that it produces what it names. The words are not merely conveying the news, rather the words are performing actions, including constructing people's identities in particular ways. As Vera and Feagin suggest, the denigration of these people "involves the use of the media as an instrument of symbolic violence" (2004, 70). The effect of the media goes well beyond mere reporting. The impact is nothing less than producing people who can be assaulted and people who will be protected.

In what follows, I make three claims concerning media representations of issues of inequality, especially racism. I refer throughout to the sexual assault case that happened in 2001 close to Tisdale, Saskatchewan, and went to trial at Melfort, Saskatchewan, in 2003. It involved a small 12-year-old Saulteaux girl and three large white men. I reference the work of Bridget Keating, who makes the claim that journalistic coverage of this trial "sexualizes and denigrates the 12-year-old girl through . . . the use of language . . . enactments of naming . . . and the *reproduction* of colonial mythologies within the textual account" (2008, 4). The trial and the reporting of it are not unlike what has happened in other cases involving Aboriginal women as victims and white male perpetrators. In spite of many similarities, the cases are treated as if they are one-off events and quite separate from everyday occurrences. At some point in these cases, no matter how heinous the crime, the roles of victim and perpetrator get reversed, even if for a short time. The court and the media also repeat the original violation when they treat the victims as if they are outside the law and not deserving of full respect and rights.

1. Media reporting is simplistic in its focus on individual events.

When racism in Canadian society is acknowledged at all, it is addressed as if it were an isolated, one-off event that most people would recognize and condemn. What is not acknowledged is that inequality occurs through systems of oppression that operate through the institutions that I have mentioned, including media and education. Speaking in more complex ways about systemic inequality or institutionalized racism is unfamiliar and easily dismissed because of the narrow definition of racism. As Canadians, we have little practice in naming systems that would help us understand how oppression is made to seem merely like an acceptable, if unfortunate, occurrence. Many issues are seen in terms of black or white, did or did not happen, and most rely on discourses that are well rehearsed. Discourses that would otherwise interrupt this way of thinking are not well-known and would not necessarily be tolerated in a commercial interest that is not known for expansive concepts or nuance.

The sexual assault case in Tisdale was reported in electronic and print media as a one-off situation, as an occurrence that is, at the same time, both singular and routine. The singularity of the treatment follows centuries of global colonization in which white men have been informed repeatedly of their ritualized entitlement to the women of the colonized other. This dehumanization of a racialized woman through ritualized access is indeed what constitutes and defines much of the racialization process. Therefore, when neither the legal process nor the media seem to notice that this charge has a very long history, it mistakenly treats the event as a one-off occurrence done by "some of our boys" who, unfortunately, should have known better.

Bridget Keating makes the point that the media description of the girl produced the effect of the girl as a Lolita, "the Nabokovian construct of a 'nymphet,' an oversexed girl who possesses sexual power over men" (2008, 59). The production is evocatively and erotically charged because of the repeated and historic production of the colonized female as the beautiful and always available, always desiring, seductress. A reporter needs very few words to sketch this image because the girl has already appeared in the colonizers' dreams of seduction handed down as a colonial legacy. The familiarity and ease of reporting this event is made possible by its colonial history; ironically, it is a familiarity that contradicts the media presentation of the event as a singular act of aggression.

Media are central to the societies of which they are a part. The story of the sexual assault is not unique, not even to the men who are involved. The story has taken place thousands of times. This racist event is embedded in the social fabric of Saskatchewan settler society. The reporting of the story in a particular way becomes part of the settler narrative, that it is possible to do this kind of thing here. The connection between this assault and the violence perpetrated on the missing women is rarely mentioned because we lack the language to discuss larger systems of oppression, including hierarchies of racism, sexism, class discrimination, and homophobia. The systemic inequality that is central to this process cannot be named when racism is considered a one-off event.

2. Media are not neutral even though this is the claim of the fifth estate in a so-called free and open liberal democracy.

In spite of claims of media neutrality, media reporting represents a particular view that reflects the dominant liberal society back to itself in positive and affirming ways. Claims of media neutrality may be understood in the narrow way that similarly recognizes racism only as individual acts of meanness. The fact that media is not separate from the society of which it is a part suggests that it has a point of view. Furthermore, the claim that media reporting is free and open in a liberal democracy can lead citizens to accept uncritically that its hegemonic practices are benign and even good for us. Canadians are more likely to identify with public media than to be suspicious of it, at least until we are embarrassed by criticism from the United Nations and exposed by Amnesty International (2004).

Moreover, in a liberal democracy, to safeguard its neutrality, media invites its consumers to be watchful of biases in reporting. It opens itself to criticism in letters to the editor and other forms of feedback. While I am watching for obvious bias against marginalized groups, however, I—as a white, middle-class woman—am less observant of how I take up the messages about dominant society; I am less likely to notice how dominance, such as white privilege, is positioned in the discourses. For white people like me, the seduction of the media is that I imagine I can spot bias when I see or hear it. Surely I can see when bias that reflects homophobia, sexism, or racism is taking place. Or so I think.

What I do not see so well is when I am being produced in ways that confirm my sense of self as a powerful white woman, as one who is in charge. This is the other side of observing the obvious bias in the media, observing the underlying assumptions with which I am more or less comfortable and therefore oblivious to. The bias that is harder for me to observe is how the life I am able to lead as a white person is reported and confirmed in ways that are positive, normative, and respectable.

What is not examined and goes unnoticed is the "collective sense of racial entitlement and racial superiority" (Vera and Feagin 2004, 73) that tells me that I am okay here. These are seductive and hegemonic practices found routinely in media, schooling, social services, the law, and all other institutions in a democratic society. What has come to be considered normative and correct is rarely scrutinized the way the lives of marginalized people are. The inherent bias in the media makes some people feel very much at home and others angry and dispossessed.

This "collective sense of racial entitlement and racial superiority" (73) was very much a part of the reporting at the trial of the three Tisdale men accused of sexually assaulting the 12-year-old girl. The sense of collective entitlement was on full display in the media in the case I have been describing. White, masculine entitlement was performed by the white actors in their initial assault on the girl. The assumption of fairness and entitlement was available to the white participants involved in the trial and the white reporters who delivered the story to the public. The men, in their early 20s, were referred to familiarly by the attorneys and judge as "boys." The jocularity between judge, attorneys, and defendants can be read in the transcripts (McNinch 2009). Resting side by side is the presumption of legal neutrality and the familiar notion that "this is the way we do things here." This contradiction was never part of the reporting because it is through silence that inequality is kept in place. Bringing assault charges against the men is not simply shedding light on a one-off assault by three large white men against a small Indigenous girl. The charge also sheds light on the sense of entitlement that is otherwise kept in place by silence.

If the notion of critical race theory (Parker, Dehyle, and Villenas 1999) could have been applied here, the image would have been different. Critical race theory claims that the assumptions on which law rests are inherently racist in a white supremacist society, regardless of the best of intentions to read the law in the way of justice. Critical race theory, if it had been applied to the case and its reporting, would have taken into account the many points of bias that may not in fact have been against the law as it is currently constituted and practiced. Critical race theory, however, and a critically informed media, would have recognized and reported on the inherent bias of the law as the starting point for the discussion.

For evidence of inherent bias in procedures and practices, one can look for examples of what cannot be talked about and questions that do not get asked. Two easy illustrations concern the effects of alcohol in the Tisdale assault case. There was considerable deliberation about whether the men believed the girl had consented to having sex, regardless of the fact that her consent as a minor is not legally defensible. This underage girl had also been given alcohol to drink and admitted to consuming quite a lot. The alcohol, however, was not considered to have impaired her ability to consent.

For the defense, excessive alcoholic consumption was central to the claim of innocence on the part of large, grown men. The effect of the alcohol was that they were too drunk to penetrate the girl. The alcohol that could impair the erections of three men was somehow not considered a deterrent to the girl's ability to consent. Alcohol was used as a mitigating factor for the actions of three large men but not for a very small girl who, by years alone, is much less experienced in managing its effects.

The so-called neutrality of media reporting impairs the assessments made of the stories that get reported. The lack of neutrality in the media has a way of exploiting and furthering the constructed differences in our society so that there is some false notion that some rights are entitled to protection while others are not.

One consequence of the failure of law and media to ask questions that disrupt entitlement is that members of the dominant culture may mistakenly imagine their entitlement is earned. Consequently, they will read stories of missing women in quite a different way. The seduction by the media suggests that people die of bad luck, indifference, statistical probability, or difficulties they have brought upon themselves.

In the Canadian context of a liberal democracy that operates under the notion that equal opportunity is available to all, inequality is seen as one's own fault, rather than as part of a system that benefits only certain people. For access to protection and resources, women are encouraged through patriarchy to align themselves in places where they are ironically most vulnerable, namely, with masculine systems of dominance. This alignment and misplaced allegiance has the effect of silencing women from speaking about the abuses that take place right in our own homes and communities. Those of us who are white women ignore at our peril the issues that significantly affect Indigenous women. We make a huge mistake when we claim solidarity with women far away whom we have never met if we neglect the many opportunities to stand with First Nations, Métis, and racial minority women right here where we live. We disarm ourselves with our silence.

3. Depictions of the "other" are ambivalent and often polarized.

Representations of minority peoples are often contradictory and polarized to the extent that, on the one hand, they are invisible even when they are very much present, and on the other hand, they are sensationalized to the point of becoming a fetishized, abject other.

This ambivalent, often polarized, view offers a particularly skewed version of disaster. Whether an Indigenous or racial minority person is the victim or perpetrator of a crime, the person will be depicted in a surprisingly similar way: he or she will be the pathetic other who has yet again brought some disaster on himself or herself. There is only one difference. The person will be depicted as a person to be either feared or pitied. In each case the problems of a minority person are read as representations of inherent difference that resides outside of "normal" society. The indifference and silence surrounding the plight of missing women fits with the cruel assumption that women have brought these disasters on themselves. They are not simply victims; these are outcomes and consequences that had been anticipated. How else can we account for the apathy towards their disappearances?

In the case of the assault in Tisdale, Keating points out that one reporter depicts the girl as aggressor (2008, 100n6). The fact that the combined weight of the assailants exceeded that of the girl by at least six to one did not prevent the court and the media from accepting the assailants' intimation that the girl had been the one who initiated sexual contact, who egged them on, who was the aggressor. And even if that case didn't logically hold, it was necessary to make the suggestion that, at a minimum, she was responsible for the behaviour of the men simply because she accepted a ride home with them, as if they could not be expected to be accountable for their actions. It was her fault. Ironically, while her alleged intentions to seduce the men can be held up for scrutiny, the men's racism and sexism is never allowed in discussion, a point that underscores the taken-for-granted sexism and racism that permeates the event, court case, and its reporting, as well as the social context of which it is a part.

In contrast, the girl is alternately portrayed as the victim, albeit the victim of her own family, including the mother with whom she had a fight and a male member of her household with whom she had been interfered with sexually. She is placed in the ambivalent position of being, on the one hand, a sexual aggressor—a Lolita and seductress—over whom grown men have no control. On the other hand, she is depicted in the media as a pitiable little girl trapped in the circumstances of her birth. By fixing her in this in-between space—this "no man's land" of no control—the media positions her as an ambivalent outsider, someone who cannot be understood and is beyond the bounds of "normal" society. She is *not* depicted as someone whose human rights have been violated, even though this is her legal status.

Ironically, one of the most significant factors of human rights violations, however, is that victims are thereby placed outside of normal society where "normal" people are not seen to be violated. The condition of people with less social, material, or economic power is exacerbated by the representation that violence is who they really are. This is the plight of the missing women. Their victimization does not receive the coverage it deserves because they are already set outside of society, with their violation as proof of their difference. Their presence is nonetheless felt in the occurrence of everyday violence that continues to haunt colonized peoples, as in the case of the Tisdale assault. When people's legal rights are ignored, belittled, and continually eroded, they become people who are outside civil discourses found in the law, education, and media.

In conclusion, I know that the action of laying out and denouncing systems of discrimination does not change the discrimination. It does not mean that they will not be dislodged and discredited at all if they are not named. Instead, other factors, besides institutionalized racism, will be held up as so-called causes of inequality. There have been many voices raised at this conference concerning the plight of missing women. All of the voices are necessary because of the myriad aspects to the exploitation and violence that we oppose.

ENDNOTES

1 Mary Eberts, Counsel for the Native Women's Association of Canada (NWAC), stated in the intervention at the assault trial in Tisdale, Saskatchewan: "While all women are vulnerable to sexual assault, certain women are more vulnerable because they suffer additional types of discrimination on the basis of, among other things, race, age, disability, or economic status. Sexual assault is an abuse of power, and women who have, or are perceived to have, diminished social status by reason of, for example, race, sexual orientation, disability or poverty are more likely to be victims. Thus, sexual assault is often another incident of oppression along a continuum of disempowering and dehumanizing experiences." (NWAC intervention in the case, October 20, 2004).

REFERENCES

Amnesty International Canada. 2004. *Stolen sisters: A human rights response to discrimination and violence against Indigenous women in Canada.* AI Index AMR 20/003/2004.

Keating, Bridget. 2008. "Pocahontas: History, territory and ekphrasis in the representation of an Indigenous girl." Master's thesis, University of Regina.

McNinch, J. 2009. " 'I thought Pocahontas was a movie': Using critical discourse analysis to understand race and sex as social constructs." In *"I thought Pocahontas was a movie": Perspectives on race/culture binaries in education and service professions,* ed. C. Schick and J. McNinch, 151–76. Regina: Canadian Plains Research Center.

Parker, L., D. Dehyle, and S. Villenas, eds. 1999. *Race is . . . race isn't: Critical race theory and qualitative studies in education.* Boulder, CO: Westview Press.

Stoler, A. L. 1997. "Making empire respectable: The politics of race and sexual morality in twentieth-century colonial cultures." In *Dangerous liaisons: gender, nation and postcolonial perspectives,* ed. A. McClintock, A. Mufti, and E. Shohat, 344–73. Minneapolis: University of Minnesota Press.

Vera, H., and J. R. Feagin. 2004. "The study of racist events." In *Researching race and racism,* ed. M. Bulmer and J. Solomos, 66–77. London: Routledge.

"She was not into drugs and partying. She was a wife and mother":
Media representations and (re)presentations of Daleen Kay Bosse (Muskego)

HOLLY A. MCKENZIE

Dedication
Thanks to Daleen Kay Bosse (Muskego) and her family:
Jeremiah, Faith, Pauline, Herb, and Dana (among others).
I am saddened by your story and empowered by your actions.

During the last year of my undergraduate "career," I, like many other students, wrote an honours paper.[1] While deciding on the topic for my honours project, I struggled with how to make my research relevant and important to the "real world" as well as to academia. As I reflected on important issues in Canada, I kept returning to the issue of racialized and sexualized violence. As a white-settler, anti-racist feminist activist, I have been involved in vigils to raise awareness about the large number of missing and murdered Aboriginal[2] women, and I wanted to conduct research that would work towards the elimination of violence against all women, especially Aboriginal women. Inspired by the research of Bridget Keating, Natalie Kallio, and Charla

HOLLY A. MCKENZIE is a white-settler woman who grew up on a farm near Trib-une, Saskatchewan. She obtained her B.A. Honours (Women's and Gender Stud-ies) and Bachelor of Health Studies in June 2009 and is now pursuing her M.A. (Canadian Plains Studies) at the University of Regina.

Vall,[3] I decided to conduct a case study examining mainstream media representations of Daleen Kay Bosse (Muskego), who was a First Nations woman from Onion Lake Cree Nation (and so much more).[4] My research examines whether mainstream media representations of Daleen contribute to (or deconstruct) Indigenous women's social and economic marginalization and, therefore, their vulnerability to violence. I also recommend anti-racist, anti-sexist techniques and tools that can be integrated into journalism educational practices as one voice in the dialogue towards more appropriate and representative material about Aboriginal peoples, especially women.

During the final stages of my honours research, an assignment in my Community-based Research Methods class presented me with the opportunity to remember the importance of conducting research that is activist in nature. Dr. Carrie Bourassa had challenged our class to participate in a photovoice project and then reflect upon its use as an "alternative" research methodology. It was a very creative assignment. I had tried to save time and "fit it into" my honours project, but technicalities thwarted this attempt and at the last minute I was left without a focus or inspiration. The day that the first part of the assignment was due, in a last ditch effort to find direction, I went on a walking tour of the University of Regina and First Nations University of Canada. It was at the First Nations University of Canada that the sight of *Bison Sentinels* stopped me in my tracks. This artwork was created by Adrian Stimson for the "Missing Women: Decolonization, Third Wave Feminisms and Indigenous People of Canada and Mexico" conference as a memorial for the (too) many Aboriginal women who have been murdered or gone missing. When I saw *Bison Sentinels,* I remembered how many people (Indigenous and non-Indigenous, women and men) are currently working to eliminate violence against women, in particular, violence against Aboriginal women. *Bison Sentinels* is an act and a representation of resistance, the valuing of women who have so often been devalued, the remembering of women who have for so long been forgotten. Immediately, I took a picture of *Bison Sentinels* for my photovoice project. However, not only is this picture of *Bison Sentinels* a part of my photovoice project, but in that moment (and still today) it became a very powerful reminder that my honours paper cannot just be for me. Rather, it has to be for the community, for the women who have disappeared, been murdered, and otherwise victimized.

Through remembering the importance of advocacy and activism, my location as a researcher shifted. In the later stages of my honours research, I realized that I was now researching as a white-settler, post-colonial, post-structural, feminist, *advocacy* researcher. Meredith Cherland and Helen

Harper explain that advocacy research is openly transformative and openly political. "It is research and scholarship for transformation and a more compassionate and equitable world."[5] Advocacy research is "research that stands in solidarity with oppressed peoples and communities and works to improve their material, economic and political circumstances."[6] Further, advocacy research is conducted in order "to improve conditions for *all* of us, including those who are in privileged positions."[7] As a white-settler woman who is awarded certain privileges within neo-colonial Canada because I am the descendent of colonists, advocacy research offered me a framework that reflected my intentions and allowed me a position as an activist and advocate as I conduct research. Therefore, it is with Daleen's and other Aboriginal women's stories in mind that I wrote my honours paper and this chapter. It is for them.

Violence Against Aboriginal Women and Mainstream Media Representations of Indigenous Women

My honours paper is about how mainstream media sources (re)present[8] Aboriginal women and particularly Daleen; however, it is also about the link between violence and these representations. Within neo-colonial Canada, dominant institutions, such as mainstream media, are predominantly controlled by white-settler men. Since the mainstream media functions as a source of information for white-settler communities about marginalized groups such as Aboriginal women, further understanding how Indigenous women are represented in the print media provides insight into white-settler attitudes towards Aboriginal women.[9]

The groundbreaking report *Stolen Sisters: Discrimination and Violence against Aboriginal Women in Canada* was released by Amnesty International in 2004.[10] *Stolen Sisters* brought to light how white-settler society's attitudes towards Aboriginal women contribute to Indigenous women's vulnerability to violence at the hands of strangers and acquaintances within white communities. *Stolen Sisters* reveals that Indigenous or non-Indigenous men may be motivated by racism and/or sexism in their attacks against Aboriginal women. However, these men may also choose to attack Indigenous women based on the assumption that they will not be held accountable by the justice system because of the indifference of white-settler society to the well-being and safety of Aboriginal women.[11] Other factors contribute to Aboriginal women's vulnerability to violence within these communities, such as historical (and present day) colonialist, racist, and sexist government policies. These policies have led to the social and economic marginalization of Indigenous women and, effectively, their exclusion from Canadian society. This marginalization has pushed a high number of Aboriginal women into homelessness, sex work, and other circumstances of extreme poverty.[12]

Contributing to both white-settler attitudes towards Aboriginal women and Indigenous women's social and economic marginalization is what Kim Anderson refers to as the "Indian princess" and "Indian squaw" images that colonizers have created.[13] This colonial imagery homogenizes and hypersexualizes Indigenous women as either the "Indian princess," who works with white men and recognizes the "inevitability of progress," or the "Indian squaw," who is drunken, licentious, dirty, and insolent—the "beast of burden" of her society.[14] Through imagery of Aboriginal women as princesses/squaws who either help white men or whose removal is necessary for the progress of society, violence against Indigenous women becomes justified in the colonial imagination. Emma LaRocque points out that the "image of the sexually loose 'squaw' renders all Native girls and women vulnerable to gross physical and/or verbal abuse."[15] Further, Keating argues that representations of Indigenous women as squaws or princesses "incites, permits and sanctions" violence against Aboriginal women.[16] Often, people will refer to the "Indian princess" and "Indian squaw" as stereotypes; however, I believe that this infers that the "Indian princess" and "Indian squaw" images are the exaggeration of a few characteristics of Indigenous women rather than a creation of the colonial imagination. In order to draw attention to their origin within the colonial mind, I refer to the "Indian princess" and "Indian squaw" as the princess/squaw motif.

The princess/squaw motif is not unique to Canada's social landscape, as it has also been employed by the dominant white culture in the United States.[17] Nor is it a recent phenomenon. During the colonization of Turtle Island (now Canada), the colonizers' speeches, written materials, and visual images began to (re)present Aboriginal women as either Indian princesses or squaw-drudges.[18] However, which side of the princess/squaw motif was/is most prevalent in certain locations and time frames depends on how colonialist power relations were/are operating.

Sarah Carter states that (re)presentations of the beautiful Indian princess were not common in the Canadian west during the late nineteenth century.[19] Rather, during this time period (when European Canada was consolidating its control over the Canadian west) many colonial writings and images presented Indigenous women as squaw-drudges.[20] This side of the princess/squaw motif was used at many times for many reasons. For instance, often the squaw image was used to justify white men's violent acts against Indigenous women. In 1889, when Rosalie, a Cree women, was killed by William "Jumbo" Fisk in Calgary, the majority of Calgary's townspeople agreed that "Rosalie was only a squaw and that her death did not matter much."[21] Through this naming of Rosalie as a squaw, Rosalie is (mis)understood[22] as disposable, someone who is less than human. It is evident that the princess/squaw motif justified the victimization of Rosalie and other Indigenous women.

Very little research analyzes recent newspaper representations of Aboriginal women; however, researchers such as Kallio, Keating, and Vall have examined how Aboriginal women are represented and (re)presented in mainstream media sources. Kallio, Keating, and Vall have found that recent mainstream newspaper representations draw upon (and recreate) narratives of sexism, racism and colonialism. Although there are several different strands of these narratives, one common strand that all three researchers found was the casting of Indigenous women as sexualized deviants.[23] For instance, Kallio examined how the *Saskatoon StarPhoenix* represented a 12-year-old Cree girl who was violated by three 20-something white men from Tisdale. Kallio's analysis suggests that the mainstream media's use of the princess/squaw motif casts this 12-year-old Cree girl as contributing to her own victimization.[24]

Representations of Daleen Kay Bosse (Muskego): A Case Study

I chose to examine how Daleen was represented and (re)presented in the *Leader-Post* and *StarPhoenix* for a number of reasons. First of all, I felt a connection to Daleen. When I began my research I, too, was a twenty-five-year-old woman and university student. However, I suspected that if I had gone missing, the media response would have been very different *because of my white privilege.* Secondly, the princess/squaw motif is often used to naturalize Aboriginal women's higher rates (or individual Aboriginal women's circumstances) of poverty, drug and alcohol addictions, and sex trade work, often referred to by the mainstream media as "high-risk lifestyles." In examining how Daleen was represented, I was able to explore whether the princess/squaw motif was present, even though Daleen did not live (what is termed) a "high-risk lifestyle." At the same time, I am in no way suggesting that the princess/squaw motif justifies Aboriginal women's higher rates of poverty, drug and alcohol addictions, and sex trade work. Rather, like Amnesty International and Carrie Bourassa, Mary Hampton, and Kim McKay-McNabb, I argue that these situations are a result of racist, sexist, and colonialist policies and practices.[25]

I used feminist critical discourse analysis to examine the *Leader-Post* and *StarPhoenix* representations of Daleen. According to Michelle Lazar, feminist critical discourse analysis is "a political perspective on gender" concerned with denaturalizing "interrelationships of gender, power, and ideology in discourse."[26] In my analysis, I examined the mainstream media representations not only in relation to themselves and each other, but also in relation to the intersecting narratives *on* racism, colonialism, and sexism, as well as their possible effects. I used the guidelines set out by Norman Fairclough in *Discourse and Social Change* and John E. Richardson in *Analysing Newspapers: An Approach from Critical Discourse Analysis.*[27] Following Richardson, I posed this question in relation to these newspaper representations: do they "help to continue inequalities and other undesirable social practices, or [do they] help to break them down?"[28]

Daleen Kay Bosse (Muskego)'s Story

Daleen Kay Bosse (Muskego), a twenty-five-year-old university student, mother, sister, daughter, and friend from Onion Lake Cree Nation, lived in Saskatoon with her husband (Jeremiah) and daughter (Faith) when she went missing on May 18, 2004. On May 18 Daleen attended a Federation of Saskatchewan Indian Nations (FSIN) meeting and supper and then went out socializing with friends at a Saskatoon nightclub, Jax.[29] Daleen went missing outside of Jax while waiting for her friends to find her a ride.[30] The next morning, when Jeremiah woke up and realized that Daleen was missing, he phoned the Saskatoon Police Service. However, when the police officer came to their home, he asked only a couple of questions about Daleen. Jeremiah says, "I think he asked, 'Is she Aboriginal?' That was about it."[31] Indeed, the family feel that the police "shrugged off and brushed to the side" their concerns.[32] Frustrated with the police response, Daleen's family were the first to make "missing" posters of Daleen. They also hired a private investigator eight days after she went missing.[33]

When Daleen's parents, Herb and Pauline Muskego, first voiced their complaints about the unwillingness of the police to accept Daleen's disappearance as a serious case, the police responded by listing numerous "sightings" of Daleen. However, Herb and Pauline have never been allowed to view the security tapes of these sightings in order to confirm them and, therefore, they consider them unsubstantiated.[34] The police had also told Daleen's family that most missing people contacted home at Christmas or other special occasions. When Christmas of 2004 passed without word from Daleen, Daleen's family grew more frustrated with the police response and chose to lodge a complaint through the FSIN Special Investigations Unit.[35] Daleen's family believes that this complaint and the continuous pressure they put on the police caused a shift in how Saskatoon Police Service dealt with Daleen's case. It was at this time that the major crimes unit took over Daleen's case.[36] While the family and police continued to receive tips about sightings of Daleen over the years, her case remained unresolved until August 2008. Finally, on August 10, 2008, Chief Weighill from Saskatoon Police Services travelled to Onion Lake First Nation to meet with Daleen's parents and tell Daleen's family about new information relating to Daleen's case.[37] Daleen's body had been found halfway between Martensville and Warman, and the police had enough evidence to charge a suspect with her murder. The same day, Douglas Hales was arrested in Saskatoon and charged with first-degree murder and indignity to a body.[38] Hales grew up in White Fox and is a white-settler, 30-year-old man who was working as a doorman at Jax at the time of Daleen's disappearance.[39] Hales's preliminary hearing was scheduled to begin April 2009.[40]

The *Leader-Post* and *StarPhoenix* (Re)presentations and Representations

In early March 2009, I searched the *Canadian Newswire* database for articles containing the name "Daleen Kay Bosse" or "Daleen Bosse." I found fifty-one articles and two letters to the editor that the *Regina Leader-Post* and *Saskatoon StarPhoenix* had published. Out of these articles, thirty-four were from the *StarPhoenix* and seventeen were from the *Leader-Post*. While these articles span more than four years, the majority of *StarPhoenix* articles mentioning Daleen are found in 2008. Indeed, eleven articles were written after Hales first appeared in court charged with her murder on August 11, 2008. The majority of the *Leader-Post* articles mentioning Daleen were also written after Hales' first court appearance. During the last five months of 2008, Daleen was mentioned in seven *Leader-Post* articles. Of the thirty-four articles found in the *StarPhoenix,* only fifteen related directly to Daleen's disappearance, developments in her missing person's case, the discovery of her body, and the resulting preliminary hearings. Similarly, out of the seventeen articles found in the *Leader-Post,* only nine were related directly to Daleen's disappearance, missing person's case, the discovery of her body, and the resulting trial procedures.

The lack of *Leader-Post* and *StarPhoenix* newspaper articles even *mentioning* Daleen Kay Bosse (Muskego) creates a discourse of silence around her disappearance, her missing person's case, and Hales's murder trial. This silence was most evident in 2004. Despite the fact that Jeremiah had reported Daleen missing on May 19, there was no media coverage dealing with Daleen's disappearance in the Saskatoon *StarPhoenix* until May 28. After a short article that the *StarPhoenix* ran in the later pages of their news section on May 28, 2004, the *StarPhoenix* did not mention Daleen for another month and a half. These were the only two newspaper articles that mentioned Daleen in 2004. The *Leader-Post* ran no articles that mentioned Daleen in any way during 2004.

While this silence was pervasive during the entire four years of media coverage examined, another time this silence was especially obvious was after October 2, 2008. In the article "Murder suspect makes video court appearance," Betty A. Adam notes that "[Hales] is scheduled to return for another appearance Oct. 8." However, there were no articles covering Hales's court appearance, or lack of court appearance, on October 8: there is only silence. Furthermore, there were no other articles in 2008 or 2009 directly relating to Hales's court case. This silence fails to bring Hales's trial to the consciousness of readers and, as such, informs them that Daleen's death and how her accused murderer is dealt with is not an important event.

As "Choosing to be Missing," "Partying," "Irresponsible"

In 2004, there are only two *StarPhoenix* articles discussing Daleen's disappearance. While the fact that there were only two articles is evidence of the silence that surrounds Daleen's disappearance, how she is represented—or rather (re)presented—within these articles is also important. The first short article discussing Daleen's disappearance, entitled "Police search for missing woman" and found on page A7 of the May 28 *StarPhoenix,* begins,

> Saskatoon city police are asking for the public's helping in locating a missing 25-year-old woman. Daleen Kay Bosse has been missing since May 18. However, police said she has been seen at several different locations in Saskatoon, *and was possibly spotted around 2:20 a.m. on Thursday* (emphasis added).

It is apparent that the *StarPhoenix* received this information from a Saskatoon Police Services media release (or similar materials) about Daleen's disappearance. Within this article, Saskatoon city police are referred to as the institution that is actively looking for Daleen and that is considered a reliable source of information on her. However, Daleen's family, friends, and their actions of looking for Daleen are left unmentioned.

Within this article, Daleen is named in several different ways. As Richardson notes, words "convey the imprint of society and value judgments in particular."[41] As well, how individuals are named influences how they are perceived by the readership. Since every person has a number of identities and social groups that they belong to, the choice of how to name an individual relates them to one (or more) of these social groups. Within this article, Daleen is first named as a "25-year-old woman" who is "missing." Later in the article, she is also described as "of Native descent" and effectively named as Aboriginal. However, this description of Daleen names her as one of (many) Métis and First Nations women, rather than as a First Nations woman from Onion Lake Cree Nation. Describing individual, specific Aboriginal women in these general terms effectively homogenizes Aboriginal women. Most problematically, Daleen's identity as an Aboriginal woman who is missing is not connected to the larger issue of missing and murdered Aboriginal women. Just a few months earlier, in March of 2004, the Native Women's Association of Canada (NWAC) had launched the Sister in Spirit (SIS) Campaign in order to raise awareness about the issue of racialized and sexualized violence.[42]

At the same time, her identity as an Aboriginal woman does inform the description of Daleen's disappearance, as the presence of the princess/squaw motif is implicit within this article. In the excerpt above, the sentence "Daleen Kay Bosse has been missing since May 18" is followed by the adverb "however" and new information is added to the first statement.[43] This new information in the next sentence contradicts what the audience would have assumed from the previous statement, that is, that Daleen has been "taken," "is being held captive," or possibly has been murdered. Indeed, this new information locates her as being seen several times (according to the police, a reliable source), with one possible sighting occurring late at night. When this article refers to her as "being seen," the reader is asked to suppose, then, that Daleen has *not* been taken, rather that she has *chosen* to go missing. Furthermore, by (re)presenting Daleen as "possibly spotted around 2:20 a.m. on Thursday night," the reader is encourage to assume that she is doing what most people do at that time: partying, drinking, or using drugs. Therefore, this sentence positions her as "choosing to be missing," "partying" and, as a result, irresponsible. At the same time, Daleen is not named as mother, sister, daughter, student, wife, or even future teacher, all relevant and accurate names that reflect her identity.

The second newspaper representation of Daleen was published in the *StarPhoenix* on July 13, 2004, this time in a public appeal by Crime Stoppers to locate Daleen. This public appeal was placed on page A7 under the headline "Community Crime Report" and subheading "Missing Person." The text of this crime report appeals to the public for their "assistance in locating Daleen Kay Bosse who has been missing since May 18, 2004." The beginning of this public appeal raises questions for the reader: What happened to Daleen? Why is she missing? While this public appeal does not answer these questions directly, when it notes that Daleen "has reportedly been seen at several different locations in Saskatoon," the reader is left to suppose that she has "chosen" to go missing. Also, the Crime Stoppers appeal did not include a picture of Daleen, only a text description of her: "25 years old, weighs 170 pounds and stands 5-foot-5 inches tall. She has shoulder-length black hair, brown eyes and a medium complexion." This lack of a photograph is problematic. There are a number of women who would fit that description, so without a picture it is difficult to identify Daleen. Therefore, despite the text suggesting otherwise, the lack of a picture signifies to the reader that if they do not know Daleen, they *do not need* to look for Daleen. Rather, through reading the public appeal and not seeing a picture, the reader constructs a narrative of what happened: Daleen has chosen to go missing and the police as well as her family are concerned about her. Therefore, those who know Daleen and know where she is (or Daleen herself) should contact the police.[44]

Disrupting the Princess/Squaw Motif

Since Daleen disappeared in 2004, political and social activists have engaged the media around Daleen's disappearance specifically, as well as around the larger issue of missing and murdered Aboriginal women. In particular, Pauline and Herb Muskego began to engage with the media in order to raise awareness about Daleen's disappearance in 2005.[45] In March 2004, NWAC began the Sisters in Spirit (SIS) Campaign to "raise public awareness of the alarmingly high rates of violence against Aboriginal women in Canada."[46] In November 2005 the campaign became a research, education and policy initiative.[47] Amnesty International also brought public attention to the issue of missing and murdered Aboriginal women with the release of the *Stolen Sisters* report in October 2004.[48] As well, other Aboriginal and non-Aboriginal activists along with family and friends of Aboriginal women who have gone missing or been murdered have held vigils and rallies and otherwise organized around the issue of violence against Aboriginal women.

In 2005, how the media represented Daleen shifted, with both the *Leader-Post* and *StarPhoenix* representing Daleen in ways that disrupted the princess/squaw motif. There are a number of ways that their representations of Daleen interrogate the princess/squaw motif. For instance, articles that located Daleen in relation to the issue of missing and murdered Aboriginal women often call into question the colonial assumptions of the princess/squaw motif and make them visible. Often, direct quotes from Aboriginal and non-Aboriginal activists and Aboriginal community members also reveal that the princess/squaw motif is linked to Aboriginal women's vulnerability to violence. While some articles only listed Daleen as "one of" the many missing and murdered Aboriginal women, other articles described Daleen in two notably disruptive ways: As a "mother, sister, wife, daughter, university student" and as "not a partier," "not irresponsible," and, no, "she did not choose to go missing."

A Sister, A Mother, A Daughter, A Wife, A University Student

In twenty-five *StarPhoenix* articles and ten *Leader-Post* articles from 2005–2008, Daleen was positioned as a mother, a wife, a daughter, a university student, and a friend, as well as a First Nations woman from Onion Lake Cree Nation. In many Indigenous communities, an individual's identity is constructed around the family and familial relationships.[49] "Where you are from" (physically, spiritually, emotionally) is also integral to understanding "who you are."[50] Therefore, positioning Daleen in relation to her family and her land base effectively reclaims her traditional First Nations identity. This is done in a number of ways, including describing Daleen or directly naming Daleen as a wife, mother, university student, First Nations woman, and/or future teacher. As well, newspaper representations often visually represented Daleen's mother, father, and daughter, as well as indirectly or directly quoted Daleen's family and friends in order to represent Daleen's various relationships, roles, and "where she was from."

The following excerpt taken from the *StarPhoenix* article "Walk draws attention to missing Sask. Women" used description and naming to position Daleen as a wife, mother, and Cree First Nations woman from the Onion Lake Cree Nation:

> The 26-year-old *wife* and *mother* of a six-year-old girl had just attended an Assembly of First Nations function and then went to Jax nightclub in downtown Saskatoon. She has not been heard

from since. There is a $10,000 reward being offered by the *Onion Lake Cree Nation* for information leading to her whereabouts. (Kenyon Wallace, July 28, 2007; emphasis added)

Positioning Daleen as a Cree wife, mother, daughter, sister, university student, and future teacher effectively disrupts the princess/squaw motif and, with it, the boundaries between the Euro-western and Aboriginal community. When Daleen is named as a First Nations woman who is a good mother, daughter, wife, and university student, the white-settler reader comes to recognize the link between Daleen and herself. Daleen is recognized as both a First Nations woman and a Canadian citizen who has roles, relationships, and responsibilities similar to those of other Canadian citizens.

She was "Not a Partier, Drug-user" and "She Did Not Choose to Go Missing"

Other articles directly challenge and deny the assumptions of the media, police, and wider society about Daleen. These representations interrogate the princess/squaw motif primarily through direct quotations from her family, friends, and activists concerned with the issue of missing and murdered Aboriginal women. The reader's assumptions are both revealed and denied through the sentences that are often phrased as a negative answer to a question that was never asked.[51] For instance, in the *StarPhoenix* article, "Family awaits word on missing woman," Herb Muskego is quoted as saying, "she is not a street person, not into drugs and partying. She is a wife and mother who cared for her family."[52] Within this statement, Herb both denies the colonial assumptions that the reader may make about Daleen and positions her as a wife and mother. This direct contestation of the colonial assumptions about Daleen is not as common as the representations of Daleen as a mother, sister, daughter, university student, future teacher, First Nations woman, and friend, discussed above. However, as Stuart Hall argues, it is necessary to interrogate colonial imagery, such as the princess/squaw motif.[53] If the princess/squaw motif were left uninterrogated and instead only replaced with new, positive representations of Daleen, the colonial imagination could reduce these to the princess/squaw motif, as that is what it (mis)understands as natural.

Another Shift in Coverage:
the Deracing of Daleen and her Accused Murderer

Unfortunately, after Daleen's body was found and Hales was charged with her murder, the media coverage shifted yet again. Some newspaper representations continued to interrogate the princess/squaw motif and represent Daleen as a mother, sister, daughter, student, and Cree First Nations woman. However, other articles positioned Daleen as a mother, sister, daughter, and student *but left her identity as an Aboriginal woman unwritten.* Furthermore, only one article acknowledged Hales's identity as a white-settler (or Caucasian) man. By "de-racing" Daleen and Hales, these newspaper representations discourage the reader from connecting Daleen's murder to the victimization of Aboriginal women across Canada or to Canada's history of colonialism, sexism, and racism. The colonial construction of the princess/squaw motif and how it justified Daleen's disappearance and other Aboriginal women's victimization again becomes invisible.[54]

Deconstructing and Reproducing the Colonial Motif:
What Does it Mean?

The *Leader-Post* and *StarPhoenix* articles positioned Daleen in ways that both (re)produced and disrupted the princess/squaw motif. For instance, during 2004, both the lack of media coverage of Daleen's disappearance and the two *StarPhoenix* articles positioned Daleen as an irresponsible Aboriginal woman who had, in order to go partying, chosen to go missing. In 2004, the silence around Daleen's disappearance is partially due to the police's low prioritization of Daleen's case and therefore their lack of media releases.[55] However, while a lack of public and police interest in Daleen's case may be argued as a reason for this silence, it can also be argued that this silence and the presence of the princess/squaw motif *creates* a lack of police and public involvement.

For many people, the mainstream media is a crucial source of information, events, issues, and stories. In addition, mainstream media provides readers with information not only about events, issues, and stories, but also about people, "especially those belonging to groups with whom they rarely interact."[56] Therefore, when the mainstream media represents Daleen as someone who is not really a victim, the readers are *not* called upon to (and do not) pressure the police to search for Daleen. Equally, it was not until Daleen's family lodged a complaint with FSIN Special Investigations Unit that the police finally responded "seriously to Daleen's disappearance."[57]

These misrepresentations of Daleen were later challenged by the same newspapers that produced them. Articles from both the *Leader-Post* and *StarPhoenix* challenged colonial assumptions about Daleen's nature and revealed the princess/squaw motif as a part of the colonial imagination. Through the use of direct and indirect quotations from Daleen's family, friends, and activists these *Leader-Post* and *StarPhoenix* articles denaturalized the princess/squaw motif and rendered it *visible*. Similarly, through naming Daleen as a mother, sister, daughter, university student, and First Nations woman, Daleen is positioned as belonging to both Canada and her First Nation. As a result, the boundaries constructed between the white-settler community and the Aboriginal community collapse. This (de)construction of difference contributes to new understandings of the rights of Daleen and other Aboriginal women within Canada and their First Nations. Joyce Green suggests that Aboriginal rights and Canadian citizenship rights are not exclusionary and, rather, Aboriginal women can and should be granted access to both, as well as protection through international human rights guidelines.[58] Currently, most Aboriginal women are too disempowered to access their rights through the state or government. True access to Canadian citizenship rights and Aboriginal rights requires more than representations of Aboriginal women's belonging and the interrogation of colonial motifs. Recognition that Aboriginal women's access to citizenship and human rights is limited by social and economic marginalization and the underlying historical and current government policies is crucial. As well, the redistribution of power and resources in order to undo this marginalization is necessary. Journalistic representations can, in addition to positioning Daleen (and other Aboriginal women) as belonging to their Aboriginal community and Canada, contextualize violence against Aboriginal women, bringing the racist and sexist nature of their victimization to the public consciousness.

Recommendations for Truly Disruptive Journalistic Practices

Indigenous and non-Indigenous researchers have pointed out that (mis)representing Aboriginal women as either "squaws or princesses" has negative effects on the identity, self-esteem, and safety of these women.[59] In particular, Keating argues that representations of Indigenous women as squaws or princesses "incites, permits and sanctions" violence against Aboriginal women.[60] This case study revealed that journalistic representations can effectively disrupt and/or (re)produce the princess/squaw motif. Furthermore, since Henry and Tator indicate that the mainstream media influences white-settler Canadians' understandings of marginalized communities, I have used the findings of this case study to suggest some anti-racist, anti-sexist techniques and tools that can be integrated into journalism educational practices. As my recommendations are primarily directed at mainstream media institutions, I recommend the Sisters in Spirit "Unlocking the Mystery of Media Relations Toolkit"[61] for those activists protesting racialized and sexualized violence, and families and friends of Aboriginal women who have been victimized.

While practices of representation and interpretation are often largely unconscious, Fairclough argues that through critical language awareness, individuals can become more conscious of their discourse practices. Indeed, Fairclough suggests that through the introduction of critical language awareness into the secondary school system, youth would be able to change their own language practices and interrogate others.[62] Furthermore, it is very possible that mainstream media agents are not consciously (re)producing racist, sexist, and colonialist narratives. Rather, it is likely that they, like many members of the imaginary white-settler nation state, have naturalized racist, sexist, and colonialist assumptions. Therefore, like Tom Brislin and Nancy Williams, I argue that journalism ethics classes should challenge and interrogate these narratives that help "explain" (imaginary) white-settler Canada.[63] Ways to explore these new ethical dilemmas that deal with racism, sexism and colonialism could include: having students conduct analyses of the mainstream media, examining how gender roles and racial identities are constructed; using role-playing exercises in which students play parts that are not their natural social identity (for instance, First Nations students and women can play white men in positions of power); teaching students how to find sources and experts who are not white males and whose community's voices are currently excluded from mainstream media;[64] exploring how students can ethically engage with communities that they do not belong to. Furthermore, critical language awareness should be integrated into ethics classes in order to ensure ethical representation of sexualized and racialized others. This awareness can bring to consciousness:

* words: denotative and connotative meanings and what they mean;

* naming: how social positioning in journalistic texts is read and what implications it has;

* verb tense: who is active, who is passive and the absent referent;

* presuppositions and what they tell readers they should think.

Diversity education should not be relegated only to university programs. Rather, newsrooms should engage their staffs in anti-racist, anti-sexist, cultural awareness education. In Ann Johnston and Dolores Flamiano's study, one woman suggested that diversity training deal primarily with the racist and sexist nature of our society.[65] As well, how naturalized sexism and racism operates within an individual's own consciousness, speech, and writing should be explored. Furthermore, diversity education could discuss ways that journalists can ethically engage with Aboriginal communities, for instance, building relationships with members from those communities and becoming comfortable in those communities.[66] As well, non-Aboriginal Canadian journalists should consciously engage in a dialogue with Aboriginal community members about what stories are important to that community. Otherwise, like journalists in other locations, non-Aboriginal Canadian journalists may assume that they are the same stories that are newsworthy to the white-settler community about the Aboriginal community.[67]

In order to inform mainstream media agents of my findings, I will be summarizing this case study, as well as providing a practical, detailed list of recommendations. I will provide the University of Regina's School of Journalism, the *StarPhoenix,* and the *Leader-Post* with a summary. As well, other interested parties will be provided with a summary upon request. It is my hope that educational institutions and newspapers can use these recommendations in order to produce more appropriate and representative material when writing about Aboriginal peoples, particularly Aboriginal women. As such, this research may serve as one voice in the dialogue of "undoing" the oppression of Aboriginal women by the white-settler majority.

ENDNOTES

1   McKenzie, "(De)constructing and (re)producing the princess/squaw motif."

2   This chapter will use both the terms "Aboriginal" and "Indigenous" when referring to the Indigenous peoples of Canada, who are constitutionally recognized as "Indian, Inuit and Métis peoples of Canada."

3   Kallio, "Aboriginality and sexualized violence"; Keating, "Raping Pocahontas"; Vall, "Representations of Aboriginal women in Canadian hegemonic print media."

4   See Daleen Bosse's story on page 34.

5   Cherland and Harper, *Advocacy research in literacy education,* 3–4.

6   Ibid., 6.

7   Ibid., 6.

8   In order to draw attention to how mainstream media (and other) representations are often indeed presentations of a viewpoint, interpretation or own prejudices, I will use parentheses to communicate this, for instance: (re)presentation and (re)present.

9   Henry and Tator, *Discourses of domination,* 35–36.

10 Amnesty International, *Stolen sisters.*

11 Ibid., 2.

12 Ibid., 2.

13 Anderson, *A recognition of being,* 101–102.

14 Anderson, *A recognition of being,* 102; Bird, "Gendered construction," 76; Green, "The Pocahontas perplex," 17, 22.

15 LaRocque, "Tides, towns and trains," 87.

16 Keating, "Raping Pocahontas," 71.

17 Green, "The Pocahontas perplex"; Bird, "Gendered construction."

18 Anderson, *A recognition of being,* 101–102; Carter, *Capturing women,* 161.

19 Carter, *Capturing women,* 161.

20 Ibid., 161.

21 Smith, "Bloody murder almost became miscarriage of justice," quoted in Carter, *Capturing women,* 189 and 190. This Cree woman was only identified as Rosalie in the legal documents and newspapers. Although Fisk was eventually convicted of manslaughter, this was only after Judge Charles Rouleau refused to accept the jury's first verdict of not guilty. In fact, at the retrial, Rouleau told the jury to "forget the women's race and to consider only the evidence at hand."

22 In order to draw attention to how mainstream media's understandings (and those of other white-settler institutions) are often widely accepted misunderstandings, I will use parentheses to communicate this when appropriate, for instance: (mis)-understandings.

23 Kallio, "Aboriginality and sexualized violence," 11, 17; Keating "Raping Pocahontas," 12; Vall, "Representations of Aboriginal women," 24–25.

24 Kallio, "Aboriginality and sexualized violence."

25 Amnesty International, *Stolen sisters;* Bourassa et al., "Racism, sexism and colonialism, 23–29.

26 Lazar, *Feminist critical discourse analysis,* 5.

27 Fairclough, *Discourse and social change;* Richardson, *Analysing newspapers.*

28 Richardson, *Analysing newspapers,* 42.

29 Sisters in Spirit, "Voices of our sisters in spirit," 19; Hrynchuk, *Stolen sisters.*

30 Hrynchuk, *Stolen sisters.*

31 Ibid.

32 Hrynchuk, *Stolen sisters;* Sisters in Spirit, "Voices of our sisters in spirit," 19.

33 Sisters in Spirit, "Voices of our sisters in spirit," 19.

34 Ibid., 20–21.

35 Ibid.

36 Ibid., 22.

37 Ibid.

38 Adam, "Bosse's body found."

39 Ibid. Often mainstream media's descriptions of men who violate women personalize these men. These same media representations further objectify the women victimized. As a small measure in undoing this inequality, I will refer to Douglas Hales by his last name throughout this chapter and I will refer to Daleen Kay Bosse (Muskego) as Daleen.

40 Sisters in Spirit, "Voices of our sisters in spirit," 22.

41 Richardson, *Analysing newspapers,* 47.

42 Sisters in Spirit, "Backgrounder."

43 Halliday, *Introduction to functional grammar,* quoted in Fairclough, *Discourse and social change,* 175.

44 Richardson, *Analysing newspapers,* 71. This is what Richardson refers to as "narrative content."

45 Sisters in Spirit, "Voices of our sisters in spirit," 21.

46 Sisters in Spirit, "Sisters in Spirit—raising awareness."

47 Sisters in Spirit, "Backgrounder."

48 Amnesty International, *Stolen sisters.*

49 Silko, *Yellow woman and a beauty of the spirit,* 52.

50 Absolon and Willet, "Putting ourselves forward," 101–2.

51 Fairclough, *Discourse and social change,* 121.

52 Noskiye, March 26, 2005. I do not mean to suggest that women who live on the street, using drugs, drinking, and partying deserve to go missing or be murdered. Rather, my intention is to point out that these characteristics are projected onto Indigenous women even when they do not embody them. See Jiwani and Young, "Missing and murdered women," 895–917, for a discussion problematizing the dominant understandings that privilege "good" women who deserve our attention, sympathy, and intervention over "bad" women.

53 Hall, *Representation and the media.*

54 For a longer discussion of this shift in coverage, see McKenzie, "(De)constructing and (re)producing the princess/squaw motif," 45–50.

55 Sisters in Spirit, "Voices of our sisters in spirit," 20. At one point in 2004, the sergeant in charge of missing persons informed Pauline and Herb Muskego that they had a large stack of cases and Daleen's was on the bottom.

56 Henry and Tator, *Discourses of domination,* 5.

57 Sisters in Spirit, "Voices of our sisters in spirit," 22.

58 Green, "Canaries in the mines of citizenship," 736.

59 Anderson, *Recognition of being,* 105–6; LaRocque, "Tides, towns and trains," 87.

60 Keating, "Raping Pocahontas," 71.

61 Available at www.nwac-hq.org.

62 Fairclough, *Discourse and social change,* 239.

63 Brislin and Williams, "Beyond diversity," 16–27.

64 Ibid., 24.

65 Johnston and Flamiano, "Diversity in mainstream newspapers," 111–31.

66 Ibid., 120.

67 Ibid., 120.

REFERENCES

Absolon, Kathy, and Cam Willet. 2005. "Putting ourselves forward: Location in Aboriginal research." In *Research as resistance: Critical, Indigenous and anti-oppressive approaches,* ed. Leslie Brown and Susan Strega, 97–127. Toronto: Canadian Scholars' Press/Women's Press.

Adam, Betty A. 2008. "Bosse's body found, murder charge laid." *Regina Leader-Post,* August 12.

Amnesty International. 2004. *Stolen sisters: A human rights response to discrimination and violence against Indigenous women in Canada,* October. http://www.amnesty.ca/campaigns/resources/amr2000304.pdf (accessed 20 March 2009).

Anderson, Kim. 2000. *A recognition of being: Reconstructing Native womanhood.* Toronto: Second Story Press.

Bird, S. Elizabeth. 1999. "Gendered construction of the American Indian in popular media." *Journal of Communication* 49 (3): 61–83.

Bourassa, Carrie, Kim McKay-McNabb, and Mary Hampton. 2005. "Racism, sexism and colonialism: The impact on the health of Aboriginal women in Canada." *Canadian Women Studies* 24 (1): 23–29.

Brislin, Tom, and Nancy Williams. 1996. "Beyond diversity: Expanding the canon in journalism ethics." *Journal of Mainstream Media Ethics* 11 (1): 16–27.

Carter, Sarah. 1997. *Capturing women: The manipulation of cultural imagery in Canada's Prairie West.* Montreal: McGill-Queen's University Press.

Cherland, Meredith, and Helen Harper. 2007. *Advocacy research in literacy education.* New York: Routledge.

Fairclough, Norman. 1992. *Discourse and social change.* Cambridge: Polity Press.

Green, Joyce. 2001. "Canaries in the mines of citizenship: Indian women in Canada." *Canadian Journal of Political Science* 34 (4): 715–38.

Green, Rayna. 2007. "The Pocahontas perplex." In *Native women's history in Eastern North America before 1900: A guide to research and writing,* ed. Rebecca Kugel and Lucy Eldersveld Murphy, 10–26. Lincoln: University of Nebraska Press.

Hall, Stuart. 1997. *Representation and the media.* DVD. Directed and produced by Sut Jhally. Northhampton MA: Media Education Foundation, 1997.

Halliday, M. A. K. 1985. *Introduction to functional grammar.* London: Edward Arnold. Quoted in Fairclough, 1992.

Henry, Frances, and Carol Tator. 2002. *Discourses of domination: Racial bias in the Canadian English-Language press.* Toronto: University of Toronto Press.

Hrynchuk, Antonio (Producer and Director). *Stolen sisters.* 2007. DVD. Saskatoon: Fahrenheit Films.

Jiwani, Yasmin, and Mary Lynn Young. 2006. "Missing and murdered women: Reproducing marginality in news discourse." *Canadian Journal of Communication* 31 (4): 895–917.

Johnston, Ann, and Dolores Flamiano. 2007. "Diversity in mainstream newspapers from the standpoint of journalists of color." *Howard Journal of Communications* 18 (2): 111–31.

Kallio, Natalie. 2006. "Aboriginality and sexualized violence: The Tisdale rape case in the Saskatoon *StarPhoenix.*" Master's Thesis, Concordia University.

Keating, Bridget. 2008. "Raping Pocahontas: History, territory and ekpharasis in the representation of an Indigenous girl." Master's Thesis, University of Regina.

LaRocque, Emma. 1990. "Tides, towns and trains." In *Living the changes,* ed. Joan Turner, 76–89. Winnipeg: University of Manitoba Press.

Lazar, Michelle M. 2005. *Feminist critical discourse analysis: Gender, power, and ideology in discourse.* New York: Palgrave Macmillan.

Richardson, John E. 2007. *Analysing newspapers: An approach from critical discourse analysis.* New York: Palgrave Macmillan.

McKenzie, Holly. 2009. "(De)constructing and (re)producing the princess/squaw motif: How the *StarPhoenix* and *Leader-Post* (re)presented Daleen Kay Bosse (Muskego)." Honours' thesis, University of Regina. http://www.arts.uregina.ca/womens-gender-studies.

Noskiye, Ken. 2005. "Family awaits word on missing woman." *Saskatoon StarPhoenix,* March 26.

Silko, Leslie. 1996. *Yellow woman and a beauty of the spirit: Essays on Native American life today.* New York: Simon & Schuster.

Sisters in Spirit. "Backgrounder." Native Women's Association of Canada. http://www.-nwac-hq.org/en/background (accessed 2 March 2009).

—. "Sisters in Spirit—Raising awareness" http://nwac-hq.org/en/awareness.html (accessed 4 June 2009).

—. 2008. "Voices of our sisters in spirit: A research and policy report to families and communities." November. Native Women's Association of Canada. http://www.nwac-hq.org/en/sisresearch.html (accessed 3 March 2009).

Smith, Donald. 1989. "Bloody murder almost became miscarriage of justice." *Herald Sunday Magazine,* July 23, 1989. Quoted in Carter, 1997.

Vall, Charla. 2007. "Representations of Aboriginal women in Canadian hegemonic print media: Unmasking a gendered and racialized politics of belonging." Master's thesis, University of East London.

Reflections of a
Northern Saskatchewan Journalist

DARLA READ

Journalists often receive a lot of flak when it comes to their coverage of missing and murdered Aboriginal women. Critics make generalizations about "the media"—saying the media doesn't do the issue justice, that in many cases the media is insensitive, even that the media is racist.

It's not to say those criticisms don't ring true; in many cases, I'm sure they do. And as a journalist myself, in many cases, I agree with criticism of the media around the issue. As a reporter for an Aboriginal radio station and monthly newspaper, I make a great effort to keep this story in the news.

However, a person has to consider that there are many reasons why journalists aren't covering a story or are covering it in a particular way. Not every journalist gets to dictate his or her story for the day; in many cases, it is assigned. There are staffing shortages, and if there is something else the editor deems more newsworthy happening that day, the editor will send the journalist to that story instead.

DARLA READ is a journalist with Saskatchewan's Aboriginal radio station, Missinipi Broadcasting Corporation, and freelances for *Eagle Feather News*, a monthly Aboriginal newspaper. She has previously worked for other media outlets, including *The La Ronge Northerner* and the CBC.

The journalist is sometimes the easy scapegoat, but nothing is ever that simple.

And, the danger isn't in criticizing media coverage; it's in the blanket reference to "the media," making the assumption that every journalist thinks or reacts the same way to a story or, specifically, that we all cover stories of missing and murdered Aboriginal women in the same way and all feel the same emotions, or lack thereof, when covering those stories.

As a woman, the ongoing story of missing and murdered women has always been important to me, but within the past year it has come to the forefront in my work. In the past, I wasn't indifferent to the story, but I hadn't had any first-hand experience covering it. I had covered things like awareness walks and always wondered how families who hadn't found their loved ones dealt with the uncertainty, but I didn't have an understanding of their pain. I will probably never fully understand, but their stories and pain have deeply touched me this past year.

I felt that pain acutely in August 2008. After more than four years of uncertainty and following possible leads, the family of Daleen Bosse finally had answers, but not any that people were hoping to hear. Her body had been found near Warman and Martensville. Douglas Hales was charged with her first-degree murder, and at his first court appearance the provincial courtroom was packed with Bosse's family and friends, as well as reporters. There was an air of anticipation—people wanted to see the man accused of killing the young mother and university student. There was a lot of media attention around the Bosse case: her parents had held awareness walks each of the four years she was missing, and they had in the past also raised questions about how the case had been handled.

First court appearances are generally short and often uneventful, as the charges against the accused are read and then the case is adjourned to a later date. However, when the charges against Hales were read, they included another besides the murder; for those who don't recall, he was also charged with offering an indignity to human remains for setting Bosse's body on fire.

As soon as that charge was read, Bosse's mother cried out and began sobbing uncontrollably. I will never forget that moment, as I've never experienced anything like it. I can't even put it into words. For a moment, I felt Pauline Muskego's pain transferred to me and everyone in the room. It tugged at my heart, which was in my throat. After the brief appearance, we all filed out of the courtroom, reporters quick to get our gear in case anyone wanted to comment or to get photos.

Outside, supporters gathered in groups, hugging each other, crying. Some reporters took pictures, held their microphones nearby to capture these sounds. I stood back, as I couldn't bring myself to do this and didn't think my story needed those sounds. Very few reporters said anything; I don't know what others were thinking, but I was shell-shocked by what I had heard and was afraid to speak.

After determining that no one wanted to talk (and I didn't bother asking—I just stood with other reporters, signalling to people that if they wanted to talk, they could come over), I went to my car and immediately phoned my mom. She didn't answer, so I left her a message. I don't remember all of the content. I just remember saying, "People can be so mean to each other, and I don't understand why." I began sobbing into the phone to the point that I couldn't get out the words, telling her I wanted her to know how much I loved her. I later phoned back to apologize for leaving a message like that, saying I just needed to talk to someone.

All I could think about that day was the pain in the cries of Pauline Muskego. I don't have children of my own, although I do have stepchildren, and I'm getting to the age where a lot of my friends are having children. I was imagining how most parents are when they have a baby: how proud they are of their new little bundle, taking joy and pleasure in all the new things he or she does each day, boasting to their friends and family about a first smile or haircut or word. It's not my intention to put words in their mouths or to speak on their behalf, but it made me think the Muskegos, like any other parents, probably had dreams for their little girl, and even though she had grown up, married, and had a baby of her own, she was still their little girl. And they'd just been told that someone had not only killed their baby, but had set her body on fire. I couldn't fathom the pain they were going through, and thinking about this being done to someone's child choked me up with anger and sadness.

As I had in the past with any sad story, I filed my stories and moved on to the next assignment, not giving any thought to how it might have affected me. I didn't give this any thought until months later when I covered a first-degree murder trial in January 2009. Fresh back from Christmas break, my first assignment was to attend Court of Queen's Bench in Saskatoon where Brian Casement was being tried by jury in the death of Victoria Nashacappo. I've covered a lot of trials before, so I didn't do anything different to prepare, nor did I expect anything other than the regular routine of court.

I found myself consumed by the case. As I sat and heard horrific details, I focused on taking notes and not allowing myself to think too much about what I was hearing. I saved that for the end of the day after I had filed my stories. It was really unhealthy. Prior to the case, I had been eating properly and exercising regularly. That went out the window. I was so exhausted from running on adrenaline all day that, after I finished work, I sat on the couch, unable to do much of anything. I would tell anyone who would listen what I was hearing and seeing in court, which was a video-recorded confession by the defendant to what he thought was a criminal gang, which was, in fact, an undercover RCMP sting. In the video confession, he talked about this young woman who was going back to school at the time of her death as though she was a tissue he tossed aside once he was finished with it. I was disgusted when I heard him describe how he choked a 21-year-old girl to death because she didn't want to have sex with him, a nearly 60-year-old man. In the video, he demonstrated a choking motion and said he counted "one one thousand" 300 times, because that's how long it takes to choke someone to death. I grew even more appalled when, on the stand during cross-examination, he said she had asked him to choke her for sexual gratification.

I couldn't understand how Betty Ann Smith, the mother of Nashacappo, could sit in court and handle what she was hearing better than me and the other reporter. She was so stoic. (A side note: we were the only two reporters who were there every single day for the two-and-a-half-week trial. The other outlets covered it the first and last days.)

At night I had restless sleeps. I cried a lot of the time. I let things in my life slide: I've always been a bit of a nag to my fiancé about making sure we don't let the gas tank slip much below half a tank in the winter. I let it get nearly empty without thinking anything of it. I'm a person who does things on time or ahead of time, yet I forgot to renew my driver's license and did it days after it expired. My fiancé began to worry about me. He regularly encouraged me to call a counsellor. Finally I called our employee assistance program and asked to speak to someone.

The counsellor told me I needed to debrief at the end of the day. I needed to write down not so much what I'd heard, but what I had felt when I heard it. She also told me to write a letter to the accused, to the victim, and to myself, and then burn them. I did all of this. It was helpful, but I never fully dealt with how I felt. Two months later I found myself bordering on burnout after covering another murder trial and ended up seeing a different counsellor.

These stories have really made me think about my life and my career. At first, I dealt with the pain of the Nashacappo trial by looking into doing graduate studies. I wanted to look into why the general public doesn't care as much as I think it should about the issue of missing and murdered Aboriginal women, believing it stems from systemic racism. Focusing on this new challenge gave me an outlet, but it was also a frantic, frenzied search for a way to take something awful and feel like I was doing my part to change it.

I came to realize I haven't yet figured out a way to deal with the subject matter that won't take a toll on my well-being. Spending two or three years getting my Master's in this area would likely hurt me more emotionally than help me at this point. It's still something I may pursue in the future, but it's not feasible right now.

I'm even considering getting out of journalism down the road. I am torn: I want to tell these stories because I believe they are so important. However, I also recognize it is hurting me psychologically because I struggle with distancing myself. My counsellor told me that I am experiencing empathy and taking on the pain of victims. While it's fine to do that, eventually you need to find a way to let that go and move on.

Sometimes happy stories come out of these tragedies, and I think it's important to take note of the positive. In May, Daleen Bosse was awarded the degree she was working on when she was murdered. At the time, she had completed her third year in Education and was entering her fourth year of studies. At the University of Saskatchewan's convocation, she was awarded her Bachelor of Education posthumously. Her eight-year-old daughter, Faith, as well as her mother, accepted it on her behalf. After the ceremony, Pauline spoke of how honoured she was that people would still recognize her daughter even though she had passed on.

It was nice to see something like this come out of something so horrible. The University of Saskatchewan, to my knowledge, did nothing to highlight this event, which was a big deal and a great story. The week of convocation, the university's communications department sent out a release to media, highlighting people reporters might want to interview. Granted, we can't interview Bosse, but she wasn't even mentioned as someone noteworthy getting a degree or award. I looked for it on their website as well and couldn't find it anywhere. I know the impetus was the Indian Teacher Education Program, but thought perhaps since it was the University of Saskatchewan convocation, it would make mention of such a special event.

Another criticism of media is that we often don't tell the happy stories. I assure you that if we had all known about this, many or all media outlets in Saskatoon would have been at convocation to interview Bosse's family.

All of us can play a role in stopping the violence that happens to Aboriginal women. The answer lies in all pillars of society, and we can help whether we work in education, government, media, or any other field. Everyone needs to work on making our world an inclusive, respectful place. We need to treat each other as brothers and sisters, and when an awful act is perpetrated against one of our sisters, we all need to stand together to say emphatically that this is unacceptable. We need to stop hurting each other.

I know I am constantly in awe of how families of missing and murdered Aboriginal women handle themselves. I wonder if I would have such courage if I ever found myself in such a position. When I compare myself and my pain to those who are living it, what they are going through seems unfathomable. Until we can reach a point where no family has to suffer through not knowing where a loved one is or why someone brutally killed her, let's draw strength and support from one another . . . and as long as I am working as a journalist, I promise to approach the story with sensitivity and compassion, and do my best to keep it in the news.

Inheriting What Lives On:
The "Terrible Gift" of Sarah de Vries's Poetry[1]

AMBER DEAN

Many Indigenous women in Canada, Mexico, and beyond are presently seeking justice on behalf of the women of their communities who have been disappeared or murdered over the last few decades. Some of their important work was highlighted at the "Missing Women" conference that sparked this book, including the Native Women's Association of Canada's Sisters in Spirit initiative.[2] Recently, I had the good fortune to meet Gloria Alvernaz Mulcahy, whose documentary, *Indigenous Women in Action: Voices from Vancouver*, powerfully represents Indigenous women's resistance to violence and the legacies of colonization. I asked Dr. Mulcahy what she thought those of us who are not Indigenous could do best to contribute to ending these patterns of racialized violence. She wisely suggested that we need to begin to focus on the connections *between* our communities in order to understand more fully the violence. Colonization is, of course, a shared history, and those of us who have descended from white settlers have a particular responsibility to investigate how our contemporary lives are bound up with

AMBER DEAN is a doctoral candidate in the Department of English and Film Studies at the University of Alberta, tracing what lives on from the women disappeared from Vancouver's Downtown Eastside by examining representations of the women in media, memorials, and art.

that history. Many individuals and groups are committed to doing this work, but many more troublingly continue to resist or disavow such a responsibility. I believe that recognizing our responsibility to enter into relations of inheritance with the women who have been disappeared or murdered is one way that we can start to unravel how we are all implicated in these acts of violence. But what might it mean to enter into what I am calling a "relation of inheritance" with women who we did not know in life—women whose lives were sometimes very different from our own?

For social theorist Roger Simon, what we come to know belatedly about events of mass violence might most appropriately be labelled a "terrible gift" (2006, 187). A "terrible gift" is a form of knowledge that we might be tempted to turn away from but which may, if we engage it in a relation of inheritance, also be read as a kind of gift, albeit a difficult one. It is a kind of knowledge that is "terrible" not because it is bad or not worth knowing, but because it is hard to bear. Such knowledge is also a gift, though, because it offers us an important opportunity. As Simon explains: "[s]uch a gift sets the demanding task of inheritance, a process with the potential to open a reconsideration of the terms of our lives now as well as in the future" (2006, 188). Simon describes his use of the concept of "inheritance" as follows:

> A practice whose outcome is not guaranteed in advance, the work of inheritance is an inescapable consequence of the actions of another who has sent you something and that implicates you in the necessity of a response (even if that response is ultimately to ignore or destroy the bequest). (194)

For the past several years I have been conducting research on representations of the women who have been disappeared from Vancouver's Downtown Eastside neighbourhood, and I have noticed that several of those women sent me (and us) some things during their lives that were urgent then, and are even more urgent now that the women who sent them have been disappeared or murdered.[3] I believe that these things they have sent to us set each of us the task of inheritance, although how and even whether we take up that task will necessarily be different for different people. One such "terrible gift" has been sent in the form of a poem written by Sarah de Vries, a woman who was disappeared from Vancouver's Downtown Eastside on April 14, 1998. Sarah de Vries's poetry invites us to enter into a relation of inheritance with her, even if we did not know her in life. Her poem asks something of us, and it sets all of us the demanding task of rethinking how we see ourselves and our relationships or connections to others.

In the summer of 2003, a year before I left Vancouver to pursue my doctorate at the University of Alberta, Maggie de Vries published a memoir titled *Missing Sarah,* which is a book about the life and disappearance of her sister, Sarah de Vries. Sarah de Vries was adopted by the de Vries family as an infant, and her biological parents were "of mixed race—black, Aboriginal and Mexican Indian as well as white" (de Vries 2003, 1). Adopted in 1970, she was placed in a white family at the tail end of what has been called the "sixties scoop." Maggie de Vries tells us in her memoir that Sarah was placed for adoption voluntarily by her birth mother when she was ten months old. Nonetheless, as Maggie acknowledges, Sarah's adoption fits the pattern of its time: her racial and cultural background were deemed irrelevant, as was any ongoing contact with her birth family. Thus, the individual, personal event of Sarah de Vries's adoption is contextualized by the colonization of Indigenous peoples in Canada, enacted in part through residential schools and discriminatory child welfare policies that intensified in the sixties but are ongoing today—as Maggie de Vries writes, today "Aboriginal groups fight the loss of their children after generations of having their children taken from them" (2003, 9). Sarah's adoption is a part of this legacy, and in fact we learn in *Missing Sarah* that Sarah's father was himself adopted (2003, 3), suggesting that this is a history with a very long legacy indeed, one that is at once both personal and social.

Missing Sarah (2003) tells an important story about Sarah de Vries's life, one that recounts many happy times and the strength of Sarah's generosity and her relationships with others. It adds context and nuance to what most people who did not know Sarah de Vries in life first learned about her: namely, that at the time of her disappearance she struggled with an addiction and she did street-level, survival sex work in Vancouver's Downtown Eastside. Sarah de Vries is one of the women listed on the joint Vancouver Police/RCMP Missing Women's Task Force's official list of missing women, and Robert Pickton has been charged with her murder. Maggie de Vries and her family were extremely influential in getting officials finally to take the disappearances of women from the Downtown Eastside seriously. *Missing Sarah* (2003) is an important and timely book and is particularly poignant, for me, in its description of what it is like to witness a loved one struggling with an addiction to drugs and in how eloquently Maggie de Vries captures the sensations of living with the anguished uncertainty and ongoing, penetrating grief that arises when a loved one is missing over such a long period of time. *Missing Sarah* importantly also introduced me to some of the writing of Maggie's sister Sarah.

It is not my intention to put Sarah de Vries in the position of representing all the Indigenous women from her neighbourhood (or from across the country) who have been disappeared or murdered. De Vries led a particular, individual life, and she is not the only woman who left important traces that have the power to hail those of us who did not know the women in life into relations of inheritance. I worry that writing at length about Sarah de Vries's poetry risks (re)producing a kind of hierarchy among the women who have been disappeared or murdered, implying that some of their lives are more worthy of attention than others. Nothing could be further from the truth. And yet, it remains true that despite the best efforts of hosts of investigative journalists, there is simply more information available to the public about some of the individual women's lives than there is about others. Dirk Meissner of the Canadian Press reports, for example, that information about Diana Melnick, another woman disappeared from the Downtown Eastside, is "scarce." "Where's her family?" he asks, "Where did she grow up? How did she end up on the streets? The answers aren't easily found. What's left are the . . . bare facts provided by police and court documents."[4] By contrast, countless newspaper stories have been published on the life of Sarah de Vries (as recounted by various family and friends), the story of her disappearance was featured in an episode of the television program *America's Most Wanted,* and her sister has, as mentioned, published an award-winning memoir full of memories of Sarah de Vries's life and some of her own writing. This striking difference in the availability of information about the women's lives makes it possible to write about some of their lives with more attention to detail and particularity than is possible for others. At present, this is an irresolvable dilemma that points to the ongoing importance of investigating the facts surrounding the women's lives and disappearances—the details of "what happened"—*as well as* contemplating "what lives on from that happening" (Brown 2001, 150), which is what my own research is all about.

Because of the comparative wealth of information available, the particulars of Sarah de Vries's life have occasionally been employed as stand-ins for "Vancouver's Missing Women," signifying beyond the specific details of her life story in ways that both oversimplify that story and overdetermine how that story is likely to be received. De Vries, too, has frequently been represented in ways that "fix" her as a particular sort of person. Her sister Maggie de Vries writes, for example, about her dismay at witnessing an image of Sarah caught on film by a CBC news crew; an image she knew the CBC was going to use in an upcoming documentary about the "missing women." Maggie clearly articulates the problem with representations that narrowly fix their subjects in this way:

Ironically, that last moving image [of Sarah] freezes her. CBC will include it in their documentary. They will call it the last image of Sarah de Vries, and viewers will think, oh, that's how she was before she died. She was out of it. They won't see the time she spent preparing that day—bathing, selecting an outfit that stood out and worked together, getting her makeup just right. They won't hear the conversations she had that day, animated, connected.... (258)

Although in the end Maggie expresses satisfaction with the way her sister is represented in the documentary, her concerns about how this image fixes her sister Sarah in a very narrow and particular way deserve attention. Many family members and loved ones of women who have been disappeared or murdered have expressed dissatisfaction with the narrow focus of media representations—with how those representations so often communicate so little about the richness and complexity of the women's lives, or about the social dimensions of the injustices they experienced.

When I write about Sarah de Vries, or other individual women, I try to strike a balance between acknowledging and recognizing that I am talking about a complex, individual human life, and at the same time exploring how that life has come to signify something to a broader public, many of whom never knew anything about that individual woman before she was killed. This is no small task. Conveying a deep respect for the individual woman's life mixed with an awareness that what most of us can learn about that life now is already constrained and mediated by an array of forces, frameworks, and representations may well be the best that I can offer. Faltering, stumbling, indeed *failing* in the attempt to represent a life in all of its complexity may perhaps be an important ethical strategy when it comes to such efforts at representation.[5] That is, it seems important to acknowledge that we can never come fully to know someone through representations of his or her life. But this shouldn't be taken to mean that we are freed from a responsibility to *try* to know him or her, or, perhaps more importantly, to try to discern what it is he or she may be asking of us.

The poem by Sarah de Vries that I have called a "terrible gift" (Simon 2006, 187) addresses her readers through a direct challenge to what de Vries describes as an indifference to the murder of another woman who at the time of her death did sex work in Vancouver's Downtown Eastside. Consider this excerpt from the poem:

Woman's body found beaten beyond recognition.
You sip your coffee
Taking a drag of your smoke
Turning the page
Taking a bite of your toast
Just another day
Just another death
Just one more thing you so easily forget
You and your soft, sheltered life
Just go on and on
For nobody special from your world is gone (in Maggie de Vries 2003, 233)

De Vries's lines, "Just another day / Just another death," repeated throughout the stanzas of this poem, reflect the impact of sensing that one's own death might pass as anonymously and unremarkably as just another day gone by. It is precisely this too-easy connection between "just another day" and "just another death," as well as de Vries's insight about how vulnerability to such a connection is so very unjustly and unevenly distributed and lived, that I seek to expose and ultimately contest. De Vries's insights help me to imagine how things might have been, and might yet be, otherwise, or, in other words, might be different from how they are now and have been in the past. An attention to the "terrible gifts" left by de Vries and other women like her allows me to—indeed, *demands* that I—begin to imagine a present (and future) that might be otherwise. And, perhaps even more importantly, such an attention also demands that I begin to engage others in such an imagining, too.

Sarah de Vries's poem, so clearly addressed to a "you," functions in the way that Simon describes as the something that is sent (from the past) and that has the potential to implicate her readers (in the present), necessitating a response. This poem (and a host of other cultural artefacts through which the lives and/or the addresses of disappeared or murdered women are traceable) sets in motion a relation of inheritance, even though I did not know her in life. And certainly I am not the only one who sees myself as addressed by Sarah de Vries's "you," which leaves me wondering: what might it mean if we read de Vries's "you" as addressed to "us," both individually *and* collectively? It is clear to me through her mode of address that de Vries asks something of me (and of us); as her sister Maggie de Vries relates in the prologue to her memoir, "[w]hen [Sarah] wrote, she imagined readers. She imagined you" (2003, xiii). Of course, *what* precisely Sarah de Vries asks of her readers is not entirely clear, but her address beckons us into a relation of inheritance the character of which I have spent much of the last several years trying to discern.

Sarah de Vries herself bore witness, during her life, to the unjust, violent deaths of many women from her neighbourhood. Her poem bears witness not only to the terrible murder of another woman who had touched her life (see Maggie de Vries 2003, 233–234), but also to a sentiment of disinterest in the woman's death among some whose lives are less susceptible to such violence: "*You and your soft, sheltered life / Just go on and on / For nobody special from your world is gone*" (in Maggie de Vries 2003, 233). It is clear in this poem that Sarah de Vries was well-acquainted with the consequences of living a life that is frequently cast as disposable or unimportant. In her own reading of de Vries's poem, one that draws on Shoshana Felman's work on witnessing and testament, Geraldine Pratt makes the following compelling argument:

> The terrible burden of Sarah de Vries' poem comes from the fact that she is testifying (before the fact) about an event (murder) that she cannot witness. She speaks in proxy for herself, and her authority undoubtedly comes from her very own death. (2005, 1072)

De Vries's poem is thus at once both an indictment of how another woman's death has been cast as unimportant or inconsequential, and a testament to what de Vries recognized as the humanity and value of the life of the murdered woman (and thus, to that of her own). But the indictment de Vries makes is not of a generalized or anonymous "society;" it is directed to a "you," and it is my argument that this form of address is important because it challenges readers to take up ourselves the role of witness that de Vries enacts in the poem. If readers accept her mode of address as a challenge directed towards us personally, then it seems likely that the poem is an example of what Roger Simon calls the "terrible gift" (2006, 187) of those materials that testify to events of mass violence.

If we see Sarah de Vries's "you" as addressed to us, her poem then has the potential to call into question and potentially refashion how we understand our relationship or connection to her and to the women who have been disappeared or murdered. This relationship shifts in such a way that it becomes based not on our being bystanders to their loss, but on our becoming what I (following Simon) call an "inheritor," not of the losses themselves but of what lives on from them. As feminist theorist Wendy Brown argues:

> We inherit not 'what really happened' to the dead but what lives on from that happening, what is conjured from it, how past generations and events occupy the force fields of the present, how they claim us, and how they haunt, plague, and inspirit our imaginations and visions for the future. (2001, 150)

But what might it actually mean to inherit what lives on from the women who have been disappeared or murdered, and who are we to claim such a relation of inheritance?

"If we are open to recognizing this text as intended for and sent to us as a bequest," writes Simon, "it is likely that many of us will regard it as a terrible gift" (2006, 297). As already discussed, such bequests are "terrible gifts" because they are difficult and onerous, and because what they ask of us is no small task. The testimony found in materials like de Vries's poem "arrive[s] in the public realm making an unanticipated claim that may interrupt one's self-sufficiency, demanding attentiveness to another's life without reducing that life to a version of one's own stories" (Simon 2006, 188). We may well be tempted to turn away from the challenge posed by the poem, and it is likely that many will attempt to do so, for the challenge demands nothing less than "a reconsideration of the terms of our lives now as well as in the future" (Simon 2006, 189). Yet despite whatever individual decisions we might make about how to respond to such testaments, their challenge persists. Our best efforts to shirk or forget the challenge posed by the poem's mode of address will at some point give way, and it seems likely that the "you" addressed in the poem has the power to haunt us until such time as we are ready to take up the difficult gift of its inheritance.

What, then, does a relation of inheritance require of us? First, and perhaps most importantly, it requires that we identify "how we are in this story, even now, even if we do not want to be" (Gordon 1997, 190). So even if the stories of the disappeared or murdered women are not "our" stories because we did not know the women in life, and even though it remains necessary to *acknowledge* that these are not our stories and that proximity to the women in life does change our relationship to the stories, it is nonetheless still important to come to see that we are all in these stories, too. This does not mean that we are responsible for the disappearances or murders of the women in the same way that those who directly committed violence against them are responsible. But it does mean that we are all *in* these stories, in differing ways, and it is part of our inheritance to figure out just how.

To enter into a relation of inheritance with de Vries and other disappeared or murdered women, many of whom left testamentary traces similar to de Vries's poem, requires nothing more and nothing less than "altering one's ways of being with others" (Simon 2006, 198). This seems at once a tiny and an overwhelming request; tiny in that it is impossible to know how such a small and personal shift could contribute much of anything; overwhelming in the enormous overhaul of one's everyday life that such a shift potentially demands. Accepting the challenge of de Vries's address means relinquishing the hold that the common story we tell about people as rational, free-willed and freely choosing individuals has on our relations to others, or giving up the idea that what "I" am is possible independently of "you." It means realizing and accepting that what we are left with, then, is "*the tie* by which those terms ["I" and "you"] are differentiated and related" (Butler 2004, 22, emphasis in original). Thus, altering one's ways of being with others involves realizing that what I thought "I" was may in fact be a very significant factor in why some lives are left so much more exposed to suffering and violence than others. For example, starting this process of reconsideration requires those of us who find ourselves in Canada today as the descendents of white colonizers to begin to account for the many ways we have benefited from colonization, and the many ways that the various privileges that adhere to our white skin continue to depend on and require the increased vulnerability (to poverty and violence, among other things) of women like Sarah de Vries. We need to challenge the common assumption that personal failings are responsible for the women's disappearances or murders, or that our conventional narratives of individual tragedy or accountability are adequate for recounting these stories.

Altering one's ways of being with others in the interests of forming relations of inheritance also requires rethinking the relationship between the past and the present, for if we imagine that the lives of disappeared or murdered women are rooted solely in the past, then it is difficult to conceive of how they might make claims on us today. Being open to inheriting what lives on from the women means beginning to account for how past injustices are everywhere evident in the present and are therefore not "past" in the way this term is conventionally understood. It means starting to uncover and expose how the state-sponsored system of terror known as colonialism is indelibly tied to the present-day, ongoing disappearance or murder of Indigenous women across the country. And while our Canadian governments and many Canadians themselves prefer to locate colonialism in our nation's distant past, I argue that it is actively remade again and again in the present, belying its past-ness.[6] For the tactics of colonialism are undoubtedly implicated in extraordinary violence towards and neglect of Indigenous persons in Canada—in what some have importantly labelled "Canada's genocide."[7]

I am not alone in making this claim, for the link between colonization and the contemporary disappearance or murder of Indigenous women is being made by many scholars and activists. Beverley Jacobs and Andrea J. Williams (2008) of the Native Women's Association of Canada, for example, have argued that the disappearance and murder of Aboriginal women in Canada is a direct legacy of the residential school system and the discriminatory effects of the federal Indian Act, while Andrea Smith (2005) compellingly argues that sexual violence was deployed historically, and continues to be deployed, in the interests of American Indian genocide.[8] Sherene H. Razack persuasively argues that when Pamela George, a Saulteaux woman from the Sakimay First Nation in Saskatchewan, was murdered in 1995, the violence she experienced was "fully colonial—a making of the white, masculine self as dominant through practices of violence directed at a colonized woman" (2000, 96). And, at the recent conference on missing women that led to this book, connections between colonization and the disappearance and murder of Indigenous women in both Canada and Mexico were a central theme. So although in Canada state actors have not (yet) been singled out as *directly* responsible for the disappearance or murder of Indigenous women, the material and symbolic dimensions of colonization are heavily implicated in these disappearances, which exposes the *social* dimensions of the women's disappearances and murders and suggests that a very broad array of actors and forces are (or ought to be) implicated in these events.

Crucially, rethinking the relationship between the past and the present and starting to recognize how the past is not "past" does not mean that we can or ought to try to live *in* the past, which is where a preoccupation with righting past wrongs could lead. Instead, as Simon, Rosenberg and Eppert (2000) urge, we need to learn to "live *in relation with* the past" (4), which involves continually asking how the past matters *now*. Instead of attempting to measure how past wrongs might best be repaired, then, which secures those wrongs squarely in the past, how might we instead attempt to measure "the mass and force of the past in the present," as Wendy Brown (2001, 139) urges us to? How might the reparations required for *this* sort of measurement be radically different? I would suggest that such reparations would require not only providing compensation and support for those who suffered the injustices of residential schools or the "sixties scoop," but *also* repairing the *ongoing* injustices that contribute to such a greater risk of poverty or violence for Indigenous women today. Support for this kind of reparation requires recognizing the connections between the past and the present, rather than seeing them as separate or distinct. It also requires not just legal changes or financial support, which remain important, but also rethinking our relations with one another, and how we see each other.

In her poetry and journal writing, Sarah de Vries repeatedly asserts the personhood of the women from her neighbourhood who are being disappeared or murdered. By doing so, she communicates her awareness that such women, women not unlike herself, are so routinely cast outside this category of "person" through how little attention their deaths receive, through how their murders are so often framed as what de Vries described as "normal," expected, "a daily part of life" (in Maggie de Vries 2003, 159). At the end of the poem I have been discussing, de Vries again reasserts the personhood of the woman she knew who was murdered:

She was somebody fighting for life
Trying to survive
A lonely lost child who died
In the night, all alone, scared
Gasping for air (in Maggie de Vries 2003, 234)

Here de Vries is drawing our attention to more than just the terribleness of this woman's death (and, inadvertently, her own), for the lines of her poem suggest that the woman's struggles to survive began long before the moment of her murder. We get the impression that the woman was "trying to survive" and "fighting for life" for some time prior to the violent encounter in which she was killed. So, although de Vries succeeds in conveying the horror of the woman's murder, she also draws our attention back to that key issue of how we *see* the woman, not just after her death but also *in life,* and by doing so she points us to something to be done and to a set of past and present injustices that demand our attention. And this, more than anything, is the gift that we stand to inherit.

Simon describes the inheritance of testamentary materials as a "terrible *gift*" for a reason. Aside from binding us to an onerous combination of "thoughts and actions" (2006, 198), challenges like those posed by Sarah de Vries's poem can also be viewed as a gift, not in the sense that they offer some sort of consolation for the lives that have been lost, but because in their claiming of us they offer the possibility of hope. Gifts like these are addressed to whomever might take on the responsibilities involved with their acceptance, and as such, although they are accepted or not by individuals, they possess a social dimension. That de Vries's poem is addressed to a "you" suggests that it could be a terrible gift for any one of "us," and thus a "we" who might accept her bequest is created. The "we" in this instance becomes those of us inclined to dedicate "an attentiveness and shared reference" (Simon 2006, 195) to the testimony offered in the poem. The creation of this "we" is important, for "no single beneficiary can be said to be capable of rendering the full meaning and significance of this testament" (195). Instead, *we* must accept this gift, taking it up in different ways, in order for its hopeful potential to be fully realized.

That hopeful potential cannot be wrought by just one who is open to inheriting what lives on from the women's lives. Nor can its meaning or definition of "hope" be predicted or deciphered in advance. What such gifts and the relations of inheritance they provoke gesture hopefully towards is a future, for while we are often encouraged to imagine that the future is always ahead, always open, always just over the horizon, what rethinking the relations between present and past teaches us is that there actually *is* no future without a reckoning with the past-as-present. Instead, without such a reckoning, we are left with what Simon describes as "the endless repetition of a violent past" (2006, 203). Thus, the hope offered by such terrible gifts exists precisely in and through the relations of inheritance into which they hail us. Such relations require us to begin to imagine our connections to others otherwise, to begin to contemplate and then enact what social analyst Avery Gordon compellingly describes as "something to be done in time and for another worlding" (1997, 190). In this future time, we learn that our lives are bound up with each other's in messy, complicated, unshakeable ways. We begin to see others, living and dead, that we have often learned how to avoid seeing. We learn to become responsible for circumstances that are not of our making, but that we inherit anyway, and that the formation of such "responsible memorial kinship[s]" (Simon 2006, 203) requires our urgent attention. We stop dreaming about bright futures and begin to imagine a different present, and in that present women are no longer being vanished or murdered because we have come to recognize how their lives are not all their own making, how responsibility for their disappearances and murders cannot be found solely in the perpetrators or the police or government, although they all must be held accountable. But responsibility is a larger matter: it is yours and it is mine, and we find it because we are committed to figuring out just where we are in this story and what that means for how we go about our lives today. And, of course, this is necessarily just one partial, incomplete imagining for a possible future; imagining otherwise must become a collective project. By imagining us—indeed, by calling an "us" into being as witnesses to the myriad injustices that culminated in her disappearance and murder—Sarah de Vries's address challenges us to consider how these injustices continue to inflect all of our lives, differently, daily, and to find ways to live, differently, with difficulty, based on this knowing, in the aftermath of her murder and in a present still consumed by the disappearances and deaths of those who continue to live and die under similar circumstances.

ENDNOTES

1   For ongoing conversations that inform and support my writing, I am especially grateful to Kara Granzow, Daphne Read, and Sharon Rosenberg. Any shortcomings in this essay, however, are all my own. Many thanks also to Brenda Anderson for inviting me to participate in the "Missing Women" conference at the University of Regina in August 2008, and for the invitation to contribute to this collection. My title owes a debt to Roger Simon's (2006) essay, "The Terrible Gift: Museums and the Possibility of Hope without Consolation." This essay would never have been possible if Sarah de Vries had not sent us the "terrible gift" of her poetry, or if her sister Maggie de Vries had not published that poetry in her book, *Missing Sarah* (2003), and so I am eternally grateful to them both. Sarah de Vries poetry © Maggie de Vries. Reprinted with permission.

2   More information can be found on the Native Women's Association of Canada's website at http://www.nwac-hq.org/en/background.html (accessed 28 April 2009).

3   I have been conducting this research for my doctoral dissertation, "Haunting matters: Tracing what lives on from Vancouver's disappeared women," University of Alberta, 2009.

4   This quotation is taken from Diana Melnick's profile in *Missing Lives: A Special Report from the Canadian Press*. The entire series is available online on the CBC's website at http://www.cbc.ca/news/background/pickton/missinglives.html (accessed 26 March 2009). Meissner's sense of what would qualify as relevant or important information about Melnick's life differs somewhat from my own, but nonetheless his point about an overall lack of information is well taken. It seems important to note, though, that a recent posting on the guestbook of the website Missingpeople.net provides an important counterpoint to Meissner's findings. A woman who states that she is Melnick's adopted cousin writes: "I looked all over the web to see if there was more information on Diana, and it is suggested that no-one knows anything about her . . . which is not true. For whatever reason, the family has decided not to enlighten the public, which I do respect, but I just couldn't help but want others to know, that yes she was loved and is missed and we still think of her often . . . and there's many of us who have been following the news from the very beginning." http://www.e-guestbooks.com/cgi-bin/e-guestbooks/guestbook.cgi Message #385 (accessed 23 September 2008).

5   For more on the significance of representation as failure, see Butler 2004, 144.

6   For a more in-depth development of this argument, see my forthcoming essay, "Space, Temporality, History: Encountering hauntings in Vancouver's Downtown Eastside" in

The West and Beyond: Historians Past, Present, and Future, ed. Sarah Carter, Alvin Finkel, and Peter Fortna (collection currently under review by Athabasca University Press).

7 See, for example, the work of Kevin Annett, much of it available online at http://www.hiddenfromhistory.org (accessed 14 May 2008).

8 See also the Native Women's Association of Canada's "Sisters in Spirit" campaign. Information is available online at http://www.nwac-hq.org/en/background.html (accessed 10 July 2008).

REFERENCES

Brown, Wendy. 2001. *Politics out of history.* Princeton, NJ: Princeton University Press.

Butler, Judith. 2004. *Precarious life: The powers of mourning and violence.* London; New York: Verso.

Canadian Press. 2007. *Missing lives: A special report by the Canadian Press.* http://www.cbc.ca/news/background/pickton/missinglives.html (accessed 26 March 2009).

De Vries, Maggie. 2003. *Missing Sarah: A Vancouver woman remembers her vanished sister.* Toronto: Penguin Canada.

Gordon, Avery. 1997. *Ghostly matters: Haunting and the sociological imagination.* Minneapolis: University of Minnesota Press.

Jacobs, Beverley, and Andrea J. Williams. 2008. "Legacy of residential schools: Missing and murdered Aboriginal women." In *From truth to reconciliation: Transforming the legacy of residential schools,* ed. Marlene Brant Castellano, Linda Archibald, and Mike DeGagne, 121–40. Ottawa, ON: Aboriginal Healing Foundation.

Mulcahy, Gloria Alvernaz. 2007. *Indigenous women in action: Voices from Vancouver.* London, ON: Balance Productions.

Pratt, Geraldine. 2005. "Abandoned women and spaces of the exception." *Antipode* 37 (5): 1052–78.

Razack, Sherene H. 2000. "Gendered racial violence and spatialized justice: The murder of Pamela George." *Canadian Journal of Law and Society* 15 (2): 91–130.

Simon, Roger I., Sharon Rosenberg, and Claudia Eppert, eds. 2000. *Between hope and despair: Pedagogy and the remembrance of historical trauma.* Lanham, MD: Rowman and Littlefield Publishers.

Simon, Roger I. 2006. "The terrible gift: Museums and the possibility of hope without consolation." *Museum Management and Curatorship* 21 (3): 187–204.

Smith, Andrea. 2005. *Conquest: Sexual violence and American Indian genocide.* Cambridge, MA: South End Press.

KEYNOTE ADDRESS
"MISSING WOMEN" CONFERENCE, FRIDAY, AUGUST 15, 2008,
LED WITH ISABEL ARVIDES.

Women of Juárez

LOURDES PORTILLO

I would like to thank all of the many people who have organized this important and historical gathering, especially Elizabeth Matheson who supported and inspired this international gathering almost three years ago, when we presented the film *Señorita Extraviada* to the community at the Dunlop Art Gallery. It was Elizabeth who saw the similarities in crimes committed against the Canadian Indigenous women and the women murdered in Ciudad Juárez in Mexico.

I am honoured to be before you, the audience, who are interested and engaged in bringing about justice. We are here to create a community that is larger than we are as individuals. We are here creating a transnational link that will bring about more awareness about what is happening to young, Indigenous, poor women. This presentation is in honour of all the young women who have lost their lives, and also in honour of all the mothers and fathers who have dared to speak out in their defense and will never give up their struggle until justice is served. What marks all of us is a moment of lucid recognition that something is just not right. Those moments where something clicked and we became part of the solution. Those moments are precious and they change the course of lives.

LOURDES PORTILLO is a prize-winning filmmaker born in Chihuahua, Mexico, and now living in the United States. Her films focus on the representation of Latina/o identity, human rights, social justice, and Latin American realities.

As an artist there is one moment that inspired me to pursue a sense of justice in my work. One of the stories my mother would tell us was about when she was 14 years old—she was walking down the street in Mexico, where we were from. She saw a man in front of her who was beating his small children. My mother, without thinking, pulled the children away from him and told him that that was not the way to correct a child. She surprised even herself. The man was outraged by her boldness and called a policeman. You see, in Mexico, he felt that he had the right to beat them, being their father. The policeman agreed with him and took my mother to the police station until her parents came to get her. She never regretted what she did and would tell us children about it with pride.

I believe it is these small anecdotes that leave deep impressions on us, that propel us to action. This story in many ways was not only an inspiration to bring about justice in my own work, but later illuminated my films and gave me a clear picture of how justice works in Mexico. Many years later, living as an immigrant in the United States, I became aware of the power that the media had over our collective consciousness. I saw how we were manipulated to believe certain things, and how information was kept from us. There was an enormous desire to create a chronicle of our times and at the same time to build a better society. It was then that I decided to become a documentary filmmaker, an independent, with a voice that spoke the truth to power. In those days of civil rights struggle we all thirsted for the truth and for recognition of the situations we all found ourselves in, of exclusion and marginalization. My films express a profound need to tell stories of our people, stories that are seldom told in our society, and even less in the cinema.

We all recognize how important it is to have a visual chronicle of our times and our experiences. The journey that many have undertaken and succeeded in is an inspiration to the younger generations. It traces the way and creates a road, which acknowledges our efforts, our victories as well as our defeats. The story of my mother as a young woman facing a man who was abusing his children has resonance through my films. It inspires me to seek justice. Today in Saskatchewan, where many Indigenous girls have been brutally murdered, there has been no justice or peace for the families. I bring this humble message in a small story that can inspire you to join the many who want to stop these crimes that are perpetrated on poor young women all over the Americas. To me a moment of recognition of the crimes that are occurring against women all over the world is a sign, a moment of awareness that we must recognize as a systematic aggression towards all women. Our gatherings and solidarity will strengthen that awareness and bring about action. Here, at this conference, we have been able to join hands and face the problem and resolve to bring about justice, together from all the Americas.

Thank you.

Perspectives from the Regina Police Service

MICHELLE SOLOMON

Missing persons investigations pose a very difficult challenge for police investigators. Being missing is not a criminal matter, yet police have to explore every possible explanation for a person's failure to return home or to have contact with family and friends. Through a thorough investigation, and often with very little information, police try to determine if the file may contain a criminal element. Most missing person reports filed with police involve chronic, repeat runaways; these make up approximately 72 percent of all missing person reports at the Regina Police Service and, of these, most return safely in less than a week.

In most instances, missing person files start off with little information as to what happened or why the subject disappeared. In many cases there is no evidence to explain the subject's disappearance. It stands to reason that there is at least one person who knows, that being the subject himself or herself, but that person isn't present to offer information to police. People go missing for a variety of reasons: some people don't want to be found, wanting to start new lives elsewhere; some succumb to unforeseen accidents; some are driven by drug or alcohol addictions; some suffer mental

MICHELLE SOLOMON spoke as the Missing Persons Coordinator for Regina City Police. She was also part of the planning committee for the conference.

health issues and can't remember how to come home. In some cases, the missing person doesn't have a choice because *someone* has prevented her or him from coming home.

Most members of the public do not realize that police are restricted by privacy laws, which do not allow police to just "tap into" someone's personal information. Police require a criminal code warrant, but getting the warrant can be a challenge, too. In order to obtain a warrant, a criminal code offence must have occurred or must be suspected to have occurred. At the onset of a missing person file, police may not have the grounds to believe there has been a criminal code offence.

Police Services must take every missing person's file seriously. The safe return of the missing person is our priority. Police have learned a great deal over the years; we recognize the importance of working with and alongside other police agencies, communities, and families to find answers. Though history created distance in relationships between police and Aboriginal communities, time has allowed healing. Recognition of the need to work together, especially when it comes to missing persons, is of utmost importance.

It is virtually impossible for an officer really to know a missing person from a report. Families and friends are a tremendous source of information about the missing loved one. Communication is essential and can answer many questions. The lines of communication need to remain open and differences must be set aside in order to work on finding and bringing a missing loved one home. Trust is crucial as well; at times, families fear they will be judged if certain information surfaces, or they withhold information out of embarrassment, yet time is of the essence in locating missing persons. Even though information may appear to be disconcerting it may be vitally important to police. It may help provide some real answers or at least some understanding.

Although police do not have the daily struggle families experience in trying to cope with the absence of their family members, we do see how it affects families. It is very upsetting not to have the answers they need or what they want to hear. We must all bear in mind that we share the same goal. We want answers. We want to bring missing persons home . . . and bring them home safely. As former Regina Police Chief Cal Johnston once said, "as members of a just society if there has been any criminal interference in a person's disappearance, it grossly offends our society, our community and each and every one of us." It is our job and commitment to hold those offenders accountable for their actions. That is why police stress that if anyone has any information regarding a missing person, he or she should contact their local police service. All families need closure, and police are committed to providing it to them.

Communication with young persons is essential and can prevent chronic running behaviour. Talk to young people about the dangers of running away. Most sexually exploited youth were first exploited while on the run. Each time a youth goes missing, that child is at greater risk of becoming a victim of some type of violence; risk of death increases as well. It should also be noted that children who have been abused are more at risk of running away. When a person goes missing, he or she is most likely either running from something or running to something. Reduce the risk of running by providing stable support for children and youth through early intervention. Speak with young persons, identify their underlying issues, then address those issues. It will help reduce the risk for repeat occurrences.

Society's language and how it regards missing persons need to change. Labelling a child or youth a "child/youth prostitute" gives the perception that they have chosen to be abused. What should be said is "prostituted child/youth." Merely reversing the words explains what these youth truly are: victims of child abuse. Prostitution is not a chosen occupation. Even though this behaviour may have started out as a survival method, the fact that sexually exploited children have to "survive" on the streets is an indicator that they cannot return to a safe place. In their experience, being on the street is safer than the places that normally should provide shelter and security. Society needs to recognize these youths and children as victims. Opportunities and programs need to be available to address their underlying issues, to protect them from further violence, exploitation, addictions, poor health, disease, and premature death.

The province of Saskatchewan now has a website dedicated to all Saskatchewan missing people. The information on each long-term missing person provides a link to the families, to encourage anyone with information on a case to come forward and to let our communities know that these files are not closed or forgotten. A missing person's case, or any criminal investigation, does not simply come to an end after a certain period of time. The website is provided by the Saskatchewan Association of Chiefs of Police and can be found at www.sacp.ca/missing/.

Even one missing person is too many.

An Academic Role in Activism

CYNTHIA BEJARANO

We have listened to several people throughout these past few days, and I know it is a difficult set of topics to sit through and discuss. But I am grateful that there are still so many people on a Saturday afternoon for this session. I would really like to thank the Elders who are here, the organizers for their diligent work, the dignitaries present, volunteers, and all the students who have come together here in Canada to create what is, for many of us at the U.S./Mexico border, a space where we can share our stories and where we can build solidarity and create alliances. We need these spaces to re-energize ourselves and to cultivate the friendships and "sisterhoods" that I hope will be built together during this three-to four-day period.

We had a very similar conference in 2006, an international conference at my home institution in Las Cruces, New Mexico, which is 50 miles from the U.S./Mexico border. I know how much time and care and atten-

CYNTHIA L. BEJARANO, a native of southern New Mexico and the El-Paso/Juárez border, is an assistant professor of Criminal Justice at New Mexico State University. An advocate and activist working with the families of disappeared and murdered women in Ciudad Juárez, she works closely with people at Casa Amiga, the rape crisis centre in Ciudad Juárez, and is the co-founder of Amigos de las Mujeres de Juárez, an NGO dedicated to assisting the women of Juárez in their fight for justice.

tion it takes, and months and months and months of planning to organize a conference of this calibre, so thank you so much.

I can share with you, as I think my *compañeras*—my teachers and elders from Ciudad Juárez—shared with me as well, that during the opening ceremony, the beating of the drums and the singing by the Cree dancers, I felt called out in a very meaningful way, the spirits of the girls and the women that we carry in our hearts from Ciudad Juárez, Mexico and Chihuahua City, Mexico, as well as the other women, both Indigenous and non-Indigenous, who have been killed throughout Mexico and throughout Latin America. . . . I am very saddened and I am very, very angry. I have been carrying anger in my heart for over a decade now since I began working on this issue as an activist, as an academic, as a woman, and as a human being, and it saddens me that throughout the Americas, in the twenty-first century, in 2008, we are still dealing with the persecution of our peoples, colonization, poverty, structural violence, and institutional violence. It is a disgrace that these issues invariably become the common thread that brings us together to this conference to discuss the violence inflicted in the places we call "home": the reservations, the reserves, the *colonias* [shanty towns], the ghettos, the *barrios* [communities] that represent the locations where we live or where we are forced to live.

I am from a very small, poor border community that is on the state line of Texas and New Mexico. I grew up in this poor community with little infrastructure and fewer resources. I am from a very small family—two siblings and my mother and father. My father was probably the only person in about a three-mile radius who had a college degree. He was one of 15 siblings who went to college. The irony was that he was a social worker helping others, yet we experienced the multiple layerings of poverty that exist in our communities. I had my family as mentors, noted in my community as respected elders, and I had the modelling of a father who never hit the girls, who never hit my mother, who always said, "I wear the pants in our family, but your mother tells me which pair to put on." I also had a strong mother who tolerated very little, and these examples helped me to gain confidence and self-esteem and really to understand the violence that was pervasive in my community. I share this because there was a great deal of violence and a great deal of poverty in every corner where I grew up, but I am grateful for those experiences because this foundation of "knowing" taught me how to "bear witness" to atrocities and to react to them.

I am here bearing witness to the atrocities that have occurred in Ciudad Juárez and Chihuahua. My family origins are from the great state of Chihuahua, the largest state in the country of Mexico. My family is from Ciudad Juárez and the surrounding areas just outside of Ciudad Juárez that have been overtaken by cartel violence. I think it is important to share my story since everyone preceding me at this conference has done so. I first became involved in the advocacy for families of the murdered and disappeared girls and women in 1998 through the book, *Juárez: The Laboratory of our Future* by Chuck Bowden. In this book, I was exposed to some of the most terrifying images of murdered women in Ciudad Juárez, and unfortunately, to the harsh, violent reality of what transpires in Ciudad Juárez. Within this book, there were two images that really impacted me. One was of a group of women who were holding a banner that read *Demandamos Justicia* [We Demand Justice] and the other was of a mummified 16-year-old girl's body that was abandoned and found decomposing in the U.S./Mexico Peace Park, the *Chamizal* National Park, where 600 acres are shared between El Paso/Ciudad Juárez, yet separated by a reinforced fence twice over and cement-lined water canals and stadium lighting. Her body had been left there for many months, and I have forever remained haunted by that image. As horrific as it is, as painful as it is, I keep that memory with me to remind me why I, a U.S. citizen and fourth-generation Mexican American, am involved. I feel strongly that if I don't act now, the same thing could happen to the women that I love and to the women in my community, because it is happening to the women down the road from where I live, down the road only fifty miles from where I call home.

I wanted to bring some photographs to you. I know we are a world away, we are a world apart from each other, but we have so many shared experiences, and I know that you can see the reflection of what happens to the women in Ciudad Juárez through the images I am about to share, because they parallel the images of your own communities, and I have come to learn this throughout the years. Ultimately, poor women are disposable.

I would like to start with this first slide [Slide 1]. I felt it was important to illustrate the region that we are talking about, and what we are discussing here is a particular location at the U.S./Mexico border. I am not sure if you have a similar landscape like this at the U.S./Canadian border, but there are many twin cities between the U.S. and Mexico. The area we are discussing is the tri-state area that is located between Texas, New Mexico, and Chihuahua. This slide depicts Lomas de Poleo, which is the community that Paula Flores[1] lives in.

I met Paula in 1998. She was the first family member I met who was advocating for justice in her daughter's murder. I first met her at her house situated less than a mile from the U.S./Mexico border. You can see the mountains of El Paso, Texas, from her front door and also New Mexico, and it's absolutely surreal to think that you have a third-world and a first-world country living so closely together, and yet hundreds and hundreds

Slide 1.

of women have been killed in Juárez with little effort or involvement from El Pasoans and Juarenses. There is no uproar, no long-lasting and visible joint investigative police operation between the two countries, yet since 1993—and of course we don't know if more girls and women were killed prior to that—there have been close to 600 women who have been killed in Ciudad Juárez alone. Ciudad Juárez has a population of roughly 2.5 million people, not including transient people who are trying to cross the border into the United States. Some records have shown between 400 and 4,000 young girls and women are still disappeared; they are still missing. And the office of disappeared people and missing people in Ciudad Juárez will not really give an accounting of those women and girls still missing. Last year, I recall a statistic that was circulated for some time was that *thirty-seven,* only thirty-seven women were missing, and that was the official record coming from that office.

So there are several types of people that are drawn to this city who eventually end up residing there because they have limited options or no other option. Ciudad Juárez is a city of migrants, where people attempt to cross into the United States. If they are not able to, they are left in a difficult and stagnant situation where some, like Indigenous people from the southern Mexican states like Chiapas or Oaxaca, may not know the Spanish language. If they cross illegally into the U.S., they are deported from El Paso through Ciudad Juárez and are literally left at the bridge, literally just left at the bridge to make their own way "home." I mention this because it might help to understand the poverty, the sense of helplessness, the sense of hopelessness, and the vulnerabilities that we are talking about in Ciudad Juárez, where you have the local population and the transient population struggling to make ends meet. And I will add that we don't hear these stories. . . .

We don't hear the stories of the migrant women who are trying to get across to the U.S. to bring their families for a better future, because there is a trend in the past several years for young girls to try to traverse the border unaccompanied. And now the price of admission to cross the border is to be raped by their smuggler. This is commonplace. It is so commonplace that women are now taking birth control pills before they decide to cross into the United States. And the rapists and the smugglers, as their reward, as their souvenirs, hang the women's bras and underwear on bushes and trees to mark their prize.[2] So we have the women who make it across after a possible rape, or the women who don't make it across who look for work and it is a question of survivability. And I applaud Danielle,[3] if she is still here, for her words, because we truly do not understand desperation for survival until we actually find ourselves there. And many of us, including myself, are fortunate enough never to find ourselves in those situations.

This is typical housing [Slide 2]. This is one extreme that you find in shantytowns across Ciudad Juárez. At the other extreme you find gated communities and country clubs—where *maquiladora* owners, managers of *maquiladoras,* alleged cartel members, government officials, and authorities live, and in some instances you might even have these communities side by side.

Slide 2.

Sagrario, Paula's seventeen-year-old daughter who was killed in 1998, is truly the reason why I became involved in advocacy for families of the feminicide victims, because her image haunted me for so many years. Paula doesn't know this, but I kept her photograph pinned up in my home office for three years. It was a different photograph than this one, a black-and-white flyer that was circulating of Sagrario. It was one of the 4,000 that was circulating in Ciudad Juárez for many years. I lived in Arizona while working on my Ph.D., and because of Sagrario's murder, I and other colleagues came to her house in September and October of 2001 and said, "How can we help? We feel powerless. We live on that side of the border [the American side]. I am Mexican. She is Mexican. He is Anglo and so on and so forth, but we are sisters, we are brothers of this border community and we need to do something." And so we held our first meeting as a local group called *Amigos de las Mujeres de Juárez* [Friends of the Women of Juárez]. Shortly after our first meeting, where we stared at each other, not really knowing what to do, there were reporters waiting outside the university (where the first meeting took place), and they wanted to have a response from this new organization that was just established about the eight bodies that had been found in a cotton field in Ciudad Juárez adjacent to a very busy intersection. I remember feeling appalled and incredulous, as you can imagine. So, this became part of my birth as an activist in this pandemic since 1998; my involvement was fortified in 2001, and although it stemmed from Sagrario's case, it grew to so many other cases and the haunting of other faces of more girls and women.

Sagrario is representative of just one small fraction of what's been transpiring in Ciudad Juárez and Chihuahua. And this senseless killing is ongoing and it is continuing throughout the border area. I received a call from a woman from LAWG, the Latin American Working Group, a few days ago, that three women's bodies had been found near McAllen, Texas; one was a U.S. citizen. They were killed in a similar fashion and in the same way the women in Ciudad Juárez had been killed. There have been hundreds of theories that have circulated. You heard some of these "theories" yesterday about the snuff films, satanic cults, drug traffickers who party and then sacrificially kill women. Someone or some group celebrates by successfully sequestering and raping a woman because they can. Another theory that I feel there is a great deal of credibility to is that there is a group of men, of very powerful individuals that Isabel[4] talked about, who literally picked people up in the middle of the road. That's happening in Ciudad Juárez now. All of this leads to the culmination of hundreds and hundreds of missing women and young girls. Ciudad Juárez has become a narco-militarized police state.

Since August 12, 2008, at the beginning of this week, 769 people have been killed in Ciudad Juárez. *Seven hundred and sixty-nine people have been killed.* Women have continued to go missing and are killed, but the local press in Ciudad Juárez and Chihuahua, and in El Paso, Texas, no longer closely reports the missing women because there is/was an "informal" moratorium on the feminicides. "It no longer sells newspapers" is what I was told by a female reporter from the U.S. and by a Mexican reporter last year on July 5, 2007, when these same mothers of murdered and disappeared women started a movement to protest in front of the police headquarters the first Thursday of each month. During that time, a Mexican female reporter said to me, "Why are you here? The women who are being killed now are fat, they are ugly, they are prostitutes, *son prostitutas.*" The female reporter further asked me, "What does it matter to you? It is not the same situation," meaning that young attractive girls were not being killed lately. . . . So the media does good and the media does bad. There have been 17 cases of feminicide in Ciudad Juárez this year so far.[5]

And I apologize to the families that are here for the detail that I am about to give on some of these cases of feminicide this year, but I think it is necessary for all of us to open our eyes and to be enraged and to be angry because that is what is going to carry us through this, and the violence must stop!

One of the victims of this year was eight and a half months pregnant and the fetus was also lost in the crime. Seventeen of the victims could not be identified. In each case where a perpetrator was suspected or found guilty, the individual was male. Several of the cases included the sexual violation of the female murder victims, including the case in which a 10-year-old girl was found completely nude in her home with a bag of condoms next to her deceased body. Many of the victims were murdered with knives or guns. Many were stabbed multiple times in the neck, back and chest. Other victims sustained multiple bullet wounds also to the neck and head. One 20-year-old victim was stabbed three times in the neck and eight times in the back. Another victim was shot to death and found with 31 bullet wounds throughout her body. Almost half of the victims left more than one child behind. While some of the female victims were killed and left in their own homes, others were left in open fields surrounding Ciudad Juárez. One victim was killed in front of her own home. Another was thrown out of a moving car. And another was found in a bloody hotel room where 95 bullet shells were also discovered. In one case where the identity is still unknown, a female body was found in Ciudad

Juárez where the victim was determined as having been dead over a month. (translated from Juárez newspapers by Sally Meisenhelder for *Amigos de las Mujeres de Juárez*)

There is a campaign in Ciudad Juárez by authorities called *El Mito de Ciudad Juárez* [The Myth of Ciudad Juárez]. Slogans saying "We must clean up the bad image of Ciudad Juárez" exist and there is a process of erasure that is transpiring now in that city. You don't hear about these cases except for those few journalists who have been exposing these stories and women's rights individuals who have been documenting these stories bravely. The women have received death threats. The women have been beaten. Family members have been killed. And that is something that is not talked about.

Sagrario worked at a *maquiladora* named Capcom. Another theory that has circulated and was documented in the film *Señorita Extraviada,* directed by Lourdes Portillo, is that there were lookouts in the *maquiladoras* who would identify good-looking girls. Photographs were taken, their images were placed in an album and then men would select the girls and say, "That one, that one, or that one." Someone earlier during the conference asked about human trafficking and I do believe that this could be a transnational trafficking issue that takes on many manifestations. This is something we need to open up our eyes to.

This is the memorial that families placed in front of the cotton field where eight bodies were found in 2001 [Slide 3]. And at least three of these cases of the murdered girls are now at the InterAmerican court, as I was mentioning to those of you who were here yesterday. And, interestingly

Slide 3.

enough, the cotton field is located right across from the Maquiladora Association office (AMAC) which is the circular building in the background. In 2003, our organization helped organize—along with WOLA [the Washington Office on Latin America] and LAWG, the Latin American Working Group, and Mexican Solidarity Network (all based out of Washington, DC, and Chicago)—a Hispanic Congressional Delegation to Ciudad Juárez. The press was going wild with this. Mexican government officials were quite upset that the Caucus member delegates were there, and it was the first time that they were able to meet with families of the murdered and disappeared girls. There are several organizations that have worked gallantly, tirelessly, in Ciudad Juárez and Chihuahua City. In Chihuahua City, which is three and a half hours away from Ciudad Juárez, there have been more than 25 victims—16 young girls and women have been killed and nine are still disappeared. And I work, our organization works, very closely with this organization, *Justicia Para Nuestras Hijas* [Justice for our Daughters], which is comprised of the families of murdered and disappeared girls and women in Chihuahua City. We have also worked with *Voces Sin Echo* [Voices without Echo], right before they discontinued their activities, but they still continue the work of the organization to some degree. There is another organization, *Nuestras Hijas de Regreso a Casa* [May our Daughters Return Home], which is an organization in Ciudad Juárez. Another is the *Centro de Derechos Humanos de la Mujer* [Center for Women's Human Rights] in Chihuahua City, *Mujeres de Negro* [Women in Black] from Chihuahua City, and countless others from Chihuahua and across Mexico that work to end violence against women. The *Observatorio Ciudadano Nacional del Feminicidio* [National Citizens Observatory of Feminicides] out of Mexico City is another, and *Mujeres Catolicas por el Derecho de Decidir* [Catholic Women for the Right to Decide] is another organization. Collectively, these groups have held multiple protests and activities.

Yesterday, someone mentioned during his or her talk that, unfortunately, it seems that the only way that governments hear the voices of local people is if you bring an outsider in, if you bring a foreigner in. That has been the pattern of solidarity and movement within this "stop feminicide" movement in Chihuahua, which is one of the reasons why we, as a U.S.-based organization, have been so involved. Bringing members of Congress from the United States really got things mobilized. It angered officials in Ciudad Juárez; something that has always been said about activism stemming from outsiders entering Ciudad Juárez is that any time there is a large march or protest it is popularly believed that another women or girl is killed in counterprotest of the anti-feminicide event taking place in

Ciudad Juárez. This myth, or truth, has always weighed heavily on my heart because it always seems to be that another woman is found, another woman is disappeared. . . . I remember the day we brought the congressional delegation in 2003, and Eva Arce was at some of these events, and the police came and said, "We have identified your daughter's body, we found a skull," leading Eva to believe that her daughter's body had been found, and of course it wasn't her daughter. It really frightened us, though, that another woman had been found in this gritty city.

And again, a series of photographs just so you can get a sense of some of the work that has been done in Ciudad Juárez. This photo was taken during a protest that we were at with the families of the murdered and disappeared girls and women, and this is an AFI police officer, which is a federal police officer who is supposed to be non-corruptable. He was photographing, videotaping rather, the activists who were at this one protest and the families involved. There were other individuals in plain clothes who were taking down license plates of everybody and anybody that was at this one protest at the cotton field. And one of our members of *Amigos de las Mujeres de Juárez* walked up to one of them and placed a pin, a little plastic pin that our organization has become famous for making, that in previous years raised thousands and thousands of dollars for organizations working in Chihuahua. The police officer was quite put off by it, so it was one way of disarming him and momentarily disempowering him, which was a form of resistance.

During other events, international marches and protests across the U.S./Mexico border have brought up to 7,000 people from the U.S. and abroad to march from El Paso, Texas, to Ciudad Juárez, and our organization made up of a few people helped contribute to these events. I want to say something quickly about coalition-building. There has been a lot of discussion about identity at this gathering and about our hurt and what we carry as people of colour, as Aboriginal people here, as Indigenous people throughout the Americas, and coalition-building. Solidarity-building for me means that we have to traverse some of these borders, some of these racialized and class-based and gendered borders. I can attest to this since my partner in *Amigos de las Mujeres de Juárez* is a white woman from Pennsylvania, who has been very committed and one of a handful of fierce activists that I know. We have come close to finding ourselves in frightening situations, and the only thing that has saved us, I think, has been her whiteness, interestingly enough. But there is some strength in coalition-building and that is what we need.

That's what we need to be able to curb the violence, to bring an end to all of the violence.

Slide 4.

These are the *Mujeres de Negro* [Women in Black], who carried a cross, either walking beside the cross carried on the back of a pickup truck or actually carrying it from Chihuahua City to Ciudad Juárez [Slide 4]. The cross is about eight feet tall and is made of railroad ties. That's 323 kilometres, I believe, to Ciudad Juárez. There is a cross that is now erected on one of the bridges as you cross from El Paso to Ciudad Juárez. And earlier it was mentioned that the cross has been boycotted by prominent Juarenses because it has really disrupted local economies and local business owners. The street it is on, *Avenida Juárez,* is a heavily trafficked tourist area which is right next to the red-light district, *El Mariscal,* in Ciudad Juárez. Many have complained about the cross that these women carried. They carried a cross walking, wearing that black tunic for most of the 323 kilometres to Ciudad Juárez.

Slide 5.

This is the cross [Slide 5] that they erected at the foot of Ciudad Juárez, one of the apertures coming into the city. And this has become a very sacred site for the families of the women and girls of Chihuahua. Several protests, several vigils and memorials have been held here. These protests have completely stopped traffic entering into the United States. We have held marches for International Day of the Woman, and several other recognizable memorials in all of Mexico have been held here.

This dress [Slide 6] was made by Irene Simmons, who is a phenomenal human rights activist and artist out of Phoenix, Arizona. You may have seen some of her dresses here. . . . I am not sure if those dresses [Cynthia referring to dresses in the back of the room] are part of her collection, but her dresses really spoke to the families and to the activists within the tri-state area, really dramatically impacting these border communities. At my university, we had 200 of the 450 of these dresses made. Community members came together and brought donated dresses and decorated donated dresses and last July 4, 2008, Irene accompanied me to Ciudad

Slide 6.

Juárez to have a workshop with some of the families, and the next day they wore these same dresses to march and protest in front of the police headquarters in Ciudad Juárez.

I share this image because these two individuals were scapegoated for the death of a 16-year-old in Chihuahua City. This is Ulises Perzabal, a native of Mexico City, and his wife, Cynthia Kiecker, who is a native of Minnesota. They made their life in Chihuahua City for several years and were picked up by police one night after a party, well actually they were sleeping. The police accused them of killing Viviana Rayas. They were both tortured, and torturers threatened to rape Cynthia while in prison if she or Ulises did not confess to the murder of Viviana. After the torture, both Cynthia and Ulises agreed to sign forced confessions. They were incarcerated for close to two years in the Cereso prison in Chihuahua City. I am hearing from folks in Mexico that there is a movement by state officials to question and bring Cynthia and Ulises back to Chihuahua and potentially re-incarcerate them after the torture and hell they lived with for three very long years while incarcerated and questioned. These are not the only two scapegoated victims, which is the other story of the feminicides in Chihuahua. There are people who have been incarcerated for the deaths of these girls and women, and they were falsely accused.

One young man, David Meza, was accused of killing his cousin and he served three years in prison. Another, Gustavo Gonzalez Meza "La Foca," died mysteriously in his prison cell. I say mysteriously because he called his wife before he had surgery for a hernia, a hernia surgery, and he hemorrhaged throughout the night and claimed he did not know why he was being operated on. He was one of two bus drivers accused of killing the girls/women from the cotton field case. The Egyptian, Abdul Latif Sharif, who became quite infamous for allegedly orchestrating the feminicides, was found dead in his prison cell last summer after repeatedly shouting out and telling people that he was being fed medication against his will. *Medication against his will*—"they are trying to kill me" is what I heard he would loudly claim.

So this is the other story of the feminicides that I feel is important to share. And interesting enough, too, about this "other" story is that the families of the murdered and disappeared girls have come together in solidarity with the families of these individuals [scapegoated victims] to ask for justice. This unlikely pairing of people became so unprecedented that this helped to facilitate the feminicide cases entering the Inter-American Commission and then InterAmerican Court, because they had not seen a case like this where the accused and the family of the murdered women and girls are coming together, coalescing to fight for justice and demand answers from their government. And this is commonplace.

This [Slide 7] is an official flyer about a missing girl put up by the Chihuahua government. This is what it looks like: Carolina, only 14 years of age. I know of at least four teenage girls who have disappeared since January 1, 2008, in Ciudad Juárez. And the feedback from at least one of the families is:

Slide 7.

"I can't speak to you any more or the other women in Ciudad Juárez or Chihuahua. The authorities told me not to speak to you any more because the killers, the kidnappers will definitely kill my daughter. I am really sorry."

Amigos de las Mujeres de Juárez has worked in conjunction with other organizations, and we have fundraised for seven years. We have raised money to pay for passports, Mexican passports and visas to allow families to travel abroad to share their stories. We have paid for trips to Mexico City for families to speak to the administration, whoever the administration was at that time. We have paid for conferences. We have paid for postcards and office rental spaces for groups in Juárez and Chihuahua City; the group from Chihuahua, *Justicia Para Nuestras Hijas,* has a postcard that they use similar to one I have seen on tables here that have the image of a young women who has been missing or killed and a message from her mother asking government officials to stop the feminicides and to do something about it. I know that Chihuahua officials have been bombarded by these postcards and they are pissed as hell every time they receive one. So we have done our job. We have worked to make the cross-painting campaigns possible. Paula very eloquently yesterday talked about the former mayor who threatened to arrest anybody who painted crosses, and yet these brave families have done this repeatedly. These families continue to re-paint crosses that have faded, as volunteers join them to paint and even to search for young missing girls.

The police are allegedly connected to the same individuals wreaking havoc and violence in that city, so community members have to support one another, and there have been many, many volunteer groups that have emerged to volunteer to go to the desert to search for missing women and girls. This combing of an area for missing women and girls is called a *rastreo,* literally a raking of an area.

We live in a very arid desert and sandy landscape, and individuals will gather together on a weekend and will go and search for bodies. At one point I remember hearing that boys, young boys, who were out with their parents searching for bodies had said—and this is how distorted things have become—that they were searching for women as if it were a children's game. Kids would say, "If I see something before you see something I win!" The police have never found a woman's body. The families or passersby in an area have found the bodies of women and girls. Girls have been deposited in dumpsters or on roads in the middle of the city. This isn't something that is exaggerated. I wish it was. This is something that demands our attention. And we really need to support each other through these atrocities and make a stand for one another.

PESQUISA

¿La has visto?
PM

Evelyn Rocío Morales Batancourt, de 16 años de edad, se encuentra desaparecida desde hace dos semanas.

La adolescente mide 1.55 metros de altura, tiene el cabello café castaño, ceja depilada arqueada, tez morena y es de complexión delgada.

Cualquier información que se tenga respecto a su paradero por favor comunicarse a los teléfonos 629-33-00, extensión 5-6487.

▲ Slide 8.   ▼ Slide 9.

This picture [Slide 8] was brought to me at my office at New Mexico State University by a custodian originally from Ciudad Juárez who said, "This young girl is the cousin of one of my *comadres* [good friend or someone who baptizes a person's child], one of my friends, can you please try to do something about it?"

These are the telephone poles [Slide 9]; the city is inundated, inundated, with flyers of missing girls. *Inundated.* These are two flyers. This photograph, I think I took in 1999 or 2000. . . . *Inundated.* When you look at the date of disappearance, it isn't 2000, 2001, it's 2008, it was 2 weeks ago. It was last week. It was last month.

Not all of the girls and women who have been killed were *maquiladora* workers. Several were students. Some women did work in bars. There were some women who were prostitutes. There were some women who were teachers. But the unifying factor was that they were all poor. They lived within these layerings of poverty that I have mentioned. And these are some of the volunteers from the community who came out to paint crosses. And these photographs are from the "Redressing Injustice" exhibit by Irene Simmons that really brought together our communities to feel, to cry, to share stories of women in the U.S. who have been abused. We have so much in common and we can't forget the common bonds that bring us together.

Slide 10.

This is what the crosses look like [Slide 10]. Witnessing these crosses swaying in the wind during our 2006 conference asking for justice for the women of Juárez was one of the most haunting, most significant, and memorable experiences I have had. We had a candlelight vigil and some of the families were there, and activists, and everybody who has been involved in this movement who was asked to participate in this conference, and as the wind moved through the dresses you really felt the spirits of the girls that we carry with us, which is why the drumming by the Cree men and the dancers and the entrance of the Elders welcoming us during the opening ceremony was so profound for me.

I think I will leave it with that and I will look forward to tomorrow's opportunity to build on our strengths, our capacity building. I encourage everybody here to do what Lourdes Portillo says she does with her students and what I do with mine, which is to encourage them to go out and share stories with five people, ten people, whether they want to listen or not, because so many times I am really tired—and excuse me for using this language—but I am goddamn tired, I am goddamn tired of carrying this with the families, with the other activists, with the organizers, with people who are there constantly, day in, day out, worrying about arrests, worrying about rape, worrying about any kind of violation under the sun. And as humans we have to share that responsibility. We have to share the responsibility for the murdered and disappeared here in Canada and go back to our communities and talk about the atrocities and really take ownership of this. Bring men. I know there are men out there in your community who care, who remember they came from a woman, who remember they have daughters, remember they have sisters. Bring Elders to these events. Re-educate people about the girls who are missing, about what leads them to survivability, to escapism, to alcohol, to drug use, to prostitution, to other things that are not healthy for us, as we have discussed as aspects of structural violence during this conference.

We need to educate the people around us. Please maintain that sense of continuity, because too many times I have seen people who come and go and take a story and leave and never retell it and say, "Wow, I will never go back to Ciudad Juárez. I am terrified." I am terrified, too. And the women who live with it day in and out are terrified. And the women who live with it here in Canada are terrified, but we have to shoulder some of that burden, too. And please help me and join the struggle. Join the movement. Get involved. Remember to take care of yourself in the process. To heal in the process, but remain angry and use that anger for good. Thank you.

The presentation was followed with questions from the audience:

QUESTION: My name is Pierre Guy. You said that the problem of missing women in Ciudad Juárez would be an international one because fake IDs were issued in the U.S.. Considering that the U.S. is fencing the border between Mexico and the U.S., do you think that the U.S. government or maybe the government of Texas would care to intervene in this domain?

CYNTHIA BEJARANO: The common response by my government—*my* government, the U.S. government—(sometimes it is very difficult, almost always difficult to claim) is that Mexico is a sovereign nation. And we have had multiple discussions about establishing a bi-national task force to investigate the potential linkages between human trafficking and sex trafficking and the disappearances and murders of women. There have been some very highly, highly committed members of Congress, like Congresswoman Hilda Solis from Los Angeles and Senator Jeff Bingaman from New Mexico, who have actually had resolutions passed to support, to raise their voices in solidarity with, the families of the murdered women and girls. I think when we talk about border states, many legislators are aloof to the problem. It's a black eye for Mexico and since we are twin cities, we are sister cities, it's a black eye for the U.S. side of the border, as well. And we do approach legislators; we have multiple conversations at the state and federal level. Currently, unfortunately, what is occurring is the establishment of a narco-state in Ciudad Juárez and Chihuahua City, where the feminicides have taken a back seat to the drug cartels and the 800 murders in Ciudad Juárez since January 1, 2008. And this is why I get back to the same point, that Mexico will not listen and respond to the feminicides until you as Canadians raise your voices to your own legislators and say, "I was at a conference this weekend and I am really upset. I heard that hundreds and hundreds of women are disappeared in a city that borders the United States. What are you going to do about it? What sort of conversation can you have? When you are talking about NAFTA, what sort of measurements do you have to protect women? When you are talking about trade agreements, can you look into this and I will be back next week with a group of 100 to talk about what you are doing to safeguard the rights of women in Mexico and the U.S. and Canada." And I think it has to start there and I go back to maintaining that level of continuity, because it doesn't work when we are really agitated and we become agitators and we are angry for six months and then it dies down. And the momentum dies and the legislators, regardless of what country they are from, are going to say, "Well, I am going to move on to the next subject." So the U.S. can certainly do much much more than what it has done to this point. But the Mexican government, especially the state government, has put a stop on any intervention, any investigations by state police, by police investigators at the state and federal level, from the United States.

QUESTION: I want to say thank you and I hear your tiredness and I want to say I am in this for the long term, too. I am a member of Amnesty International; I know about Ciudad Juárez, from that source and from others. But in terms of what to do, one of the pieces of information that I don't have is who are the companies, the Canadian and American companies, that operate the *maquiladoras?*

CYNTHIA BEJARANO: This is a very sensitive issue. With the *maquiladoras,* I want to reiterate that about a third of women and girls who are missing or have been murdered worked in a *maquiladora* when they were killed or disappeared. That does not necessarily mean that a woman did not work at another point in her life in a *maquiladora;* that's a question I asked Eva Arce about Sylvia. Her daughter, for instance, was a street vendor selling jewelry at the time of her disappearance, but at one point she did work at a *maquiladora. Maquiladoras* in Ciudad Juárez come and go. There are several European companies that reside in Ciudad Juárez, U.S.-based, Canadian-based *maquiladoras* that reside in Ciudad Juárez, but slowly they have shut their doors. And the labour unions, the independent labour unions in Ciudad Juárez and Chihuahua have been very involved in this movement of stopping violence against women. And they have told, retold stories of how *maquiladoras* from one day literally to the next will lock and shut their doors. And people are left without jobs and they flee. And so one of the mechanisms or strategies of retaliation has been by the businessmen, businesswomen, officials at the local and state level in Chihuahua, is to say, "It's their fault, those women. Those rabble-rousers, those *Viejas escandalosas* [exaggerating women]. Those scandalous, exaggerating women are the reason why, they are the reason why 50,000 people lost their jobs. They are the reason why half the *maquiladoras* have left Ciudad Juárez." As it is, people that work in *maquiladoras* have to supplement their income, which explains prostitution, working as street vendors, the informal economy, even the underground market as well, because it is a struggle to survive. So as you can see there are multiple places where I can perhaps leave some information with the organizers, after I leave and after we leave, where we could potentially indentify some Canadian *maquiladoras* that work in Chihuahua, and there are several hundred in Chihuahua City as well that are less publicized, or perhaps you can approach them and say, "We heard about this problem. What are you doing to safeguard your workers? Are you testing women? Are you issuing out pregnancy tests before you hire a woman? Are you checking sanitary napkins every month? Are you forcing them to exercise every work day from 7–7:30 to raise the energy of the workers? To produce more commercial goods?" because this is what is happening. "How are you ensuing their safety and the working conditions and health conditions?" OSHA [Occupational Health and Safety Administration] does not exist in Mexico. Free trade, NAFTA, the agreements to safeguard women's health and workers' rights do not exist. So those are the questions perhaps you can begin from.

QUESTION: Thank you for coming and sharing your, these, images with us. Last year I was a member of a delegation from the Anglican Church of Canada sent to Mexico to meet with our partners there. And while we were there, we had a meeting in Chihuahua City with the members of Justice for Our Daughters. And I can tell you that that meeting was a searing experience for all of us. So I would like to say that one of the things that we were asked to do was to come back to Canada and talk to our communities about what was going on in Chihuahua and Juárez. And since we came back in March of 2007, I have been out in this province talking to people and I think in the space of last year I have talked to over 1,000 people in this province to try and spread that word because it is so important that this story get out. So thank you again and I hope that we will be able to stand by this problem.

CYNTHIA BEJARANO: You have reminded me of, in Chihuahua City (and I will leave with this, because there is something you can do, I just remembered) of a company, a Canadian-based company out of Chihuahua City that just evicted 400 families from their *maquiladora* housing. There is sometimes a partnership between local governments and the *maquiladoras* to provide, to furnish their workers with housing. And I spent a good part of my sabbatical in Chihuahua City this year working with the *Centro de Derechos Humanos de la Mujer* [Women's Centre for Human Rights], which recently received death threats and had some of their offices broken into and literature burned. It's the first of its kind in the state of Chihuahua and these women working at the Centre helped to begin the organization *Justicia Para Nuestras Hijas* [Justice for Our Daughters], and I recall one afternoon being at the *Centro de Derechos Humanos de la Mujer,* the Women's Centre for Human Rights, and someone rushed in screaming a word that I had never heard before in Spanish—*desalojo*—and it was an eviction that was happening at this housing project by a Canadian company that had just closed its doors. They were losing business, so they closed their doors in Chihuahua City and they evicted 400 families. And the following day human rights activists who are just the most incredible, brave, courageous people—including the women in Juárez—that I have ever known in my life, stormed the governor's palace with at least 100 families in tow. And so I will make a promise to let Brenda and Carla know the name of that Canadian-based *maquiladora* and please give them hell!

ENDNOTES
1   See Paula Flores' story on page 30.
2   http://www.truthout.org/article/price-admission-migrant-women.
3   An Indigenous Canadian activist.
4   Isabel Arvides, a Mexican journalist, also addressed the conference.
5   Up to August 2008.

PRESENTATION
"MISSING WOMEN"CONFERENCE, THURSDAY, AUGUST 14, 2008.

The Sisters in Spirit Initiative:
Native Women's Association of Canada

JUDY HUGHES

The Native Women's Association of Canada (NWAC) is founded on a collective goal to enhance, promote, and foster the social, economic, cultural, and political well-being of Aboriginal women within the Aboriginal community and Canadian society. NWAC is recognized as the national voice of Aboriginal women in Canada. NWAC engages in national strategies aimed at legislative and policy reforms that promote equal opportunity for Aboriginal women.

One of the priority areas that NWAC is engaged in is combating gendered racism that results in Indigenous women experiencing violence, becoming missing persons, or being murdered. In 2005, NWAC undertook the Sisters in Spirit initiative 2005—2010. Sisters in Spirit (SIS) is a five-year research, education, policy and communications initiative designed to increase public awareness, understanding, and knowledge of the impact of racialized, sexualized violence against Aboriginal women that often leads to their disappearances or deaths.

The overall goals, objectives and outcomes of the Sisters in Spirit initiative are:

JUDY HUGHES is the president of the Saskatchewan Aboriginal Women's Circle Corporation and works with the Native Women's Association of Canada Sisters in Spirit Campaign.

- to reduce the risks and increase the safety and security of all Aboriginal women and girls in Canada;

- to address the high incidence of violence against Aboriginal women, particularly racialized, sexualized violence, that is, violence perpetrated against Aboriginal women because of their gender and Aboriginal identity; and

- to increase gender equality and improve the participation of Aboriginal women in the economic, social, cultural, and political realms of Canadian society.

To address the alarmingly high number of missing and murdered Aboriginal women and girls in Canada, the work of the SIS initiative addresses research, education, and awareness activities aimed at increasing the safety and well-being of Aboriginal women and girls. A key component of the SIS research agenda is the gathering of qualitative and quantitative information. In order to get an understanding of the root causes, circumstances, and trends surrounding murdered and missing Aboriginal women, it is necessary to talk to family members of the woman to get a picture of their lives. A literature review was undertaken to understand further the issues surrounding racialized, sexualized violence. The literature review focuses on documents pertaining to violence against women, Canadian and International law, socio-economic issues affecting Aboriginal women, and women and justice issues. Key informant interviews, case studies, and survey research were also conducted.

The research database contains information on over 200 indicators for each Aboriginal woman. These include: (a) demographic information about the individual woman, her life experiences, and her family situation; (b) incident, suspect, and trial information; and (c) social determinants of violence and marginalization such as attendance at residential schools, poverty, and experiences of racism, as well as factors associated with the response of the legal and justice system to the individual Aboriginal women and their families.

The database, case studies, and other qualitative methods will be used to present a fully realized picture of the reality of gendered racism against Indigenous women in Canada. What we can report to date:

- Number of cases in the database: 504 women have been confirmed as either missing or murdered. Of these 504 individuals, one-third of the women have been identified as missing, and two-thirds are identified as having been murdered.

- Decade in which the incident occurred: in general, more cases have been identified in more recent decades. There were 14 cases identified for the 1970s, while 57 cases have been found for the 1990s and 104 cases have been identified since 2000. This is likely due to constraints associated with conducting research on past events, not due to an increasing number of incidents in more recent years.

- Age ranges of women who are missing: 47 percent are under the age of 25; 19 percent are between 25 and 34 years of age; 21 percent are between 35 and 44 years of age; 13 percent are over the age of 45.

- Age ranges of women who were murdered: 49 percent are under the age of 25; 26.3 percent are between the ages of 25 and 34; 17.3 percent are between the ages of 35 and 44; and 7.4 percent are over the age of 45.

- "Clearance" of cases appears to be low for women who were murdered. There is data for only 60 percent of the cases of murder so far. Of these cases, 40 percent have had a charge laid; 57.9 percent are not cleared—that is, there has not yet been a charge laid. This contrasts with only 15 percent of homicides in Canada within the jurisdictions of Canada's largest police forces that are not cleared.

I would first like to take five minutes to talk about two other elements of the SIS initiative: education and communication.

Education

The SIS initiative has an education component. Activities undertaken here include:

- development and dissemination of the Violence Prevention Toolkit, launched on December 10, 2007;

- holding ten community-based workshops in ten communities identified as high-risk communities to raise awareness and present information on violence against Aboriginal women and girls, to meet with other stakeholders to establish networks, and to share information; and

- holding ten workshops in communities across Canada for social service workers and justice system workers/professionals on violence against Aboriginal women.

The criteria used to identify "high-risk communities" for the ten community workshops included: the existence of a large female Aboriginal population, proximity to an urban centre, availability of at least one Aboriginal service provider or organization, concentration of First Nations population, and quantitative/qualitative evidence of a concentration of missing/murdered women incidents. The ten communities targeted in Year III for this activity were Fredericton, Thunder Bay, Winnipeg, Regina, Saskatoon, Edmonton, Yellowknife, Nanaimo, Prince Rupert, and Kamloops. There will be another ten communities targeted in Year IV for the workshops with social service workers and justice system workers/professionals.

Communication

The SIS initiative has a communication component. Activities undertaken here include:

- media tracking to identify trends and issues in reporting on cases involving missing and murdered Aboriginal women and girls in the mainstream media;

- media outreach and engagement, that is, press releases, media advisories, writing stories or op-ed articles for placement, etc;

- assistance in dealing with the media to families who have missing or murdered female relatives;

- creation of public service announcements and liaison / partnership development with a national television network (CTV) to broadcast these announcements;

- liaison and partnership development with large organizations such as the Public Service Alliance of Canada to increase awareness, identify joint ventures, and gain support for the SIS initiative activities; and

- hosting an International SIS vigil annually on October 4. We encourage all communities and countries to participate and host their own vigils simultaneously. On October 4, 2007, vigils were held in 27 communities and cities in Canada, and in two international locations (Peru and Columbia).[1]

Policy

As a starting point, we know that the socio-economic barriers that combine to cause Aboriginal women and girls to be more susceptible to violence include:

- income insecurity;

- lack of employment, or involvement in non-standard, marginalized, or high-risk occupations;

- unaffordable housing, unsafe housing, crowded housing, or homelessness;

- racism and discrimination;

- inability to access justice due to poverty, powerlessness, systemic factors, or colonialist structures that exclude Aboriginal women; and

- unresolved personal, emotional or health issues that lead to addictions or other "unwell" behaviours.

Thus, the four key strategic policy areas that NWAC is concentrating on for the SIS initiative are: 1) reduction of violence; 2) housing; 3) education and employment; and 4) access to justice.

1. REDUCTION OF VIOLENCE: *Reducing violence that leads to the displacement or further marginalization of Aboriginal women— physical violence, emotional abuse, sexual abuse, and targeted violence.*

Statistical data consistently indicates the severity of the level of violence against Aboriginal women and girls in Canada:

- In 2003, Aboriginal people were three times more likely to be victims of spousal violence than those who were non-Aboriginal.

• 54 percent of Aboriginal women reported experiencing severe and potentially life threatening violence compared to 37 percent of non-Aboriginal women.

• A woman experiencing domestic violence is more likely to report the incident to police if she is young, Aboriginal, and has children who witnessed the violence.

Reduction of violence also links to the provision of adequate and appropriate victim services, reducing trafficking of women and girls, raising awareness of violence against Aboriginal women, making it unacceptable for Aboriginal women to experience violence.

BARRIERS TO EFFECTIVE ACTION

o underlying acceptance in Canadian society of some level of interpersonal violence or violence between men and women as demonstrated in mainstream media, including video games, television shows, movies, and music;

o accepted and systemic socio-economic inequalities between women and men, especially in income levels and unfunded responsibility for child care;

o lack of funding and support for organizations that address violence, especially for women who live in remote, rural, or northern communities;

o lack of options/adequate choices for women and girls who are experiencing violence.

EMERGING POLICY ISSUES

While we generally think of violence as coming from either an intimate partner/family member, or from a stranger, our SIS research is indicating another type of situation in which Aboriginal women and girls experience violence—a situation in which the violence is linked to an acquaintance. We are finding instances where, for example, a young woman has gotten into a car because she "knows" other youth in the car—although she may not know them well—that is, they are acquaintances. We are discovering that there may be a continuum of risk ranging from family at one end to strangers at the other—but that the middle section, that is, acquaintances, brings with it a particular level of risk, especially for younger Aboriginal women.

2. HOUSING: *Ensuring safe, available, and appropriate housing, both on and off reserve.*

Women who live on reserve have limited housing choices when they leave violent relationships or when their marriages or relationships break down for reasons not related to violence. Many women are forced to choose between staying in or returning to a violent home environment or leaving the reserve. Where women's shelter programs are available, second-stage housing, which is vital in the transition from emergency shelter to independent and self-sufficient living, is not readily available due to program funding cuts or highly restrictive eligibility criteria.

Housing in urban areas frequently fails to meet the criteria of being safe, secure, affordable, or appropriate. Aboriginal women tend to be isolated and may lack connections to community and social support. The availability of emergency beds and other services specifically for Aboriginal women is limited even in the largest cities. In smaller cities and towns, services targeting homeless women may be so constrained as to be virtually non-existent.

BARRIERS TO EFFECTIVE ACTION

- o lack of safe, affordable, adequate, and appropriate housing both on reserves and in towns and cities;

- o insufficient emergency and transitional housing spaces for women to meet the need for these spaces;

- o inability of Aboriginal youth to access safe and affordable housing especially for youth with pets, youth with multiple barriers, youth who are using substances, and female youth;

- o restrictions associated with rental housing, such as damage deposits, and the inability of renters to pay cash for expenses (i.e., hydro bills, monthly rent) make it difficult for Aboriginal women;

- o limited, low funds available through Income Assistance for housing rent costs make it difficult for individuals to access anything but the most insecure and unhealthy spaces.

3. EDUCATION AND EMPLOYMENT: *Improving education and employment outcomes to reduce poverty and increase the public safety and wellness of Aboriginal women.*

Issues include the feminization of poverty, institutionalized or systemic poverty, contested approaches such as living wages or guaranteed annual income, and the adequacy of Income Assistance levels, as compared with various poverty line measures. More information, communication, and education need to be provided as a way of empowering Aboriginal women. The opportunity for education and training will enable them to obtain employment and be self-sufficient in providing for themselves and their children.

BARRIERS TO EFFECTIVE ACTION

o   achieving educational and employment outcomes may require women to adopt behaviours or adapt to practices that are not consistent with their Aboriginal beliefs and values. If women are unwilling or unable to compromise these beliefs, they may be unable to access support through currently existing programs;

o   employment and training initiatives typically require applicants to be "job-ready," which may place them out of reach for Aboriginal women or youth who may require assistance to address multiple barriers;

o   eligibility for education and employment programs may depend on ability to qualify for Employment Insurance (EI), or meet other requirements such as age requirements. These can be difficult for Aboriginal women and youth to achieve. Employment training programs, for example, that require EI eligibility places them outside the reach of many women.

4. ACCESS TO JUSTICE: *Ensuring basic, fundamental standards of human rights, especially for Aboriginal women and children.*

Accessing justice to its broadest degree has been a major concern for Aboriginal women because of language and cultural barriers, lack of knowledge about the justice system, and lack of access to legal services. Police services need to acknowledge that Aboriginal women face life-threatening gender-based violence on a regular basis.

BARRIERS TO EFFECTIVE ACTION

o   Canadian values related to personal autonomy and "choice" conflict with the needs of families to investigate the whereabouts of missing Aboriginal women and girls;

o   supports and procedures are not in place for families who are experiencing the disappearance of a family member;

o   cultural differences, discrimination, and previous negative experiences with the justice system prevent families from pressing justice system officials for appropriate treatment or action.

Contested Policy Areas

This work leads to the need to discuss and come to consensus on decisions in contested policy areas, such as the decriminalization of prostitution and gender-based approaches.

Should prostitution be decriminalized?

There is a growing debate about this topic, fuelled in part by groups who wish to set up legal brothels for the 2010 Olympics in Vancouver. Pivot Legal Society in Vancouver is mounting a Charter challenge in an attempt to have prostitution decriminalized, arguing that this step will improve the safety and well-being of women working as prostitutes. Opponents argue that making the entire sex industry legal will increase the size and reach of the industry, with the benefits primarily accruing to the "business people" who run the industry, not the women who work in it.

Culturally Relevant Gender-based Analysis

A gendered approach to Aboriginal rights, including self-determination, is still lacking and in need of attention. Aboriginal women's right to equality is constitutionally protected by both section 15 of the Canadian Charter of Rights and Freedoms and section 35(4) of the Constitution Act, 1982. There is a lack of recognition of Aboriginal women's human rights; for example, Canada is a non-signatory to the United Nations Declaration on the Rights of Indigenous Peoples, which makes Aboriginal women and girls more susceptible to experiencing violence.

Government policies and laws have caused Aboriginal women to move away from their communities and to face extreme marginalization in urban areas (for example, the Indian Act, Bill C-31). The federal government has refused to amend the Indian Act to remove discriminatory provisions against Aboriginal women unless compelled to by the courts. There are currently court cases underway against the federal government because of this discrimination. The government is fighting and appealing as long as it possibly can to draw out the process.

Some government policies place Aboriginal women at more risk for violence rather than less risk. For example, reductions in welfare rates place women at risk by reducing their ability to afford housing in safe neighbourhoods, or their ability to afford housing at all.

Policy Change

Policy work of the Sisters in Spirit (SIS) initiative is focused on the social determinants identified through research that are common among Aboriginal women who have experienced violence or who are missing. This policy work may include 1) developing new or amended policies aimed at ameliorating these social inequalities and issues or 2) identifying areas in which more resources are needed to address underlying social determinants. Both are aimed at reducing the violence experienced by Aboriginal women as well as improving the overall life experiences of Aboriginal women more generally. Based on knowledge about the difficulties Aboriginal women have accessing legal solutions due to poverty, remoteness, discrimination, lack of power in political and governmental spheres, lack of knowledge of systems and their rights, etc., the policy work conducted under the SIS initiative will advance the human rights of Aboriginal women and girls in Canada.

NWAC is indebted to the women and men, youth and Elders who participate in this work. Their vision, strength, and commitment have allowed NWAC to work to reduce gendered racism. We especially thank the families who have participated in this work and who have provided us with information to help us to demonstrate the need for specific changes that will benefit Indigenous women and girls in the future.

An interim report will be published in the fall of 2008.[2]

Thank you, Merci, Meegwetch

ENDNOTES

1   Information about Sisters in Spirit vigils can be found at http://www.nwac-hq.org/
en/index.html.

2   There are now two reports available: *Voices of our sisters in spirit: A research and policy
report to families and communities* (November 2008), and *Voices of our sisters in spirit:
A research and policy report to families and communities, 2nd edition* (March 2009). They
can be found at www.nwac-hq.org/en/index.html.

SELF-CARE
and the Healing Journey

RESOLVE to End Violence in Our Society

MARY HAMPTON, WENDEE KUBIK, DARLENE JUSCHKA,
CARRIE BOURASSA, AND MEGHAN WOODS

The authors of this chapter are researchers with RESOLVE (Research and Education for Solutions to Violence and Abuse). RESOLVE is a tri-provincial Prairie research network that coordinates and conducts research aimed at ending intimate partner and interpersonal violence and abuse. Prairie*action* Foundation (PAF) funds RESOLVE, and its members are also very active promoters of this mission

MARY HAMPTON, Ed.D., is the Provincial Academic Research Coordinator for RESOLVE Saskatchewan, professor of Psychology at Luther College at the University of Regina, and a research faculty member in the Saskatchewan Population Health and Evaluation Research Unit (SPHERU).

WENDEE KUBIK is associate professor and coordinator of Women's and Gender Studies at the University of Regina.

DARLENE M. JUSCHKA is associate professor in Women's and Gender Studies and Religious Studies at the University of Regina.

CARRIE BOURASSA is associate professor of Indigenous Health Studies at First Nations University of Canada.

MEGHAN WOODS is a doctoral candidate in Clinical Psychology at the University of Regina.

to end violence and abuse in our society. We profile these networks to highlight the "invisible" commitment of members of our society who are actively working behind the scenes to support anti-violence, policy-driven research. We contributed to the "Missing Women" conference by video-taping the proceedings and sharing information about one of our tri-provincial research projects: The Healing Journey, funded by a SSHRC/CURA grant. In this chapter we present information on the over-representation of Aboriginal women who experience intimate partner violence across Canada. We also provide an explanation for this phenomenon from an Aboriginal Elder's perspective (Hampton, McKenna, and McKay-McNabb 2008) and from Aboriginal academics' perspectives (Kubik, Bourassa, and Hampton 2009). Interviewers with our Healing Journey project shared their experiences as Aboriginal women interviewing other Aboriginal women about their experiences.

Aboriginal Women and Intimate Partner Violence: Statistics

A boriginal women face greater risk of victimization and oppression than non-Aboriginal women. Aboriginal women face the highest poverty and violence rates in Canada (Bourassa, McKay-McNabb, and Hampton 2006). In 1992 eight out of ten Aboriginal women reported vic-timization by physical, sexual, psychological, or ritual abuse (Green 2000). This rate is twice that reported by non-Aboriginal women. In Saskatch-ewan, 57 percent of women who used shelters in 1995 were of Aboriginal ancestry, yet Aboriginal women comprised only 11 percent of the total fe-male population (Saskatchewan Women's Secretariat 1999). Nationally, the Native Women's Association of Canada (2007) notes that Aboriginal women aged 25 to 44 are five times more likely than other Canadian women of the same age to die violently. In 2003 Aboriginal people were three times more likely to be victims of spousal violence than non-Aboriginal people. In addition, 54 percent of Aboriginal women reported experiencing severe and potentially life-threatening violence, compared to 37 percent of non-Aboriginal women.

These rates remain unchanged since 1999; however, the percentage of non-Aboriginal women who experienced the most serious forms of violence mentioned above declined from 43 percent in 1999 to 37 percent in 2004. Twenty-four percent of Aboriginal women, compared with 18 percent of Aboriginal men, reported that they suffered violence from a current or pre-vious spouse or common-law partner in the five-year period up to 2004. Up to 75 percent of survivors of sexual assaults in Aboriginal communities are young women under 18 years old. Fifty percent of those are under 14 years old, and almost 25 percent are younger than seven years old. Eighty-two percent of all federally sentenced women report having been physically and/or sexually abused. This percentage rises to 90 percent for Aboriginal women. Research conducted by RESOLVE team members also suggests Aboriginal women in the prairie regions of Canada (Alberta, Manitoba, and Saskatchewan) are more likely to suffer from intimate partner violence than non-Aboriginal women (Ursel et al. ongoing). Researchers from the RESOLVE network have found that men of Aboriginal ancestry are more likely than men of non-Aboriginal ancestry to have been accused of intimate partner violence (Tutty, Ursel, and Douglas 2008). These statistics suggest Aboriginal women are vastly over-represented in the number of women who experience violence at the hands of intimate partners, and Aboriginal men are vastly over-represented in the criminal justice system (Ursel et al. ongoing).

The percentage of Aboriginal peoples in Canada is estimated at four percent of the total population (Statistics Canada 2006), with a slightly larger percentage in the Prairie provinces. The categorizing of "Aboriginal" as a way of self-identifying cultural background is contentious. The literature consistently struggles with defining terms such as "culture," "ethnicity," "race," and "visible minority." This confusion suggests that research that categorizes people by culture or ethnicity is inherently problematic. "Identity" is an important issue for Aboriginal peoples of Canada as an act of power and as an expression of self-definition (Kubik, Bourassa, and Hampton 2009). It is important for individuals to declare their own identity rather than be victimized by a governmental definition of identity that further racializes and discriminates against various groups. The institutional racialization of and discrimination against Aboriginal peoples, and Aboriginal women in particular, allows the violence to continue and contributes to the problem of "missing" or "taken" Indigenous women across the world.

In the Healing Journey study (Ursel et al. ongoing), 668 women were recruited from shelters and other services for abused women in the three Prairie provinces in Canada. These participants also struggled with identifying themselves by "cultural background," yielding a wide range of cultural identifications. To code these responses, Bourassa, Hampton, Juschka, and Kubik suggested possible cultural categories that might emerge in participants' self-identified cultural background in response to the question, "What is your cultural background?" The project coordinator (Woods), in collaboration with other research assistants, categorized responses, and inter-rater reliability, measured using Cohen's kappa, exceeded .70. Table 1 on the following page includes detailed results of participants' self-identified cultural background in this study.

Cultural Identification Coded Category	Frequency of Identification in Manitoba, Saskatchewan, and Alberta (N = 668)	
First Nations (responses include First Nations, Treaty Indian, and any identification with their First Nation, such as Cree	6.7% (n = 45)	
First Nations plus identification with a Non-Aboriginal Culture (responses include First Nations as well any other identification such as European, Caucasian, or Visible Minority)	0.1% (n = 1)	
Métis (responses include Métis and Half-breed)	6.4% (n = 43)	
Métis plus identification with a Non-Aboriginal Culture (responses include Métis as well as any other identification such as European, Caucasian, or Visible Minority)	1.3% (n = 9)	49.5% (n = 331) identified as having some Aboriginal cultural background
Aboriginal (responses include Aboriginal, Native, and Aboriginal plus Canadian)	30.7% (n = 206)	
Aboriginal plus identification with a Non-Aboriginal Culture (responses include Aboriginal as well as any other identification such as European, Caucasian, or Visible Minority)	3.9% (n = 26)	
Inuit plus identification with a Non-Aboriginal Culture (responses include Inuit as well as any other identification such as European, Caucasian, or Visible Minority)	0.1% (n = 1)	
European (responses include identification with one or more European countries)	29.4% (n = 197)	
Caucasian (responses include Caucasian, White, and Caucasian plus identification with a European country)	4.6% (n = 31)	50.3% (n = 337) identified as non-Aboriginal or other cultural background
Canadian (participants identified themselves as Canadian)	10.7% (n = 72)	
Visible Minority (responses include Asian, African, Caribbean, Mexican, and any visible minority as well as identification with a European country)	4.6% (n = 30)	
Other Cultural/Religious Affiliation (responses include Mennonite, Catholic, Jewish, Mixed Ancestry, and American)	1.0% (n = 7)	

Table 1. Frequency of responses to "What is your cultural background?
(For example: Aboriginal, Asian, African-Canadian, Polish, Ukrainian, etc . . .)"

Based on these analyses, 331 of these 668 women (49.5 percent) in the Healing Journey project self-identified as being of Aboriginal ancestry. These results, in conjunction with previously noted rates of victimization experienced by Aboriginal people, demonstrate that Aboriginal women are over-represented as victims of intimate partner violence. Participants from the Healing Journey project were recruited primarily through shelters in the Prairie provinces, and Aboriginal women and women who live in poverty appear to be over-represented in shelters for women who are abused by intimate partners (Taylor-Butts 2005; Tutty 2006). Given that there is a paucity of shelters for women on First Nations reserves (Assembly of First Nations 2009; Taylor-Butts 2005) the number of Aboriginal women who are using shelters is large. This imbalance could contribute to the over-representation of Aboriginal women in the Healing Journey sample recruited from shelters in the Prairie provinces. However, it appears that Aboriginal women are the largest group of women in the Prairie provinces who are abused by their intimate partners.

Aboriginal Women and Intimate Partner Violence: The Problem, Why Does This Happen?

We suggest that the problems of violence against Aboriginal women are a direct result of long-term and institutionalized societal discrimination. Racism, sexism, and colonialism intersect to create a system of "multiple oppressions" that leaves Aboriginal women victimized (Bourassa, McKay-McNabb, and Hampton 2006). A report published in 2007 by the Native Women's Association of Canada (NWAC) indicates that systemic violence is rooted in colonization. Women were devalued and seen as inferior to men, a situation that was contradictory to the traditional equitable roles of women in Aboriginal communities. They note:

> European colonizers viewed women very differently. European women were subordinate objects deemed to be property of the men. They were suppressed and oppressed. The attitudes and treatment white men used to subjugate white women were shifted to Aboriginal women, displacing and dispossessing them from their positions of power and influence. (NWAC 2007, 3–4)

The introduction of the Indian Act in 1876 had profound effects on the identity of Aboriginal women. The Act promoted the process of disenfranchisement or losing one's Indian status. For example, under Section

12(1)(b) of the Act, Indian (First Nations) women could lose their status if they married a non-Indian (First Nations) man. Women could not own property, and once a woman left the reserve to marry she could not return because non-Indians could not reside on the reserve even if a divorce had occurred. This also applied to her children. From the government's perspective, these women had been assimilated and had lost their Indian status. However, if an Indian (First Nations) man married a non-Indian woman, he not only retained his Indian status, but the non-Indian woman would gain status under the Act and so would their children (Kubik, Bourassa, and Hampton 2009).

The goal of the Act was assimilation of First Nations people so that lands and resources would be freed for exploitation and development (NWAC 2007). Although the Act affected First Nations people directly and affected women in particular, it also affected Inuit and Métis people indirectly:

> All Aboriginal women experience extreme marginalization and suffer from inequalities related to their social, economic, cultural, political and civil rights. These inequalities breed violence, such as post-colonial structural inequalities, family violence, racialized and sexualized violence, and gender violence. They also lead to poverty, lack of access to adequate housing, including the lack of access to matrimonial property rights, lack of access to justice, low education and employment rates, low health status and little or no political participation. (NWAC 2007, 4)

Moreover, Aboriginal communities internalize these notions of inequality and take on the role of the oppressor (Adams 1999). NWAC also points out that these new roles were internalized in communities and where violence was once rare prior to contact it became a common occurrence as a result of colonization (NWAC 2007). A recent study commissioned by Health Canada (2008) confirms that the root causes of violence are perceived to be "loss of identity and way of life, continued impact of residential schools [and] a learned cycle" (3).

The residential school experience continues to have intergenerational impacts (Indian and Northern Affairs Canada 1996). One of the outcomes of the residential school experience is the high incidence of violence against Aboriginal women (Day 1995; Hart 1997). NWAC (2007) notes that sexual abuse rates are higher among Aboriginal women, while violence against Aboriginal women is three times higher than non-Aboriginal women (4). The links between poverty and violence can be easily drawn. Violence against Aboriginal women often leads to substance abuse and additions, which can then be compounded by further victimization. Because many Aboriginal women do not have a way out of this cycle they often turn to their only alternative: survival sex and the sex industry. It becomes a vicious circle that is extremely difficult to escape.

Aboriginal women face the highest poverty and violence rates in Canada. According to Statistics Canada (2006), 24 percent of Aboriginal women (as compared to 8 percent non-Aboriginal) experienced spousal violence from either a current or previous marital or common-law partner in the five-year period prior to the survey. They were also twice as likely (36 percent) compared to other women to experience abuse from either a current or previous marital or common-in-law partner. These multiple economic, social, and political barriers result in Aboriginal women having "lower incomes, less formal education, poorer housing, lower health status and a greater chance of becoming lone parents" (Kubik, Bourassa, and Hampton 2009, 24). Gaps exist between Aboriginal women and Aboriginal men as well as non-Aboriginal men and women, with Aboriginal women experiencing a lesser status than all men and all non-Aboriginal women.

Emma LaRocque argues that discrimination and stereotyping of Aboriginal women contributes to the high rates of violence against Aboriginal women. She argues that the portrayal of Aboriginal women as "squaws" is a dehumanization of Aboriginal women and girls and makes them particularly vulnerable to physical, psychological, and sexual violence (cited in NWAC 2007). A further major factor that leads to the victimization of Aboriginal women is the continuation of negative stereotypes of Aboriginal women as promiscuous and sexually available (LaRocque 2005; Martin-Hill 2003). Martin-Hill (2003) notes that the ideology of the sexually available and subservient Aboriginal woman leads to the internalization of colonial stereotypes that then offers a justification for sexual violence against Aboriginal women. Tolman (1999) suggests that gender-based violence is a learned behaviour, linked to male power, privilege, and domination in society and the family in general.

In 2004, Amnesty International released its report *Stolen Sisters: A Human Rights Response to Discrimination and Violence Against Indigenous Women in Canada*. This report documents how the social, political, and economic marginalization of Aboriginal women has led to a heightened risk of violence, particularly for Aboriginal women living in poverty or working in the sex trade. The report discusses how the violence against Aboriginal women is often met with indifference and systematic prejudice by police forces, the media, the government, and society in general. The report documents many of the lives, stories, and situations of the estimated more than 500 Aboriginal women who have gone missing over the last 20 years (NWAC 2007). It calls for Aboriginal women to have the same protection and human rights as others in society guaranteed by law.

Global connections

What is at stake in these times of neo-liberalism and globalization, where human lives, particularly those lives marked by gender, race, class, and geopolitical location, have lesser value that the products humans secure or produce through their labour (e.g., oil)? We can ask about the relationship between our governments and multinational corporations and take note that one outcome has been the exploitation of citizens who do not approximate the ideal human—white, Euro-western, elite, and masculine—and who instead signify as exploitable and expendable.

Linked to the control of scarce and valuable resources is masculinity. In the twenty-first century most of us would have no difficulty agreeing that masculine hegemonies of multiple forms dominate our social bodies. There are powerful women, yes, but they are not in great enough numbers to have an effect, and certainly they are not all feminists. Indeed, I suspect getting a hearing with regard to politics and economics, national and international, is difficult for women, particularly Aboriginal and Indigenous women, because when it comes to politics, economics, and governance they are considered to be unauthorized "knowers." They are unauthorized knowers because of a gender/sex ideology that says women are better caretakers than politicians or economists. But who said daughters, mothers, sisters, aunties, and grandmothers cannot be politicians, economists, and caretakers? Are they not already?

Cynthia Enloe (2004), a feminist activist and political theorist, comments that there are a number of ways in which women are silenced; the public-private divide, no matter how that is manifested, and violence against women, all kinds of women. The potential and realized violence women face is found in their homes, their communities, streets and pathways, markets, jails, other countries. The list is endless. When it comes to violence there is apparently no public-private divide, although certainly public areas remain more threatening for women, particularly Aboriginal women in neo-colonial, racist, and settler societies. Violence directed against a group for whatever reason—religion, gender, race, ethnicity, aboriginality, indigeneity—is a means by which to control said group, a means by which to exploit their labour (reproductive or productive) and a means by which to expropriate their resources. All of this can be governmentally supported, condoned, ignored, or trivialized, particularly when it serves the interests of the unseen profiteers concealed behind the robes of some of our politicians.

To get to the bottom of the violence against women, particularly women marked as "raced" in a colonialist and racist society, we must begin to ask different and harder questions, questions that look at the gender ideologies and ask how they play into domination and exploitation; that ask what social mechanisms are in place that continue to normalize violence against women, be it in the home or on the streets of our cities; that ask what kind of masculinity and femininity is fostered upon Aboriginal and Indigenous peoples and how they respond; and, finally, that ask what kind of masculinity and femininity is proposed for those who would desire to be dominators. These kinds of questions can be generated in our own communities and homes to look at domestic violence and ask again what kind of gender relations exist between men and women that promote a normative masculine violence against a normative feminine victim and what kind of social relations exist between Aboriginal peoples and settler peoples that promote a normative masculine and racist violence against a normative feminine and raced other? What we can learn by asking these questions is that there is a connection between the violence enacted against those marked by race and gender in the streets of cities, in towns, villages, and homes: this violence, then, is gender-coded and systemic, as it is woven into the very fabric of our social bodies.

Aboriginal Women and Intimate Partner Violence: The Solution

The evidence presented above makes the problem clear: Aboriginal women are targets for violence and abuse in our society. Education is a key to the solution. Knowledge of the history of colonialism and the marginalization of Aboriginal people, particularly women, could help eliminate many of the gender stereotypes that exist. A solution that has been proposed by several studies is to reduce economic and status differences between people based on categories such as culture, race, age, gender, and disability (Saskatchewan Women's Secretariat 1999). The elimination of poverty across all groups in Canada would help to eliminate many of the ongoing disparities that continue to exist today. Current research by the Centre for Policy Alternatives (2006) documents that the gap between the rich and the poor continues to widen.

The Sisters in Spirit campaign and Amnesty International have made recommendations for action, including: implementing the recommendations of the Royal Commission on Aboriginal Peoples (Indian and Northern Affairs Canada 1996); sustaining funding for culturally appropriate services; increasing recruitment of Indigenous police officers (particularly women); protecting women sex trade workers' fundamental rights; developing education programs addressing the history of colonialism and marginalization of Indigenous people; and upholding international human rights instruments relevant to the prevention of violence of women. The Royal Commission on Aboriginal Peoples also makes specific recommendations that could be translated into public policy. For example, they emphasize that health services need to be realigned to be more responsive to the needs of Aboriginal women. They note: "The importance Aboriginal women attach to healing cannot be overstated, and their role in achieving wellness needs to be acknowledged and incorporated in all aspects of the design, development and implementation of health and social services" (Indian and Northern Affairs Canada 1996). They make three key recommendations:

4.2.1 The government of Canada provide funding to Aboriginal women's organizations, including urban-based groups, to (a) improve their research capacity and facilitate their participation in all stages of discussion leading to the design and development of self-government processes; and (b) enable them to participate fully in all aspects of nation building, including developing criteria for citizenship and related appeal processes.

4.2.2 Aboriginal governments and organizations provide for the full and fair participation of Aboriginal women in the governing bodies of all Aboriginal health and healing institutions.

4.2.3 Aboriginal governments and planning bodies with a mandate to develop new structures for human services undertake, in collaboration with women's organizations, an inventory of existing services, organizations and networks with a view to building on existing strengths and ensuring continuity of effort. (vol. 4, ch. 2)

These recommendations point to the need for change within mainstream (federal, provincial, and local institutions and policies) and Aboriginal communities. They further advocate a holistic, inclusive approach to address the needs and concerns of Aboriginal women. Calls have also been made for the Canadian government to "organize the balance between

local specificity and national coherence needed for effective and lasting reductions in health disparities through action on social determinants of
health, synchronizing disparate elements of our multinational, multicul-
tural, and federal character" (Johnson et al. 2008, 1690). Awareness is
slowly being raised about the missing sisters, nationally and internationally.
With the leadership of organizations such as NWAC, violence issues have
become much more prominent and have been brought to the attention
of Canadians. We concur with these recommendations. The elimination
of poverty among Aboriginal women and revaluing Aboriginal women
and their culture are key areas that influence the health of Aboriginal
women. Unless this happens, the causes of poor health will never be eliminated. These, along with greater emphasis on the social determinants of
health, are long-term undertakings. In the short term, serious jail sentences
and heavy fines for those who procure, exploit, and perpetrate crimes on
underage girls and women may raise some awareness of the undervaluing
of Aboriginal women. However, the whole culture of "disposable women"
needs to change drastically before the eradication of the colonial underpinnings of the past can occur. The need to revalue Aboriginal women
(and men) and their culture cannot be overstated. The legacy of colonialism, racism and sexism will continue to affect Aboriginal women, their
families, and society negatively, while the strength and power of Aboriginal
women goes unrecognized because of the systemic indifference, oppression, racism, sexism, and discrimination that Aboriginal women face daily.

NWAC (2007) also recommends addressing root causes of violence against
Aboriginal women, noting that "colonization is at the very core of the systemic violence targeted at Aboriginal women and girls. Canada must stop
its colonial policies immediately" (12). They also recommend validation
and recognition as integral components to healing. NWAC demands that
the Government of Canada heed the pleas of former residential school students, their families, and all First Nations for a public apology. NWAC supports the call the opposition made in the House of Commons (May 2,
2007) in their motion for the House collectively to apologize. In addition,
they recommend that the government be encouraged in their efforts to
identify outstanding equality gaps, to address those gaps in a proactive manner, and to ensure that there is commitment from the highest levels for
considering the differential impacts of all policies, programs, and laws on
Aboriginal men/boys and women/girls by implementing a Culturally Relevant Gender Based Analysis so that attitudes and perceptions towards Aboriginal women will begin to change (NWAC 2007).

Finally, NWAC has asked Canada to agree to the suggestions put
forth by Aboriginal leaders towards developing a "Statement of Shared

Understanding" about the application of the *UN Declaration* in Canada that would remove any obstacle to Canada voting "yes" to the *UN Declaration* in its current form at the UN General Assembly. NWAC believes that Canada's support of the *UN Declaration* at the General Assembly will be a historical moment of pride and accomplishment built on over twenty years of hard work by Canada and many other states to affirm and to advance Indigenous peoples' human rights. Should Canada continue to oppose the declaration, this will go down in history as a blight on Canada's reputation as a human rights defender (NWAC 2007).

REFERENCES

Adams, Howard. 1999. *Tortured people: The politics of colonization.* Rev. ed. Penticton: Theytus Books Ltd.

Amnesty International. 2004. *Stolen sisters: A human rights response to discrimination and violence against Indigenous women in Canada,* http://www.amnesty.ca/campaigns/ sisters_overview.php (accessed 4 November 2005).

Assembly of First Nations. 2009. "NWAC, AFN and AFN Women's Council unite to oppose Bill C-8 on matrimonial real property." http://www.afn.ca/article.asp?id=4516 (accessed 6 June 2009).

Bourassa, Carrie, Kim McKay-McNabb, and Mary Rucklos Hampton. 2006. "Racism, sexism and colonialism: The impact on the health of Aboriginal women in Canada." In *Canadian women's studies: An introductory reader,* ed. Brenda Cranny and Andrea Medovarski, 540–51. 2nd. ed. Toronto: Inanna Publications.

Centre for Policy Alternatives. 2006. "Growing gap, growing concerns: Canadian attitudes toward income inequality." http://www.policyalternatives.ca/documents/National_Office_Pubs/2006/Growing_Gap_Growing_Concerns.pdf (accessed 5 June 2009).

Day, Tannis. 1995. *The health care sector's response to woman abuse: The tip of the iceberg.* London, ON: Centre for Research on Violence against Women and Children.

Enloe, Cynthia. 2004. *The curious feminist: Searching for women in the new age of empire.* Berkeley, Los Angeles, and London: University of California Press.

Green, Joyce. 2000. "Constitutionalizing the patriarchy." In *Expressions in Canadian native studies,* ed. Ron F. Laliberte, Priscilla Settee, James B. Waldram, Rob Innes, Brenda Macdougall, Lesley McBain, and F. Laurie Barron, 355–73. Saskatoon: University of Saskatchewan Extension Press.

Hampton, Mary Rucklos, Betty McKenna, and Kim McKay-McNabb. 2008. "Family violence from an Aboriginal Elder's perspective." *RESOLVE News* 10: 2.

Hart, Robert. 1997. *Beginning a long journey. Health Canada and the National Clearinghouse on Family Violence,* http://www.phac-aspc.gc.ca/ncfv-cnivf/familyviolence/pdfs/beginnine.pdf (accessed 27 January 2006).

Health Canada. 2008. *Aboriginal women and family violence.* Ottawa: Health Canada.

Indian and Northern Affairs Canada. 1996. *Royal commission on Aboriginal peoples.* http://www.collectionscanada.gc.ca/webarchives/20071115053257/http://www.ainc-inac.gc.ca/ch/rcap/sg/sgmm_e.html (accessed 21 February 2010).

Johnson, Shanthi, Sylvia Abonyi, Bonnie Jeffery, Paul Hackett, Mary Hampton, Tom McIntosh, Diane Martz, Nazeem Muhajarine, Pammla Petrucka, and Nazmi Sari. 2008. "Recommendations for action on the social determinants of health: A Canadian perspective." *Lancet* 372: 1690–3.

Kubik, Wendee, Carrie Bourassa, and Mary Rucklos Hampton. 2009. "Stolen sisters, second class citizens, poor health: The legacy of colonization in Canada." *Humanity and Society* 33: 18–34.

LaRocque, Emma. 2005. Violence in Aboriginal communities. National Clearing House on Family Violence. Ottawa: Health Canada. http://www.phac-aspc.gc.ca/ncfv-cnivf/familyviolence/pdfs/beginnine.pdf (accessed 27 January 2006).

Martin-Hill, Dawn. 2003. "She no speaks and other colonial constructs of 'The Traditional Woman.'" In *Strong women stories: Native vision and community survival,* ed. Kim Anderson and Bonita Lawrence, 106–20. Winnipeg, MB: University of Manitoba Press.

NWAC (Native Women's Association of Canada). 2007. *Violence against Aboriginal women and girls.* Ottawa: NWAC.

Prairie*action* Foundation (PAF). www.prairieactionfoundation.ca.

RESOLVE (Research and Education for Solutions to Violence and Abuse). http://www.uregina.ca/resolve/.

Saskatchewan Women's Secretariat. 1999. Profile of Aboriginal women in Saskatchewan. Regina, Saskatchewan: Saskatchewan Women's Secretariat. Statistics Canada (2006). Statistics Canada—Catalogue no. 97–558 9.

Taylor-Butts, Andrea. 2005. Canada's shelters for abused women, 2003/04. *Juristat,* 25. Statistics Canada catalogue no. 85–002-XIE. Ottawa: Statistics Canada.

Tolman, Deborah L. 1999. "Female Adolescent Sexuality in Relational Context: Beyond Sexual Decision Making." In *Beyond appearance: A new look at adolescent girls,* ed. Norine G. Johnson and Michael. C. Roberts, 227–47. Washington, DC: American Psychological Association.

Tutty, Leslie M. 2006. *Effective practices in sheltering women leaving violence in intimate relationships.* Toronto: YWCA Canada.

Tutty, Leslie Maureen, Jane Ursel, and Fiona Douglas. 2008. "Specialized domestic violence courts: A comparison of models." In *What's law got to do with it? The law, specialized courts and domestic violence in Canada,* ed. Jane Ursel, Leslie Maureen Tutty, and Janice LeMaistre. 69–94. Toronto: Cormorant Books.

Ursel, Jane, et al. ongoing. *The healing journey: A longitudinal study of women abused by intimate partners.* Funded by SSHRC/CURA—Social Science and Humanities Research Council/Community University Research Alliance.

Two-fold Participation:
Dialogue with Self . . . Heartbeat of Mother Earth . . .

LORI CAMPBELL

Dialogue with self . . .

What? You want me to present at the Missing Women's Conference? What's that? You want me to speak in front of a whole room full of people—on something so personal, something so hush-hush? Are you sure? It's important, you say? You are right. It is. Okay then, I will. I will do it.

Oh my gosh. What have I gotten myself into? I think I am feeling afraid. What if no one is interested? What if people laugh at me? What if everyone thinks I'm a freak? No, it's okay. It's important. I have a perspective, an experience, and a voice, and it needs to be shared.

If it weren't so hush-hush perhaps other sisters would not find themselves in the situation I was in. Perhaps if people knew that violence against women can occur, and does occur, in relationships—lesbian relationships—then perhaps it can be stopped.

LORI CAMPBELL, born to a 15-year-old displaced First Nations woman, went through a Social Services apprehension, foster care, and adoption, and then struggled extensively with discovering and reclaiming her Métis identity. She is currently pursuing a Master's degree in Adult Education, with research in Aboriginal cultural competency in post-secondary institutions as a determinant of Aboriginal student health and success.

I tell my story. My very personal story. I have never told this story in a public forum before. I see heads nodding in acknowledgement, under-standing, and empathy as I speak. I catch tiny glimpses of eye contact from women who know exactly what I am talking about. I know. They know. And they know that I know. A connection is made. A dialogue is opened. Today, it is not hush-hush. Today, it is not a secret. Don't let it be your secret—I won't let it be my secret anymore.

Heartbeat of Mother Earth . . .

I am a drum carrier—a carrier of a big drum. Yes, it is true. I sit at the big drum, and yes, I am a woman. The drumbeat is the heartbeat of Mother Earth. The drum comes from woman. I used to just listen to it, and I would cry—so filled with emotion, but so afraid to let my voice out. A shift began to happen. The balance of feeling too scared to let my voice out shifted to become one of being too afraid not to let my voice out. Who was I to get in the way of what the Creator put in me to do? Who was I to tell the Cre-ator a mistake was made—women do not sing at the big drum?

I sing with the Rainwater Singers. We are guided by an Elder—a woman Elder. We are all women at the drum. We are all doing what the Creator put in us to do. It is a woman's drum—a woman's healing drum. We sing songs of prayer—prayers for women's healing and strength—for the women, those before them and those that will come after them—for their families and their communities.

The heartbeat extends out into the auditorium. Some women are smil-ing, some are crying, and some have their eyes closed—letting the uniting, powerful heartbeat soak into their very being. Women walk towards the drum. They sit with us. Our verbal languages are not the same—but our heartbeat is. The energy is strong. It is very powerful. It is the powerful, healing energy of the united heartbeat of women connecting with the uni-versal heartbeat—the heartbeat of Mother Earth.

Kamāmakos:
The Woman Who Wouldn't Fly Away

CHELSEA MILLMAN

> As I have come to understand it from listening to the Elders and traditional teachers, the only person I can speak about is myself. That is how the Creator made all of us . . . All I have to share with you is myself, my experience, and how I have come to understand that experience.—PATRICIA MONTURE-ANGUS (Mohawk)

I am a woman. I am a daughter. I am a granddaughter, a niece, and a friend. I am Canadian, but it has been difficult for me to understand fully what that means. I have struggled with my identity as an invisible minority; my identity of being fair-skinned but having Indigenous roots. I was raised in white-bred small town Saskatchewan for most of my life and that made it difficult for me to understand my identity. There were no other Métis or First Nations kids in Watrous and when one did pass through, he was called a "dirty Indian" and she was referred to as "an Indian squaw." This racism and hatred made it difficult for me to be open with my identity, not only to the people around me, but to myself as well. I spent many years fumbling through life, not knowing who I was or what I was missing. It

CHELSEA MILLMAN, a Métis women raised in southern Saskatchewan, has been working on the issue of missing and murdered women since April 2007.

wasn't until I came to university that I found the strength to stand up and claim my identity.

I was 18 years old and I remember it as if it was yesterday. I was in my Interdisciplinary Studies 100 class and a blonde-haired, blue-eyed girl spoke authoritatively to the class about how "Natives get their school paid for" and how "they shouldn't get all of these things because it's not like any of the people who were in residential school are still alive anyway." I sat back in astonishment as the people in my class promoted colonialist views through their prejudiced, misguided group conversation regarding contemporary treaty rights and the legacy of residential school. I remember looking at my professors, thinking that they would surely jump in and tell these people how ignorant their beliefs truly were. Looking back, however, I think the Creator did not allow my professors to say anything in order to empower me to claim publicly my identity for the first time. I felt a lump at the back of my throat, I could feel my skin turning red, and my heart beat so fast I thought it was going to jump out of my chest, and I yelled, "You really have no clue, do you? Do you really think there are no residential school survivors alive today? The last school closed in 1996! And these things the government 'gives' to 'Natives' are a small price to pay for raping and pillaging Indigenous land, culture, and people!" By this point I was extremely angry. I had heard enough and I yelled even more loudly, "Would you say those things in front of an Indigenous person? Sometimes you cannot tell who is 'Native' just by looking at their skin. I AM ONE OF THOSE 'NATIVES' YOU ARE TALKING ABOUT! AND IT ANGERS ME WHEN YOU DO NOT THINK BEFORE YOU OPEN YOUR MOUTH!" I was very angry and, now that I look back, I didn't handle the situation well. At the same time, however, I felt empowered. It was the first time that I publicly claimed my identity. It was the first time that I didn't care about what people thought. It was also the first time that I knew what I wanted to do with my life. From that point on I began to claim my identity as a Métis woman and I also began to feel proud of that identity. Research and writing about/for First Nations and Métis women became my passion, and my goals in life all revolve around that identity.

With claiming my Métis identity, however, came much frustration, sadness, and sometimes anger. The legacy of residential schools and the greater impact of colonization have taken traditional knowledge away from my family. Through this time of self-discovery I knew what I wanted and so desperately sought after but was unable to find it. I remember feeling as if I needed something more; I needed spiritual guidance from Elders. Because I was raised by my lone mother, a woman who rejects not only my, but her own, Métis identity, I had nowhere to turn. I had no one to go to for support or guidance. During this time I went back to feeling like an invisible minority because I was rejected by mainstream society for being too open about my Métis identity, but was rejected by the Métis/First Nations community because I wasn't Métis enough.

It wasn't until I was 20 years old that I met a woman who changed my life forever. I feel as though the Creator placed me in her Psychology of Women class for a reason. I feel as though he placed me there so I could meet Mary Hampton and develop a relationship with her. Trusting relationships don't come easily for me, but this relationship did and I had to trust the inner knowing that my life would never be the same as it was before I met Mary. Mary is someone who empowered me to seek knowledge, claim my identity to a greater extent, and to pray for spiritual guidance. During the first year of our relationship I felt valued and, truthfully, I felt loved. Mary has not only been my professor and supervisor; she has been my mentor and, in a sense, she has been somewhat of a spiritual guide as well. It was Mary who guided me to Elder Betty McKenna.

The first year of getting to know Elder Betty was tough. I felt extremely nervous every time I was around her. I didn't want to make any mistakes, and I didn't want her to take my anxiety for insincerity. I felt frustrated many times because it seemed as though spiritual connectedness came so easy to some people and I had to work so hard to gain nothing. These feelings however, subsided in September 2008 after attending a Moontime ceremony hosted by Elder Betty.

Four young women, including myself, took the short prairie drive to a farmyard outside Moose Jaw, Saskatchewan, on the full moon of September 2008. I remember being slightly nervous, but I was also so excited finally to be reconnecting to my spiritual roots. When we arrived, there were approximately 20 women already sitting around a beautiful sacred fire. As we approached, the women welcomed us by making the circle larger. I felt comforted. Elder Betty began the ceremony by presenting us with traditional knowledge. She spoke of how we as women must come together in harmony. She said that we are not on the river of life alone; our sisters are there with us, even when the waters are rocky. Everyone in the circle was given a cedar branch, and as we burned these cedar branches we prayed. I prayed for my mother, others prayed for themselves, some prayed for family members, and others prayed for all who were there. As Elder Betty began to sing the Water Song, I heard drumming in the distance. At first I thought I might be losing my mind! No one was there except those of us who were in the circle, and none of us was drumming. At that point I began to cry tears of joy. In that drumming I truly heard the heartbeat of Mother Earth and I felt as though I was back home. I felt as though I was where I needed to be.

Months later I asked Elder Betty if anyone was drumming and she said, "Those are the spirits that come. They come and let us know that everything is okay. And you will only hear it on the women's Moon. [It happens] only on every September Moon but you will hear the drums. The ancestors will come and say things were good; women are together and learning [and] it's good. They give us that approval by drumming for us. It is a blessing from the spirit world. That's what that is."

My journey in university has not been only about getting a degree. It hasn't been about getting into graduate school or impressing my professors and peers. This journey has been about self-discovery, empowerment, and spiritual growth. The Creator sent me to university for a reason, but that reason was not only to get my B.A. in Psychology. He sent me here in order to meet person after person who gently guided me onto my spiritual path. He sent me to this institution because I needed to learn something; I needed to learn who I am as a Métis woman, and this university and conference space happened to be the perfect places for me to do just that.

Some people say I am lucky. They say that the Creator answers all of my prayers. I don't know if this is necessarily true, but I do know that I have lived a very blessed life. I have not always recognized my life as being this way, but over the past few months I have come to know this. I have come to know that the Creator has given me the strength finally to be proud of my Métis identity as well as everything (positive and negative) that comes along with this identity. I am empowered by my Métis identity because I now understand where my warrior spirit comes from, why I have an intense connection to the land, why I am the woman I have grown to be, and, surprisingly, why it was difficult for me to claim my identity in the past.

Empowerment, however, is not always the feeling I get from claiming my identity. Throughout the planning of this conference and feeling a connection to the larger issue of missing and murdered women, I have also felt deeply saddened, and my spirit has often become broken; my tough exterior always remained, but on the inside my soul constantly wept. You see, with claiming my Métis identity, I have also come to know *all* Indigenous women as my sisters. Every time I see a photograph of another one of my missing or murdered sisters, I see a reflection of myself within her. I allow their pain, spirit wounds, and sorrow to enter into my soul. I can almost feel the cold on their bodies as they lay in a dark place; a place where malevolent beasts have discarded them.

After speaking with Gwenda Yuzicappi, I remember calling my mother. I cried to her and told her that I felt depressed, angered, bitter, disgusted, and guilty. I felt this way because every time she looks at my high school graduation picture she can smile and remember how beautiful I looked that day. When she looks at the picture that my friend took of me drunk at thirteen, she can feel angry because I lied to her that night. When she sees the picture of me flashing the finger at fifteen, too cool to smile for the camera, she can laugh at my immaturity. When she sees me sitting on the hood of my "brand new" 1990 Chevrolet Cavalier z24, she can be annoyed when she reminisces about the heavy metal music that constantly blasted from the expensive speakers that she warned me not buy. When she sees the picture of me holding my cousin's daughter she can be excited by the thought that one day she might be the grandmother of my children. When my mother sees any picture of me, she can think about the next pose, the next special occasion, the next moment she will capture. Gwenda, on the other hand, cannot think of the next picture she will have of her daughter, and that saddens me. These are the simple, constant, fleeting thoughts that have often bogged me down in a cold, dark, deep depression.

When I saw Tara-Lynn Poorman's bright smile and intense eyes in her family-made missing person's poster I felt an intense sickness that, in many ways, continues to exist within me today. I feel this way because on the day she disappeared I was flying to a warm Caribbean island with my family and closest friends. I saw a younger, more beautiful version of myself within her dark brown eyes. I heard more innocent, but nonetheless radical, words flowing from her slightly pursed lips, and I felt a warmth within her that I have always strived to have. This saddened me because, as I was travelling to participate in the most important day of my life thus far (my wedding), her life was ending. When I was having a fun-loving time, one of my Indigenous sisters was taken from us. My mother got to see me marry the man of my dreams, but Shellyn Kay will never even meet the man or woman of her daughter's dreams. As I was drinking mojitos on the sandy beach of Varadero, Tara-Lynn was being punished by the media for celebrating with alcohol as most teenagers do. As I lay in the warm comfort of my new husband's arms, she lay alone in four feet of snow. The happiest day of my life was the saddest day of Shellyn's, and that saddens me. These are the images that haunt my dreams, causing me to lie awake, paralyzed, sweating, trembling, and feeling as though it is me who is dying.

Although I am empowered by knowing who I am and where I come from, I also know that in Canada my identity means that I am worthless in many people's eyes. With this identity comes a deep, searing heartache for my Indigenous sisters who have disappeared or been murdered. During the planning of this conference I had to distance myself from the group many times. I often felt angry because my time and my energy were being consumed with room rentals, catering orders, and politics, when my spirit was aching for something more. Sometimes I looked at the women around the table and I thought that although they had passion for the issue because they were women and because they were people, I also felt that they would never understand the issue because (many) were not Indigenous. I often felt as though some people just did not understand this issue because their white privilege clouded their view of reality. I also felt that along with this came a colonization of Indigenous spirituality where some people refused to acknowledge the wrongs committed against Indigenous culture by the Christian church. I also felt as though an appropriation of Indigenous culture sometimes occurred and some people were content with blaming ignorance for their repeated cultural/spiritual blunders. Soon, however, the conference came and went and these problems didn't bother me as much as they once did.

I have come to understand that this is my life. I am never going to escape this issue. I cannot escape it, and even though it causes me much pain and anxiety, I do not want to run away from it. Sometimes it is this pain, anger, disgust, and frustration that push me to do "something." I once told my husband that, although I often feel as though working on this issue is damaging me, I cannot stop, because if my passion ever dies a piece of me will die as well. I do not know where my path will take me next. I do not know what the next step is. I do, however, know that I must keep pushing on. Although I need to continue to write and pursue academics, that is not enough. I need to pray, participate in ceremony, seek guidance from Elders, be an active activist, and attempt to instill my passion for this issue in the younger generation. I encourage you to do the same.

Activism as Healing:
People Before Profit

ERNESTA VILEITAITE-WRIGHT

The "Missing Women" conference 2008 was an eye-opener to many. People presenting were both humbling and inspirational. The conference made people evaluate the issue of missing Indigenous women in Mexico and Canada and inspired activism. It was a huge step towards the creation of our non-profit organization, People before Profit: Empowering Communities through Women. It was a logical step after the new and disturbing knowledge gained from the conference. The goal of our non-profit is to empower communities through women: locally, nationally, and internationally. We believe that women are the social fabric of community. Women are also often at the bottom of the priority list when it comes to education, nutrition, health, etc., especially when the finances in the family are scarce. Through fundraising we aim to provide support to the marginalized groups while standing in solidarity with them. We intend to continue the work that the " Missing Women" conference started, which is creating conscious awareness of women's struggles across the world as well as creating a global community.

ERNESTA VILEITATE-WRIGHT was born in Panevezys, Lithuania, and came to Canada in 2005. A devoted activist on behalf of human and animal rights and the well-being of our planet, she is co-founder and board member of the non-profit organization People Before Profit: Empowering Communities through Women.

To date, we have assisted a local family in raising money to help with a reward when their daughter went missing. We have also raised money for a "squatter settlement" in Mexico to hire a kindergarten teacher, and we are currently in the middle of raising funds to assist artisan groups from Peru in selling their jewelry in Canada. People Before Profit believes that we are not only assisting these groups, but also continuing to raise awareness within our local communities regarding the effects of multinational corporations squeezing out marginalized groups from their land, their livelihoods and their cultures. By our local actions, we stand in solidarity with women around the world.

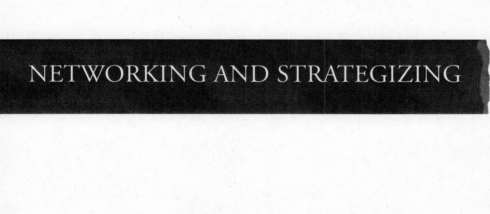

NETWORKING AND STRATEGIZING

Common Themes from Conference Participants

WENDEE KUBIK

The " Missing Women" conference was structured in such a way as to give the conference participants an arena to voice their suggestions, ideas, recommendations, experiences and solutions to the problem of missing women in Canada and Mexico. Conference attendees joined affinity groups that included healing, law/policy, community, academic, family, youth, media, and faith. Each group met for approximately three hours and was facilitated by a conference organizer or volunteer. The affinity groups concentrated on a number of guiding questions. These questions focused on the conference itself (what was most and least helpful); people's experiences around the issue of missing women; the strengths the group brought to the problem; what positive action is presently being taken; areas that need improvement, what we can do to bring about change, and how we can make this happen; and prioritization of these actions.

While several common themes emerged from the affinity groups as a whole, the overarching theme was people working and joining together.

WENDEE KUBIK is associate professor and coordinator of Women's and Gender Studies at the University of Regina. Her research interests focus on farm women, women's health, Aboriginal women, women and work, gender analysis, changing gender roles, participatory action research, food security, and global health issues.

Suggestions were made that people need to become more connected and that communities need to be built. Men were seen as needing to be part of the solution (for example, taking responsibility and teaching sons how to treat women). It was suggested that women need to come together through mechanisms like consciousness-raising, petitions, walks and rallies, and that this should include women from different places and countries. Being active by using our voices and incorporating activism against injustices were mentioned by several participants. There were suggestions that youth need to be involved, and ways to do this pointed to teaching and empowering students and youth. Traditional First Nations teachings were also suggested for youth. Along this line was the recommendation that grandmothers be involved.

Other groups of people who were mentioned were politicians, the police, and the media. It was noted that coalition-building with politicians was important and that politicians who were unaware of the issues surrounding the missing women need to be targeted specifically with education and action plans. Suggestions were made that the police need to be more approachable and more involved in the missing women's cases. In order to do this it was felt that the police need to involve and work with the families more. There were feelings among some of the participants that the media portrayed the missing and murdered women in a negative (victim blaming) and stereotypical fashion. The solution was to try and change the way the media portrays missing and murdered women or at least point out some of the racism/sexism and stereotypical images of women in some of the media reports.

Another suggestion to instigate social change, mentioned by several groups, was to focus on art and art installations. Many groups suggested large-scale art projects that could be linked to women specifically. Examples were given, such as an exhibit of dresses in Mexico, banners, shoes, and silhouettes of some of the missing and murdered women.

Besides this major theme of working/coming together, a second theme also arose out of the discussions of the affinity groups: education. Education was seen as the other key to solving the problem of murdered and missing women. Some spoke of workshop-type education, while others spoke of formal education. Teaching of teachers and connecting with universities was another thrust of this theme. The education of men was seen as very important.

The following is a brief summary of the action items voiced by each of the affinity groups. Suggestions for solutions to combat the large number of missing and murdered women were given as well as discussions of what some of the perceived problems are that need to be addressed.

Academic Affinity Group

Action items

- A stronger connection with the legal system

- More police involvement

- Support for the families and people who have stories to tell

- Writing in multiple voices (meaning from various perspectives: family, academic, police, etc.)

- More involvement with universities regarding research/ information exchange

- More stories need to be heard and support shown for the storytellers

- Careful research and dissemination of the facts, including research into the similarities and differences of the disappearances

- Responsibility and empowerment of the community is important

- Organize forums for sharing

- Rallies and demonstrations need to be held

- Expansion and clarification of the term "missing" (e.g., murdered)

Perceived problems that need to be resolved

- It was felt by some that the police are not as committed as they should be to finding the women or resolving the murders

Community Affinity Group

Action items

- Police need to work more with community organizations

- Healing and forgiveness need to occur

- The media needs to portray the missing/murdered women accurately (not stereotypes or with racist/sexist language)

- Programs that teach about racism and sexism

- More use of Domestic Violence Court

- More use of "John" School

- Art exhibits to raise awareness

- More marches and rallies held to raise awareness

Faith Affinity Group

Action items

- Police need to work more with community organizations

- Various funds from church groups could support healing

- First Nations leadership is needed, plus working with Elders

- Indigenous theology is needed

- In general, more dialogue with Indigenous people

- Acknowledgment of residential school trauma and its links to problems in society

- Faith groups must not try to force people to convert

- Building of social justice coalitions and working with Amnesty International, Sisters in Spirit and Status of Women

- Build on organizations that are already working on the issue

- Coalition of churches to work on the issue is needed

- Networking and maintenance of email updates is important

- Education

Perceived problems that need to be resolved

- Some members of faith-based organizations can be racist

- Focus on trying to get people to convert to Christianity

- White settler invader language needs to be eradicated

Family Affinity Group

Action items

- More resources are needed to find the women

- Families need to connect

- Groups needed to support the families

- More search and rescue teams to find the women are needed

- Educate the community and raise profile of the issue in general

- Teach our own family members about the situation

- Advise and advocate for family members when the police stop searching

- Teach sons how to treat women

- Men need to take more responsibility

Healing Affinity Group

Action items

- Education is very important, especially for men

- By healing one person, they will heal the next

- Raising awareness through art, ribbons, healing walks

- Work with agencies and projects focusing on the issue

- Prayer

- The media must be held more accountable in terms of how the women are portrayed

- More resources and a focus on finding the women who are missing

Perceived problems that need to be resolved

- Silence and inaction is a major problem, especially by the authorities

Law/Policy Affinity Group

Action items

- More dialogue with Indigenous people and women from all countries is needed

- People need to be more connected and work together

- Activism, including rallies and art exhibits

- More victim's advocates are needed

- There is a need for allies in the provincial and federal government

- Challenge the government and ask why

- Internally examine culture and change areas of society regarding negative attitudes towards women and race

- Men need to talk and be part of the solution

- Support women politicians and target specific politicians who are not supportive

- Make use of the Internet

- Involve youth because they are the wave of the future

- Youth groups are important

- Explain traditions to youth

- Collaborate with policy makers

- Make immediate and long-term plans to focus on the missing and murdered women

- The media must be held more accountable

- Education is the key

Perceived problems that need to be resolved

- The media focuses on the victimized more than the victim

- Families need to be kept aware of the processes that the police need to go through and where the police are in their investigations

- Politicians need to be more aware

- Intersectionality: sexism, racism; all "isms" compounded together

Youth Affinity Group

Action items

- Men need to take more responsibility

- Networking is important

- Connect with teachers, youth, academics, Elders, Aboriginal leaders, government, students, school boards, non-governmental organizations, community-based organizations, refugees, and immigrants

- Need for a website on sexism and racism

- Teacher training program

- Parents need to get involved

- Have more evening programming/activities for youth

- Need to be a voice for the voiceless

Perceived problems that need to be resolved

- Racism and sexism

- We don't have the real picture of missing and murdered women; this may be due to portrayals in the media

- Need money from the government and First Nations leaders

Summary of Provincial Partnership Committee on Missing Persons

P ublic concern about missing persons, including cases of missing Aboriginal women, led to the Province of Saskatchewan undertaking a number of initiatives in fall 2005, including the creation of a Provincial Partnership Committee on Missing Persons. This committee brought together a number of organizations with interest and expertise or province-wide experience in the issue of dealing with missing person's cases to consider how to improve collaboration and support provided to families and communities of missing persons. Its mandate is set out below.

Provincial Partnership Committee on Missing Persons Mandate

VISION: Work towards a future that ensures that when people go missing there is a full response that mobilizes all necessary participants and that recognizes the equal value of every life.

GOALS:

* to raise awareness of and support public education around the reasons why people go missing;

* to promote prevention strategies;

* to encourage cooperation and partnerships amongst agencies to better support families and communities where someone goes missing; and

* to enhance capacity to respond to cases of missing persons at the family, community and provincial level.

PRINCIPLE: The Partnership recognizes that people go missing for a variety of reasons, and will work to respond specifically to each of these reasons, as brought forward by the members of the Partnership committee, while addressing the needs of all missing persons.

The Committee started its work in January 2006 and involved representatives from 14 organizations representing police, First Nations, Métis, community organizations involved with missing persons, search and rescue, and provincial government departments. The Committee established the mandate. The Committee issued an interim report in February 2007, met with some families of missing persons in February/March 2007 and issued a final report in October 2007. [http://www.justice.gov.sk.ca-/missing-persons-report] The Committee continues to meet to monitor progress on implementation of the recommendations, to support implementation of the recommendations and to identify other areas where work may be needed.

The Saskatchewan Provincial Partnership Committee on Missing Persons is a unique approach that brings together a broad range of perspectives to build partnerships across sectors and amongst differing perspectives to strengthen the Saskatchewan response to all cases involving missing persons.

Background
What do we know about missing persons nationally and in Saskatchewan?

- A 2005 consultation report released by Public Safety and Emergency Preparedness Canada indicated that there were over 100,000 reports of missing persons annually in Canada, with around 4,800 persons still recorded as missing after a year, with an average increase of 270 new, long-term missing persons annually. As well, about 20 to 30 new or partial sets of human remains are discovered each year in Canada.[1]

  Research completed by Dr. Jeffrey Pfeifer in November 2006 found that in Saskatchewan in 2005 there were 4,496 reports of missing persons filed with the police.[2] However, these reports represented only 2,956 people. This differential is the result of some individuals going missing a number of times during the year. The discrepancy between these two numbers highlights the challenge of dealing with chronic runaways. The data also reveal that:

- There is generally an equal distribution of males and females.

- The majority of missing persons are reported as white or First Nations/Aboriginal, but race is not listed for a number of individuals. As well, the number of First Nations/Aboriginal persons reported missing is disproportionate to their representation in the population—about 38 percent of cases where race is known.

- The bulk of missing persons fall between the ages of 9 and 18.

- People go missing for different reasons:
  - o 64 percent of missing person reports in Saskatchewan in 2005 involved children—mostly runaways. This high level of runaways is also found in national data. Abductions involve less than 1 percent of all missing children cases and most are parental child abductions cases. While most missing person cases are solved within 24 to 48 hours, runaways are at serious risk of physical or sexual abuse or involvement in crime while on the run.
  - o People with health concerns are at risk of going missing. For example, people with Alzheimer's disease can leave home and become lost. The projected number of people with Alzheimer's disease or related dementia will likely increase as the Canadian population ages. People suffering from mental disorder and depression may also go missing and may be at risk of suicide.
  - o People may go missing as a result of foul play or criminal conduct.
  - o Aboriginal women, in particular, are at risk of going missing as a result of violence. The Amnesty International Report, *Stolen Sisters, A Human Rights Response to Discrimination and Violence Against Indigenous Women in Canada,* released in October 2004, documents a range of concerns. Certainly, Saskatchewan data on long-term missing person cases indicates that Aboriginal women in Saskatchewan are disproportionately represented amongst missing women and as possible victims of foul play . . . an estimated 60 percent of long-term missing women in Saskatchewan are Aboriginal while representing only 6 percent of the population. A disproportionate number of these cases are also suspected to involve foul play and a number of "found" cases have involved murder.
  - o People go missing as a result of accident. Boating, hunting or other accident situations can lead to a person going missing.

- Current information on long-term missing person cases and unidentified human remains in Saskatchewan can be found in the website operated by the Saskatchewan Association of Chiefs of Police which commenced operations in April 2006.[3] The site provides the public with a convenient location to find out about the known cases and an opportunity to get involved in providing information to the authorities.

Summary of Recommendations in the Final Report of the Provincial Partnership Committee on Missing Persons (October 2007)

I. Responding to issues raised by families

RECOMMENDATION 1. Supports need to be developed to help families deal with a missing person situation. This includes simple checklists to follow of actions they can or should take; media kit or information on dealing with the media to help them understand the issues and relationship with the media; and financial and emotional support from community members or organizations.

RECOMMENDATION 2. The media should develop best practice standards in dealing with missing person cases.

RECOMMENDATION 3. Families should be assisted to develop a support network.

RECOMMENDATION 4. Existing common law and legislation dealing with missing persons and their estates should be reviewed.

RECOMMENDATION 5.1. Families of missing persons should be consulted to determine the form or forms that a provincial memorial to missing persons could take and how it would be implemented and maintained. And this topic should be raised for discussion in terms of a national memorial by the Saskatchewan Minister of Justice at the next national ministers meeting. [RECOMMENDATION 5.2]

RECOMMENDATION 6. The SACP [Saskatchewan Association of Chiefs of Police] and the Saskatchewan Minister of Justice are encouraged to raise the need for a national website or linked websites on missing persons in appropriate national forums.

II. Responding to prevention, awareness and public education issues

RECOMMENDATION 7.0. Information/education materials should be developed to provide a factual overview of all aspects of missing person situations.

RECOMMENDATION 7.1. Agencies that deal with at-risk populations should establish teams to conduct presentations on awareness, prevention and personal safety.

RECOMMENDATION 7.2. An inventory of agencies involved in missing person cases should be compiled and maintained.

RECOMMENDATION 7.3. Police should ensure that information about police policy, procedure and practices related to missing persons cases and the role that the public can play in assisting in missing person cases is generally available.

RECOMMENDATION 8. Information to increase awareness about the risks of going missing or facing missing children and youth should be available in all schools through health education programs and through school councils.

III. Improving responses to missing person cases

RECOMMENDATION 9.1. The Saskatchewan Police Commission should review its current policy and work with all police agencies in Saskatchewan to develop and implement an overarching provincial Missing Person Policy for all municipal police agencies, and encourage the RCMP to adopt the policy in Saskatchewan.

RECOMMENDATION 9.2. The policy could include the following standards:

1. A missing person report must be taken immediately when information comes to the attention of police, regardless of the length of time the person has been missing or the location where the person went missing.

2. A standardized specialized in-take form for recording a missing person report and a specialized investigative checklist should be used.

3. A common assessment tool should be developed to help assess the priority of the investigation.

4. Immediate investigation of missing persons in suspicious circumstances.

5. Once it is established that a person is missing, the case will be entered on the database of the Canadian Police Information Centre (CPIC) as soon as possible.

6. Continued communication with the families of missing people.

7. A media and public communications protocol for disseminating information about missing persons and requesting the public's help in locating a missing person.

8. The police, upon identifying a chronic runaway situation, should develop approaches to link with other agencies to support appropriate intervention.

9. All police forces should assign a police officer responsible for co-ordination of missing person files and establish a backup process to avoid gaps in effectively responding to missing person reports.

10. In order to effectively implement the above approach to recording and managing investigations on missing person cases, standardized training and practice guides should be developed.

11. There is a need for a more systematic and consistent approach to collecting data on: 1) missing person reports; 2) actual missing persons; 3) basic demographic information about missing persons; and 4) CPIC data entry.

RECOMMENDATION 10. A process is required to ensure that all suspicious and at-risk missing person reported incidents (young children, medical, elderly, high-risk life style) are fanned out to all relevant police agencies in the province immediately.

RECOMMENDATION 11. Police should establish protocols with community agencies to provide a formal system to fan out "Missing Person Information."

RECOMMENDATION 12.1. The provincial government should amend provincial legislation to permit the disclosure of information on missing persons to police conducting a missing person investigation as information necessary to protect the mental or physical health or safety of an individual. And a similar recommendation should be made to the Federal Government to ensure access to information in federal databanks. [RECOMMENDATION 12.2]

RECOMMENDATION 13. The mandate of Victim Services should include the provision of support to families of missing people.

RECOMMENDATION 14.1. The province and local government need to enhance search and rescue resources province-wide by standardizing provincial policy and providing provincial core funding to ensure volunteer sustainability.

RECOMMENDATION 14.2. The province, communities and search and rescue organizations need to work cooperatively to ensure effective Search and Rescue (SAR) responses by:

- creating a provincial SAR Advisory Council of representative and mandating agencies, for strategic and operational direction to Search and Rescue Saskatchewan Association of Volunteers (SARSAV);

- creating a standard policy regarding the use of SAR teams;

- ensuring that municipalities and communities take ownership of SAR volunteer teams;

- providing basic SAR training and equipment to volunteers free of charge;

- ensuring that trained SAR teams, SAR managers and trainers are available throughout all areas of the province;

- creating a central provincial database for all SAR events, training and personnel;

- ensuring consistent and timely involvement of SAR teams in a missing person event;

- providing specialized training for SAR volunteers, i.e., emergency management, and recognizing the need for SAR teams in a disaster event, crime scene or evidence recovery;

- developing heavy urban SAR capacity;

- ensuring support systems are in place for long-term and/or remote searches;

• ensuring liability protection for volunteers; and

• ensuring Critical Incident Stress Management support to SAR volunteers.

RECOMMENDATION 15. The various Saskatchewan police forces need to establish protocols on when and how to engage search and rescue capacity in a missing person event.

RECOMMENDATION 16. All school divisions are encouraged to develop policies and procedures for collaborating with police and/or school resource officers in missing person cases.

RECOMMENDATION 17. Research is needed to better understand the issues related to the high number of runaways and to identify prevention and intervention strategies, particularly for chronic runaways and their families.

RECOMMENDATION 18. The provincial government should fund a caseworker pilot with a police service.

RECOMMENDATION 19. The provincial government, the Federation of Saskatchewan Indian Nations, the Métis Nation of Saskatchewan, First Nations, and Métis communities and organizations should be encouraged to develop and enhance mutually supportive strategies to ensure that:

• First Nations and Métis communities have the capacity to respond to a crisis when a person goes missing;

• trained search and rescue capacities exist in all communities that incorporate and are sensitive to the culture, language, traditions and values of those communities;

• First Nations schools participate in prevention and response approaches similar to the recommendations for provincial school involvement; and

• relationships between the police (RCMP and municipal police forces) and First Nations and Métis communities are strengthened in missing person cases.

RECOMMENDATION 20. The Saskatchewan Minister of Justice should raise for national consideration with colleagues whether and how a voluntary national information base or linked information bases on potential missing persons could be created.

—Prepared by the Ministry of Justice and the Attorney General, August 8, 2008

ENDNOTES

1 Public Safety and Emergency Preparedness Canada, DNA Missing Persons Index (MPI), A public consultation paper, March 2005. http://www.ulcc.ca/en/poam2/DNA_Missing_Persons_Index_CP_En.pdf (accessed 31 March 2010). Canadian Police Information Centre (CPIC) data.

2 Dr. Jeff Pfeifer, *Missing persons in Saskatchewan: Police policy and practice,* November 2006.

3 www.sacp.ca.

Bibliography of Useful Resources

Acoose, J. 1995. *Iskwewak kah'ki yaw no wah komakanak: Neither Indian princesses nor easy squaws.* Toronto: Women's Press.

Amnesty International. 2004. *Stolen sisters: a human rights response to discrimination and violence against indigenous women in Canada.* http://www.amnesty.ca/stolensisters/amr 2000304.pdf.

Baird, V. 2007. "Trafficked." *New Internationalist* 404 (September). http://www.newint. org/features/2007/09/01/keynote/

Bowden, C. 1998. *Juárez: The laboratory of our future.* New York: Aperature Foundation.

Canada. Manitoba. Aboriginal Justice Implementation Commission. n.d. The death of Helen Betty Osborne, http://www.ajic.mb.ca/volumeII/toc.html.

Carter, S. 1997. "In sharp relief: Representations of Aboriginal women in the colonial imagination." *Capturing women: The manipulation of cultural imagery in Canada's Prairie West,* 158–93. McGill: Queen's University Press.

Dean, Amber, and Anne Stone, eds. 2007. *Representations of murdered and missing women.* Special issue, *West Coast Line* 41(1).

DeVries, M. 2004. *Missing Sarah: A Vancouver woman remembers her vanished sister.* Toronto: Penguin.

Fogel, M. (Producer/Director). *North of Dewdney: A play by the Voices of Change theatre ensemble.* Motion Picture. Canada: Acimo Productions.

Frank, K. 2007. *Highway of tears.* http://www.youtube.com/watch?v=It5AGKLNwqw.

Fregoso, R. 2001. *Lourdes Portillo: The devil never sleeps and other films.* Texas: University of Texas Press.

Goulding, W. 2001. *Just another Indian: A serial killer and Canada's indifference.* Calgary: Fifth House Publishing.

Green, J. 2007. *Making space for Indigenous feminism.* London: Fern Publishing.

Healy, T. 2008. *Gendered struggles against globalization in Mexico.* Burlington: Ashgate Publishing.

Hernández, D., and B. Rehman. 2004. *Colonize this: Young women of color on feminism.* Emeryville: Seal Press.

Hrynchuk, A. (Producer/Director). 2007. *Stolen sisters.* Motion Picture. Canada: Fahrenheit Films.

Jiwani, Y., and M. L. Young. 2006. "Missing and murdered women: Reproducing marginality in news discourse." *Canadian Journal of Communication* 31(4): 895–917.

LaRocque, E. 2002. "Violence in Aboriginal communities." In *Violence against women: New Canadian perspectives,* ed. Katherine M. J. McKenna and June Larkin, 147–162. Toronto: Inanna Publications & Education.

Kallio, N. 2006. "Aboriginality and sexualized violence: The Tisdale rape case in the Saskatoon *StarPhoenix*." Master's thesis, Concordia University.

Keating, B. 2008. "Raping Pocahontas: History, territory and ekphrasis in the representation of an Indigenous girl." Master's thesis, University of Regina.

Marcuse, G. (Producer/Writer/Director). 1999. *Pride and prejudice: The road to multiculturalism and human rights in British Columbia.* Motion Picture. Canada.

Marmon Silko, L. 1996. *Yellow woman and a beauty of the spirit: Essays on Native American life today.* Toronto: Simon & Schuster Paperbacks.

Mendenhall, M. 2008. "Our missing mothers, sisters and daughters." *Degrees: University of Regina magazine* (Fall): 14–19.

Mercredi, M. 2006. *Morningstar: A warrior's spirit.* Canada: Coteau Books.

Petit, M. (Producer/Writer/Director). 2008. *Hookers: A film of hope and survival.* Motion Picture. Canada: m.pet Productions.

Pilkington, D. 2002. *Rabbit proof fence: The true story of one of the greatest escapes of all time.* USA: Miramax Books.

Portillo, L. (Producer), and L. Portillo (Writer/Director). 2001. *Señorita extraviada: Missing young women.* Motion Picture. United States.

Native Women's Association of Canada. 2009. *Voices of our sisters in spirit.* http://www.nwac-hq.org/en/documents/VoicesofOurSistersInSpirit_2ndEdition_March2009.pdf

Price, P. 2004. *Dry place: Landscapes of belonging and exclusion.* Minneapolis: University of Minnesota Press.

Razack, S. 2002. "Gendered racial violence and spatialized justice." In *Race, space and the law,* ed. Sherene Razack, 121–56. Toronto: Between the Lines.

Rodriguez, T., D. Montané, and L. Pulitzer. 2007. *The daughters of Juárez: A true story of serial murder south of the border.* New York: Simon and Schuster.

Sanford, V. 2003. *Buried secrets: Truth and human rights in Guatemala.* New York: Palgrave MacMillan.

Smith, A. 2005. *Conquest: Sexual violence and American Indian genocide.* Cambridge: South End Press.

WEBSITES

www.missingnativewomen.ca

www.vanishedvoices.com

www.whokilledtheresa.blogspot.com

www.kare.ca

www.sextradeworkersofcanada.com

http://www.cwhn.ca/node/39432

www.highwayoftears.ca

www.missingpeople.net

www.endingviolence.org/publications/286/FinalReportSeptember2005.doc

Contributors

A. BRENDA ANDERSON teaches in Women's and Gender Studies at Luther College, University of Regina. Her interests are in the area of justice work, identity politics, and the ways in which women tell their stories, whether it be interreligious dialogue between Muslim and Christian feminists, Aboriginal women in colonized countries, women resisting globalization, and so on. Brenda co-chaired the Missing Women conference, and recently developed a course entitled "Missing Indigenous Women: A Global Perspective." She looks forward to teaching a new course entitled "Feminisms and Activism: Dancing through the Minefields."

GORDON BARNES has been active in Amnesty International for many years and is a volunteer fieldworker. In addition to participating in the "Missing Women" conference, Gordon has also been involved in the organization of other events related to this area of human rights work.

LEONZO BARRENO is a Mayan from Guatemala. He came to Saskatchewan in 1989. Leonzo has served as the Global Television Chair and as adjunct professor for the School of Journalism, University of Regina. He is the author of *Higher Education for Indigenous people in Latin America* (2003), used as a working document by a UNESCO-Latin America gathering of experts in Guatemala in April 2002. In January 2003, he testified to the Senate of Canada Standing Committee on Aboriginal People about issues affecting Aboriginal youth as the Committee aimed to develop a national "Action Plan for Change." He is currently the provincial coordinator of the Saskatchewan Association of Settlement and Integration Agencies (SAISIA).

CYNTHIA L. BEJARANO, a native of southern New Mexico and the El-Paso/Juárez border, is an assistant professor of Criminal Justice at New Mexico State University. Her publications and research interests focus on border violence; race, class, and gender issues; and Latino youths' border identities in the Southwest. Bejarano was recently awarded a $1.3 million grant to assist migrant and seasonal farm-worker children to attend New Mexico State University. She has been an advocate and activist working with the families of disappeared and murdered women in Ciudad Juárez for five years, and works closely with people at Casa Amiga, the rape crisis centre in Ciudad Juárez. She is also the co-founder of Amigos de las Mujeres de Juárez, an NGO dedicated to assisting the women of Juárez in their fight for justice.

CARRIE BOURASSA is an associate professor of Indigenous Health Studies at First Nations University of Canada. Carrie completed her Ph.D. (Social Studies) in January 2008. Her dissertation is entitled "Destruction of the Métis nation: Health consequences." Carrie's research interests include the effects of colonization on the health of First Nations and Métis people; creating culturally competent care in health service delivery; Aboriginal community-based health research methodology; Aboriginal end-of-life care; and Aboriginal women's health. Carrie is Métis, belonging to the Riel Métis Council of Regina Inc. She resides in Regina with her husband, Chad, and her daughter, Victoria.

LORI CAMPBELL, born to a 15-year-old displaced First Nations woman, went through a Social Services apprehension, foster care, and adoption. She then struggled extensively with discovering and reclaiming her Métis identity. Lori has a large community network and has several years of experience developing liaisons and partnering with various agencies in order to achieve common goals. However, she always stays focused and remembers the importance of the community at the grassroots level. She is currently pursuing a Master's degree in Adult Education, with research in Aboriginal cultural competency in post-secondary institutions as a determinant of Aboriginal student health and success. Presently, she is employed as the Science and Health Aboriginal Success Strategy Advisor for SIAST, Wascana Campus, is a sessional instructor for First Nations University of Canada and the University of Regina SUNTEP Program, and sits on the Saskatchewan Midwifery Transitional Council Committee.

MARIA CAMPBELL, recipient of the Order of Canada in 2008, is perhaps best known for her autobiography, *Halfbreed,* in which she portrays the discrimination and racism she and other Métis endured. She has received many awards for her writing, including Honorary Doctorate degrees from the University of Regina and York University. The Métis nation also honoured her for her community work, especially with women and children, with the Gabriel Dumont Medal for Merit.

AMBER DEAN is a Ph.D. candidate in the Department of English and Film Studies at the University of Alberta. In her dissertation she is tracing what lives on from the women disappeared from Vancouver's Downtown Eastside by examining representations of the women in media, memorials, and art. She is also theorizing the links between the colonization of Western Canada and the disappearances and murders of Indigenous women from Western Canadian cities. With Vancouver writer Anne Stone, Dean recently co-edited a special issue of the journal *West Coast Line* on representations of murdered and missing women.

LILLIAN DYCK is a member of the Gordon First Nation, Saskatchewan. Senator Dyck, a neurochemist, was the associate dean of programs in the College of Graduate Studies and full professor in the Neuropsychiatry Research Unit, Department of Psychiatry, University of Saskatchewan. In addition to numerous awards for her research and community service, including several from First Nations communities, Senator Dyck was awarded an honorary degree from Cape Breton University in Sydney, Nova Scotia. Senator Dyck was summoned to the Senate by former Prime Minister Paul Martin in March 2005.

KIM ERNO is an ordained Evangelical Lutheran Church in America (ELCA) pastor with more than twenty years of parish ministry experience. He has worked with various solidarity organizations related to El Salvador and Mexico. Before this assignment, he was a mission developer serving a Latino community in Washington, DC. He is the program director for the ELCA's Transformational House in Mexico City, where the Transformational Immersion Program follows a "reverse mission" process: participants do not come with tools, resources and solutions to overcome poverty and injustice; rather, they are invited to hear, learn and grow through dialog and relationship with those on the margins of life. http://www2.elca.org/mexico/program.html

JESSICA GREYEYES is a student at First Nations University of Regina. She is working towards a Bachelor of Administration degree, followed by a Bachelor of Arts majoring in Indigenous Studies and Women and Gender Studies. Her aunt first taught her how to make Star Blankets after her Mushum passed away, and now she and her Kokum continue the tradition. Jessica writes: "I started making them at a period in my life that was hard and stressful; there was something that was peaceful and serene, and I feel more connected with my heritage and my family. Being asked to work on the conference blanket was a wonderful experience and an honour."

JOHN HAMPTON is a conceptual arts and independent videographer (www.jghampton.com). He videotaped the conference when he was a student at the University of Regina. When John graduated in October 2009 he received the award for most outstanding graduate in the Faculty of Fine Arts. John has several shows in Canada and other countries, and is a member of the art collective, Turner Prize. He is a member of the Chickasaw First Nation.

MARY RUCKLOS HAMPTON, Ed.D., is the Provincial Academic Research Coordinator for RESOLVE Saskatchewan, professor of Psychology at Luther College at the University of Regina, and a research faculty member in the Saskatchewan Population Health and Evaluation Research Unit (SPHERU). She is a registered clinical psychologist in Saskatchewan and regularly teaches courses in humanistic psychology, psychology of women, developmental psychology, abnormal psychology, and introductory psychology. Dr. Hampton's research interests include intimate partner violence, cross-cultural psychology, women's health, adolescent sexual health, and end-of-life care. She has several funded research projects from the Canadian Institutes of Health, the Saskatchewan Health Research Foundation, and the Social Sciences and Humanities Research Council.

CHARLOTTE HAUK is a third-year Fine Arts student, majoring in ceramics, at the University of Regina. In May 2006 Charlotte curated an art exhibit in the Fifth Parallel Gallery at the University. This show was then moved to the conference in August. The exhibit showcased the work of students who travelled with Brenda Anderson to Mexico City for nine days to study and visit the Indigenous communities where women were resisting violence against women. The show then travelled to the Women's Center of Education at the University of Toronto as an opening for Jessica Yee's artist talk about *Highways of Hope,* her film about the murdered and missing from British Columbia. Charlotte has continued her activism through art in other films on missing women, selling mugs made for the conference, and painting a mural for the Women's Centre at the University of Regina. She has been supported in her work with a bursary from the Women's Professional Business Organization. Charlotte will curate a show at the Mackenzie Art Gallery in January 2011 and will graduate with a Bachelor in Fine Arts in fall 2011.

JUDY HUGHES is the president of the Saskatchewan Aboriginal Women's Circle Corporation and works with the Native Women's Association of Canada Sisters in Spirit Campaign. SAWCC is an organization designed to bring forth issues concerning Aboriginal women and children, and is mandated to address issues regarding the Indian Act, the Constitution, family violence, AIDS, child welfare, education, justice, health, employment and Aboriginal rights.

ALEXIS J. JOHNSON is grateful and honoured to have shared a healing space through art, nature, and awareness of a deeply felt issue. She feels that this has been a very empowering journey. She came to the conference with an open mind, and left with a full heart. In 2009, Alexis completed weaving her B.A. Hons. Psychology degree at the University of Regina. She currently resides in Victoria, BC, and shares healing through a women's circle and mentoring group. She looks forward to gaining experience in and providing holistic counselling to whomever and wherever her journey may take her.

DARLENE M. JUSCHKA is associate professor in Women's and Gender Studies and Religious Studies. In her interdisciplinary work she brings together feminist theorizing, ritual and myth studies and the new phenomenology of religion. Several of her more recently published articles include "Gender" in John Hinnells (ed.), *The Routledge Companion to the Study of Religion*, 2nd edition (Routledge, 2009), "The Fantasy of Gender/Sex: Angela Carter and Mythmaking" in Lee Easton and Randy Schroeder (eds.), *The Influence of Imagination: Essays on Science Fiction and Fantasy as Agents of Social Change* (McFarland, 2008), and "Deconstructing the Eliadean Paradigm: Symbol" in Willi Braun and Russell T. McCutcheon (eds.), *Introducing Religion: Essays in Honor of Jonathan Z. Smith* (Equinox, 2008). Released in 2001 was her anthology *Feminism in the Study of Religion: a Reader* (Continuum), while her newest text, *Political Bodies, Body Politic: The Semiotics of Gender* was released in 2009 through Equinox Press.

WENDEE KUBIK is associate professor and coordinator of Women's and Gender Studies at the University of Regina. Her research interests focus on farm women, women's health, Aboriginal women, women and work, gender analysis, changing gender roles, participatory action research, food security, and global health issues. Her current research is focused on RE-SOLVE's Healing Journey, a Canadian International Development (CIDA) project in Chile aimed at having more women involved in water organizations and looking at the health and needs of Aboriginal grandmothers caring for grandchildren.

KIERA LADNER is associate professor and Canada Research Chair in Indigenous Politics and Governance in the Department of Political Studies at the University of Manitoba. Her current community-based research into reconciliation and decolonization attempts to create deeper understanding both within Indigenous communities and between Indigenous nations and colonial societies in Canada and Hawaii.

ELIZABETH MATHESON is an independent curator, lecturer, and writer of Canadian and international contemporary art and culture. Matheson is the author of numerous reviews, articles, and catalogue essays, which have been translated into various languages and have appeared in *Art Nexus, CV Ciel*

Variable Magazine, Prefix Photo, Studium (Brazil's leading electronic arts magazine), and other publications. She has organized group exhibitions in galleries, art centres, historical buildings, and outdoor spaces, including the widely acclaimed work of Jo Spence (UK), Joan Fontcuberta (Spain), and many regional and nationally recognized artists. Her recent projects include *Back Talk: protest and humour* (2006), *Missing and Taken: A Symposium (2006), Familiar but Foreign* (2007), and *The Last Photo* (2008). As part of her independent curatorial practice, she has worked with and written on renowned Latin American artists and filmmakers, including Betsabeé Romero (Mexico, Cairo Biennial 2006 and Havana Biennial 2003), Rosângela Rennó (Brazil, Venice Biennial 2003), Oscar Muñoz (Columbia, Venice Biennial, 2005 and 2007) and Academy Award nominee Lourdes Portillo (Mexico/U.S.). Most recently, in the summer of 2008, Elizabeth Matheson was invited to speak about her curatorial practice with the aforementioned artists at the Four Corners Centre for Still and Moving Image Work in London (UK); this presentation was subsequently broadcasted for audiences at the fifth annual São Paulo Fotoweek, São Paulo, Brazil. She is currently researching an international exhibition on the role of video in contested spaces within Latin America (with artists such as Cinthia Marcelle and Narda Alvarado), entitled *Occupy, Resist and Produce* (with the accompanying essay, *Somoza's Teeth*) and has been invited to co-curate a project on transnational migration with the artist and filmmaker Humberto Vélez (Panama/UK) at the Art Gallery of York University (Toronto).

BRITTANY MATTHEWS is a young teacher dedicated to activating responsible citizenship among young people in Regina. As a member of the Regina Public School Division, she is involved in a number of justice-related initiatives, including contributing to the Equitable Opportunities committee and leading her school's ACT (Anti-Racist Cross-Cultural Team-Building) group and her school's GSA (Gay-Straight Alliance). In addition, Brittany is currently a board member for Camp fYrefly Saskatchewan, a leadership retreat for sexual minority, gender variant, and allied youth, as well as a board member for SCIC (Saskatchewan Council for International Cooperation), an umbrella organization for international development agencies serving communities locally and globally. Brittany is grateful to have had the opportunity to learn from the many strong, inspiring women and men involved in the conference.

HOLLY A. MCKENZIE is a white-settler woman who grew up on a farm near Tribune, Saskatchewan, with horses and a lot of open space. She convocated with her Bachelor of Arts Honours, majoring in Women's and

Gender Studies, and Bachelor of Health Studies in June 2009 and is now pursuing her M.A. in Canadian Plains Studies at the University of Regina. She is extremely thankful to have met and learned from many Indigenous academics, community members, activists, and Elders. Holly enjoys spending time at her family farm (especially in the summer) and reading.

MORNINGSTAR MERCREDI is a storyteller, actress, social activist, poet, playwright, researcher and multi-media communicator. She has previously published one non-fiction children's book, *Fort Chipewayan Homecoming,* which was a finalist in the Silver Birch young readers' choice award in Ontario. She has also had poetry published in the *Gatherings* anthology series. She has done extensive acting work in film, television, radio, and on the stage. Born in Uranium City, Saskatchewan, Morningstar Mercredi has lived in Alberta (Fort Chipewayan, Calgary, and Fort McMurray), in Saskatchewan (Saskatoon and Prince Albert), in British Columbia (Cranbrook, Kimberly, Merritt, Penticton, and Surrey), and in the Northwest Territories. She also settled for a time in Gisbourne, New Zealand, and Nowra, Australia. She currently makes Edmonton her home. She is honest and self-critical in her descriptions of many attempts and repeated failures. She gives enormous credit to her son, for his constant love, his determination to be honest with her, and his unfailing confidence in her ability to succeed.

CHELSEA MILLMAN is a Métis women who was raised in southern Saskatchewan. Chelsea began working on the issue of missing and murdered women in April 2007 and has continued to do so since. She recently completed her B.A. High Honours degree in Psychology and Women's Studies at the University of Regina. In her CPA-recognized qualitative thesis, "Stories from the Moonlodge: Indigenous Female Elders Share Stories of Menstruation and Menarche," Chelsea explored traditional knowledge surrounding women's power. Her broader research interests include intimate partner violence, feminist theory, race theory, spirituality, end-of-life care, Indigenous health, and animal rights.

IAN PEACH is a special advisor to the Office of the Federal Interlocutor for Métis and Non-Status Indians on secondment from the Government of Saskatchewan, where he has been employed for fourteen years. While in Saskatchewan, he was director of the Saskatchewan Institute of Public Policy, where he had previously been a Government of Saskatchewan senior policy fellow and research director. He has also been the director of Constitutional Relations in the Saskatchewan Department of Intergovernmental and Aboriginal Affairs and a senior policy advisor in the Cabinet Planning Unit of

Saskatchewan Executive Council. In his twenty years of public service, Mr. Peach has been involved in numerous intergovernmental negotiations and policy development exercises, many focused on issues of constitutional law, federalism, Aboriginal self-government, and the socio-economic equality of Aboriginal peoples. Born in Halifax, NS, Mr. Peach holds a Bachelor of Arts from Dalhousie University and a Bachelor of Laws from Queen's University. He is currently completing a Master of Laws degree, also at Queen's.

LOURDES PORTILLO was born in Chihuahua, Mexico, and moved to the United States in 1960. Her films focus on the representation of Latina/o identity, human rights, social justice, and Latin American realities. An equally important aspect of her filmmaking is experimenting with the documentary form. Her most recent film, *Señorita Extraviada* (Missing Young Woman), released in 2002, is a documentary about the disappearance and death of young women in Juárez and the search for truth and justice by their families and human rights groups. It received a Special Jury Prize at the Sundance Film Festival, the Best Documentary Prize at the Havana International Film Festival, and the Néstor Almendros Prize at the Human Rights Watch Film Festival. It premiered on POV and received more than twenty prizes and awards around the world. The film inspired a number of governmental and non-governmental organizations such as Amnesty International to conduct intensive investigations into the disappearances and murders of women in Juárez. Lourdes Portillo made her first film, a dramatic short called *After the Earthquake*, in 1979. Some of the other documentary, dramatic, experimental, and performance films and videos she has made are the Academy Award-nominated *Las Madres: The Mothers of Plaza de Mayo* (1986); *La Ofrenda: The Days of the Dead* (1988); *Vida* (1989); *Columbus on Trial* (1992); *Mirrors of the Heart* for the PBS series *Americas* (1993); *The Devil Never Sleeps* (1994); *Sometimes My Feet Go Numb* (1997); *13 Days,* a multi-media piece for a nationally toured play by the San Francisco Mime Troupe (1997); and *Corpus* (1999), a documentary about the late Tejana singer Selena.

BETTY ANN POTTRUFF is co-chair of the Provincial Partnership Committee on Missing Persons, Ministry of Justice and Attorney General, Saskatchewan.

DARLA READ has been a journalist with Saskatchewan's Aboriginal radio station, Missinipi Broadcasting Corporation, for nearly two years. She also freelances for *Eagle Feather News,* a monthly Aboriginal newspaper. She graduated in 2003 from the University of Regina's School of Journalism and has previously worked for other media outlets, including *The La Ronge Northerner* and the CBC. She is passionate about gardening, the environment, and Aboriginal issues.

CAROL SCHICK is associate professor in the Faculty of Education at the University of Regina. She is involved in anti-oppressive education in teacher preparation programs and uses feminist theories, critical race theories, and whiteness studies to live and work through tensions of post-colonial education at all levels of schooling as found on the Canadian Prairies.

TIMOTHY ST. AMAND has a Bachelor of Arts degree in Psychology and a Bachelor of Education degree in Secondary Education from the University of Regina in Regina, Saskatchewan. He is currently a learning resource teacher with the Regina Catholic School Division and works with elementary school students in the areas of reading and academic assessment.

ADRIAN STIMSON was born and raised in Sault St. Marie, Ontario, and lived on a number of First Nations across Canada, including his home reserve, Siksika Nation (Blackfoot). His formative years were spent in Saskatchewan, on the Gordon First Nation, and in Lebret. After completing his B.F.A. at Alberta College of Art and Design in Calgary, Adrian moved to Saskatoon to complete an M.F.A. at the University of Saskatchewan. Though he initially trained as a painter, he now considers his practice interdisciplinary. Adrian has been researching and experimenting with his personal blend of environmental art and activism, Indigenous knowledge, and sustainable communities.

CHERYL TOTH is the chaplain at Luther College, University of Regina. In addition to her role at Luther, Cheryl is currently working on a Master's degree in Women's and Gender Studies at the University of Regina. Cheryl has worked for many years on issues of justice and inclusion, including those affecting First Nations and Métis people. Most of this work has been with the Anglican Church of Canada, through which she was ordained over twenty-five years ago.

ERNESTA VILEITATE-WRIGHT was born in Panevezys, Lithuania, and came to Canada in 2005. She recently completed a psychology degree at the University of Regina. She is a devoted activist on behalf of human and animal rights and the well-being of our planet. She is co-founder and board member of the non-profit organization People Before Profit: Empowering Communities through Women.

MEGHAN WOODS is a doctoral candidate in Clinical Psychology at the University of Regina, supervised by Dr. Mary Hampton. Meghan's research interests include the relationship between intimate partner violence and sleep. Her dissertation is entitled "The Nature of Sleep in Victims of Intimate Partner Violence: A Feminist Longitudinal Analysis." Meghan has received funding from the Social Sciences and Humanities Research Council to complete this project. She resides in Lumsden, Saskatchewan, with her husband, Nicholas Berry.

Thank you to family members who contributed their stories, and thank you to Sisters in Spirit for allowing us to reprint these stories from *Voices of our sisters in spirit* (2008):

Eva Arce
Paula Flores
Pauline and Herb Muskego
Marta Perez
Gwenda Yuzicappi

Index

A NOTE ABOUT THE TYPE

This book is set in *Adobe Garamond Pro*, an Adobe Originals design, and Adobe's first historical revival. It is a digital interpretation of the roman types of Claude Garamond and the italic types of Robert Granjon. Type designer Robert Slimbach has captured the beauty and balance of the original Garamond typefaces while creating a typeface family that offers all the advantages of a contemporary digital type family.

Claude Garamond (ca. 1480-1561) cut types for the Parisian scholar-printer Robert Estienne in the first part of the sixteenth century, basing his romans on the types cut by Francesco Griffo for Venetian printer Aldus Manutius in 1495. After his death in 1561, the Garamond punches made their way to the printing office of Christoph Plantin in Antwerp, where they were used by Plantin for many decades, and still exist in the Plantin-Moretus museum. In 1621, sixty years after Garamond's death, the French printer Jean Jannon (1580–1635) issued a specimen of typefaces that had some characteristics similar to the Garamond designs, though his letters were more asymmetrical and irregular in slope and axis. Jannon's types disappeared from use for about two hundred years, but were rediscovered in the French national printing office in 1825, when they were wrongly attributed to Claude Garamond. Their true origin was not to be revealed until the 1927 research of Beatrice Warde. In the early 1900s, Jannon's types were used to print a history of printing in France, which brought new attention to French typography and the "Garamond" types. This sparked the beginning of modern revivals; some based on the mistaken model from Jannon's types, and others on the original Garamond types. Garamond is considered to be distinctive representations of French Renaissance style; easily recognizable by their elegance and readability.

The accents in this book are set in *Gill Sans*. Designed by the English artist and type designer Eric Gill and issued by Monotype in 1928 to 1930, the roots of Gill Sans can be traced to the typeface that Gill's teacher, Edward Johnston, designed for the signage of the London Underground Railway in 1918. Gill's alphabet is more classical in proportion and contains what have become known as his signature flared capital R and eyeglass lowercase g. Gill Sans is a humanist sans serif with some geometric touches in its structures. It also has a distinctly British feel. Legible and modern though sometimes cheerfully idiosyncratic, the lighter weights work for text, and the bolder weights make for compelling display typography.